THE
EVERYTHING
KETO DIET MEAL PREP
COOKBOOK

Dear Reader,

One of the most common objections I hear to starting a keto diet is "it's too much work," and while I can definitely empathize with that—it does take more forethought, preparation, and calculations than other nutrition plans—there's a viable solution. Meal prep.

Now I know what you're thinking: "Do I really need to spend the time meal prepping?" Take it from someone who's been there before: the answer is yes. Especially when you're following a keto diet.

The whole point of keto is to kick your body into ketosis and, unfortunately, sometimes all it takes to knock you out of that fat-burning state is one high-carbohydrate meal. If you're out and about with nothing to eat and you start to get hangry, you're significantly more likely to reach for whatever you can grab. Hey, hunger can make you do crazy things!

On the flip side, when you meal prep, you take away the unknowns, so to speak. You may spend a little more time getting organized, but you'll always know that you have a perfectly balanced keto meal or snack ready to go. You won't have to wonder where your next meal is coming from and/or if you'll be able to find something on the go. You won't have to skip a meal and spend the day hungry because you can't find anything that fits into your plan. And that peace of mind is worth the extra effort. Ease in, adjust, and learn as you go, and most importantly, have fun with it.

Wishing you a lifetime of laughter, health, and happiness.

Lindsay Boyers, CHNC

Welcome to the EVERYTHING® Series!

These handy, accessible books give you all you need to tackle a difficult project, gain a new hobby, comprehend a fascinating topic, prepare for an exam, or even brush up on something you learned back in school but have since forgotten.

You can choose to read an Everything® book from cover to cover or just pick out the information you want from our four useful boxes: e-questions, e-facts, e-alerts, and e-ssentials.

We give you everything you need to know on the subject, but throw in a lot of fun stuff along the way too.

We now have more than 600 Everything® books in print, spanning such wide-ranging categories as weddings, pregnancy, cooking, music instruction, foreign language, crafts, pets, New Age, and so much more. When you're done reading them all, you can finally say you know Everything®!

QUESTION

Answers to common questions

FACT

Important snippets of information

ALERT

Urgent warnings

ESSENTIAL

Quick handy tips

PUBLISHER Karen Cooper

MANAGING EDITOR Lisa Laing

COPY CHIEF Casey Ebert

ASSOCIATE PRODUCTION EDITOR Jo-Anne Duhamel

ACQUISITIONS EDITOR Zander Hatch

SENIOR DEVELOPMENT EDITOR Brett Palana-Shanahan

EVERYTHING® SERIES COVER DESIGNER Erin Alexander

Visit the entire Everything® series at www.everything.com

THE EVERYTHING®

KETO DIET MEAL PREP COOKBOOK

Lindsay Boyers, CHNC

Adams Media

New York London Toronto Sydney New Delhi

Adams Media
An Imprint of Simon & Schuster, Inc.
57 Littlefield Street
Avon, Massachusetts 02322

An Everything® Series Book.
Everything® and everything.com® are registered trademarks of Simon & Schuster, Inc.

First Adams Media trade paperback edition May 2019

ADAMS MEDIA and colophon are trademarks of Simon & Schuster.

For information about special discounts for bulk purchases, please contact Simon & Schuster Special Sales at 1-866-506-1949 or business@simonandschuster.com.

The Simon & Schuster Speakers Bureau can bring authors to your live event. For more information or to book an event contact the Simon & Schuster Speakers Bureau at 1-866-248-3049 or visit our website at www.simonspeakers.com.

Photographs by James Stefiuk

Manufactured in the United States of America

10 9 8 7 6 5 4 3 2

Library of Congress Cataloging-in-Publication Data
Names: Boyers, Lindsay, author.
Title: The everything® keto diet meal prep cookbook / Lindsay Boyers, CHNC.
Description: Avon, Massachusetts: Adams Media, 2019.
Series: Everything®.
Includes index.
Identifiers: LCCN 2018058741 | ISBN 9781507210451 (pb) | ISBN 9781507210468 (ebook)
Subjects: LCSH: Ketogenic diet. | Reducing diets--Recipes. | Low-carbohydrate diet--Recipes. | BISAC: COOKING / Health & Healing / Low Carbohydrate. | COOKING / Methods / General. | COOKING / General. | LCGFT: Cookbooks.
Classification: LCC RM222.2 .B648247 2019 | DDC 641.5/6383--dc23
LC record available at https://lccn.loc.gov/2018058741

ISBN 978-1-5072-1045-1
ISBN 978-1-5072-1046-8 (ebook)

Contents

Acknowledgments

To JWM.
Thank you for changing my world.
I love you.

Introduction

THE KETO DIET IS a powerful weight loss and health tool that is known for its ability to help your body burn fat, improve your blood sugar, reduce cravings, and improve brain function. Because it centers around regulating your macronutrient intake to put your body into a state of fat-burning ketosis, it's important to make sure all your meals meet the required fat/protein/carbohydrate ratios, or your body will be forced out of ketosis. So what's the secret to staying on track? The answer is meal prep.

Meal prep—or planning out and cooking (or freezing) your meals in advance—is vital to your success on any diet, but it is especially important when you are following the keto diet. When you are following a keto lifestyle even one ill-prepared, high-carbohydrate meal can knock you off your path. But when you meal prep, you are guaranteed to always have a keto-friendly meal at your fingertips.

In addition to all its great benefits—like saving time, saving money, always having something healthy to eat on hand—meal prep has a lot of added value when you're on a keto diet. Instead of scrambling to put something together at the last minute after getting home from work, you'll have a meal ready to go. Instead of grabbing something while you're out and then whipping out your nutrition calculator to analyze your potential meal's macronutrient breakdown, you'll be able to just start eating, knowing that each meal is already perfectly balanced for you.

To help make your #ketolife even easier, this book provides three hundred easy-to-prepare recipes (most of which have six servings) that use basic ingredients you'll find in most well-stocked keto kitchens. Most of the recipes are also designed to freeze well. So, if you're cooking for one and/or you just want to double up on your meals to get ahead of the meal prep curve, you can store what you need in the refrigerator and then tuck the rest away in the freezer for convenient meals down the road.

There are also some suggestions on how to store and reheat your meals. A major component in making sure meal-prepped food tastes good past the first day is proper storage and taking the time to reheat your meals slowly in the oven or on the stove, instead of in the microwave. Of course, there will be times when you might not have access to a full kitchen, but just do the best you can. That's always the goal.

It may take a little while to adjust to it—both the meal prepping and your keto diet—but once you get the hang of it, the two together are a real powerhouse.

CHAPTER 1

Keto Basics

The ketogenic diet, affectionately nicknamed "keto" by its faithful followers, is a high-fat, low-carbohydrate, moderate-to low-protein dietary regimen that aims to change the way your body fuels itself. The ultimate goal of the ketogenic diet is to kick your body into ketosis—a metabolic state in which your body turns to fat for energy instead of carbohydrates (it's usual, preferred energy source).

What Is Ketosis and Why Do You Want It?

Carbohydrates are your body's favorite source of energy (or fuel). When you take in carbohydrates, they go through the entire digestive process and eventually get broken down into glucose, a simple sugar that travels into your bloodstream where it's picked up by insulin.

Once insulin attaches to glucose, one of two things happens. The insulin either carries glucose straight to your cells to use immediately for energy or your body converts the glucose to glycogen, which is then stored in your liver for your body to use as energy when it doesn't have easy access to glucose, like in between meals. As long as you're regularly eating a significant amount of carbohydrates, this cycle will continue. When your body is using carbohydrates as its main energy source, the fat you eat gets stored in your fat cells and stays there.

The goal of the ketogenic diet is to restrict carbohydrate intake enough that it interrupts this metabolic process and your body has to use something else—or more specifically, fats—for energy.

Carbohydrates are your body's primary energy source, but in their absence, your body will turn to fat—it's second preferred source—for the fuel it needs. To turn fat into energy that your body can actually use, the liver first breaks it down into fatty acids. From there, it converts these fatty acids into energy-rich substances called ketones. When you have ketones in your blood, you've entered ketosis. Entering ketosis means that your body is effectively burning fat for energy instead of carbohydrates.

FACT

One of the physiological benefits of using fat for energy instead of carbohydrates is that your body can only store a certain amount of carbohydrates, but its ability to store fat is endless. That means that if you rely on carbohydrates for energy, you'll eventually reach a point where that energy runs out because stored carbohydrates have also run out; but your body can keep an unlimited reserve of fat. That's also why it's so easy to gain weight. Your body will store fat forever.

The Health Benefits

A lot of people are drawn to the ketogenic diet because of the promise of quick weight loss; and while it's true that weight loss can be a major benefit of the dietary plan, that barely touches the surface. Most people following a ketogenic diet also experience:

- Increased energy
- Improved body composition (less fat and more muscle)
- Decreased inflammation
- Better brain function (improved concentration, less brain fog, better memory, and so on)

But aside from these fairly immediate and short-term benefits, the ketogenic diet has also been shown to:

- Lower blood sugar levels and improve insulin sensitivity
- Improve risk factors for heart disease (cholesterol levels, blood pressure, and blood sugar)
- Slow tumor growth for some cancers
- Reduce symptoms of Alzheimer's and slow disease progression
- Reduce frequency and severity of seizures in those with epilepsy

ALERT

The ketogenic diet was originally developed to help treat epilepsy in patients who weren't responding well to medication. The diet, which was introduced in the 1920s, was intended to mimic the effects of fasting. After seeing other health benefits people were experiencing when following the ketogenic diet, the diet exploded in popularity in mainstream culture.

The Macronutrient Breakdown

The exact percentage of each macronutrient you need to kick your body into ketosis is different from person to person but, in general, the macronutrient ratio for a ketogenic diet falls into the following ranges:

- 60–75 percent of calories from fat
- 15–30 percent of calories from protein
- 5–10 percent of calories from carbohydrates

Of course, this is just a basic guideline. You'll have to play around with these numbers a little bit to determine which macronutrient ratios are right for you, but once you've figured it out, you can design your meal plan.

Easing Into the Keto Diet

You often hear people say "just jump right into the deep end" or "rip the bandage off," and while this is good advice for some things, it's probably not the best approach when starting the keto diet, especially if you're used to eating a lot of carbohydrates. By easing into the diet, or slowly lowering your carbohydrate intake over a period of time, you'll give your body the time it needs to adjust and you're less likely to experience negative side effects or a collection of symptoms dubbed the "keto flu."

ESSENTIAL

You can reduce the severity of keto flu symptoms by gradually lowering your intake of carbohydrates over the course of a couple weeks instead of cutting them all out right away. Start by reducing the amount of sugar and sweet foods you eat. Then cut out grains and other high-carbohydrate sources, like potatoes and beans. Eventually, you can work your way into a full ketogenic diet.

When you restrict carbohydrates, your hormones and electrolytes go through changes as they work to become balanced. As these changes occur, you may experience some uncomfortable symptoms. The most commonly reported are fatigue, headaches, nausea, cramps, diarrhea, brain fog, and upset stomach. Because these effects are similar to the symptoms of the flu, this stage of adapting to ketosis is referred to as the "keto flu." The duration of symptoms varies from person to person, but usually, keto flu goes away in a week.

Common Mistakes and How to Avoid Them

The ketogenic diet does take some forethought and prep work since you have to be careful to stay within your macronutrient ratios. Sometimes this mental preparation can lead to mistakes or overthinking traps. Many people find themselves dealing with the same common obstacles, but if you can catch yourself before you run into them—and prepare yourself with ways to rectify them—you'll be more successful in the long run.

Ignoring Your Macros

The macronutrient ratios are the biggest factor of the ketogenic diet. Of course, there are ranges for these macronutrients and not everyone will need the same amount, but it's important to figure out what works for you and then to stick to that. If you're eating too many carbohydrates, you'll never reach ketosis, no matter how much fat you're consuming.

Spend some time calculating your macros, finding recipes that fit into your plan, organizing your meal plan, and prepping your recipes. It may seem like a lot of work in the beginning but putting in this prep time will save you a lot of time and frustration in the long run. You may have to adjust this number as your body changes and adapts, but eventually, you'll find your sweet spot.

Avoiding All Fruits and Vegetables

Fruits and vegetables can be a significant source of carbohydrates, so many people following a ketogenic diet avoid fruits altogether and severely limit vegetable intake. You can incorporate both low-sugar fruits and vegetables on a ketogenic diet—and you should!

Fruits and vegetables are some of the greatest sources of micronutrients— vitamins, minerals, antioxidants, and phytochemicals. When you limit them, you also limit the amount of essential nutrients that you're taking in. On any diet, it's important to maximize your nutrient intake, rather than restrict it.

Of course, there are multivitamin supplements available, but the synthetic nutrients in many of these supplements are not as bioavailable, meaning your body cannot absorb them as efficiently as it can absorb the nutrients that come directly from whole foods. Instead of avoiding fruits and vegetables, work them into your ketogenic diet strategically.

Stick to low-sugar fruits like raspberries, blackberries, and strawberries and limit high-sugar fruits like bananas, apples, and pineapple. Pay attention to your portion sizes as well and don't overdo it. If the fruit you're consuming isn't part of a recipe, measure out your servings as part of your meal prep and don't eat more than your carbohydrate allotment allows.

Limit starchy and high-carbohydrate vegetables, like potatoes (both white and sweet), carrots, pumpkin, and other squashes, and instead, fill up on lower carbohydrate vegetables, like spinach, kale, broccoli, cucumbers, zucchini, celery, and tomatoes.

Thinking One Size Fits All

Although there's a general guideline for the amount of carbohydrates, protein, and fat you should be eating, it's just that: a guideline. When starting a ketogenic diet, and as your body changes and adjusts to it, you'll probably have to play around with the numbers a little bit to find the perfect macronutrient fit for you. This is when it's important to listen to your body, rather than getting caught up in what a ketogenic diet is "supposed" to look like.

While there is an overall theme of carbohydrate restriction, nutrition can be very personalized; and what works really well for someone else may not be the best approach for you. For example, some people can achieve ketosis on 45 grams of carbohydrates per day, while others need to restrict their intake to around 20 grams.

Letting Stress Knock You Out of Ketosis

Stress throws several of your hormones out of whack and the imbalance of these hormones can make it more difficult to achieve—or stay in—ketosis. One of the ways stress makes ketosis harder is by increasing the amount of a hormone called cortisol, which triggers a process called gluconeogenesis. The literal translation of gluconeogenesis is "the making of new sugar" and that's exactly what happens during the process.

When cortisol triggers gluconeogenesis, it prompts your liver to turn other compounds, like amino acids, glycerol, and lactate into sugar that your body can use for energy. This process raises blood sugar levels and decreases your sensitivity to insulin—a combination that results in glucose staying in your blood for a longer period of time. And when there's too much glucose present in the blood, it shuts down the body's production of ketones, kicking you out of ketosis.

There are the obvious stressors in your life, like working too much, worrying about money or the future, and a hectic family life, but then there are not-so-obvious stressors too. Exercising too much or too intensely, not eating enough, and not getting enough sleep are all stressors that are often overlooked.

When following a keto diet, it's not just important to stay within your macronutrient ratios, it's also vital to get your stress levels under control. You can do this by:

- Making sure you're eating enough
- Alternating between high-intensity and low-intensity exercises
- Meditating and practicing yoga
- Reducing your workload and incorporating more fun/family time
- Getting enough quality sleep

Planning out your weekly menus and prepping your meals in advance is another way to significantly reduce stress when following a ketogenic diet, especially if you're new to it.

CHAPTER 2

Meal Prep 101

Meal prep can seem intimidating at first, especially if you're brand-new to the concept, but it's an essential component to any nutrition plan. In fact, it's almost as important as the actual food you're eating, especially when you're following a diet that requires you to keep track of your macronutrients, like keto. Although it may take some getting used to, practice makes perfect, so get familiar with some meal prep tips and shortcuts, figure out an organizational system that works for you, and dive right in.

Preparation Is Key

Meal prep isn't just some obscure concept that someone started throwing around for kicks. There's lots of scientific evidence to back up its validity. Research published in the *International Journal of Behavioral Nutrition and Physical Activity* linked meal planning to a healthier body weight, an overall better diet, and more food variety.

Other meal prep benefits are:

- It can help save money.
- It can help save time.
- It can reduce stress (fewer last-minute preparations or decisions about food).
- It can reduce or eliminate temptation (or giving in to temptation).
- It gives you total control over the ingredients in your food and the macronutrient breakdown.
- It helps manage hunger (instead of searching for food when you're hungry, you have something ready to go right away).
- It prevents overeating, since meals are pre-portioned and planned out.

Meal Prep Tips and Shortcuts

When venturing into the meal prep world for the first time, it's tempting to gather a list of fancy recipes and try to incorporate as much variety as possible, but resist this urge and, instead, keep it simple. The more you can get into a regular, simple routine, the better off you'll be and the more likely you'll stay consistent.

One of your major goals should be to compile a set of go-to keto recipes. Of course, this may take some time as you experiment with different recipes and find out which ones earn a spot in the rotation and which ones don't. But having a set of regular recipes that you really enjoy and that are quick and easy to prepare will make meal prep easier, especially when you don't feel like cooking or getting creative. If you're able to accumulate tried and true recipes, you can cycle through them each month and keep things interesting while also being consistent.

When the time comes to actually prepare your recipes, carve out some time to sit down and make a meal prep calendar and a grocery list. Go through the recipes and decide when you want to eat them. Then once your calendar is mapped out, figure out what ingredients you need. Make a grocery list that's divided into categories. Put all the produce items together on the list and make a separate column for canned goods or dairy products. Organizing your items this way in the beginning will make it easier to navigate through the grocery store, so that you don't waste time going back and forth between sections because you forgot an item.

FACT

When making your grocery list, don't forget to go through your pantry and refrigerator to cross-check for ingredients that you already have. The goal is to save money, so you don't want to buy too much extra and end up throwing anything out. You can also go through the ingredients you already have before planning your menu for the week and work your menu around the things you need to use up. For example, if you have ground turkey and roasted red peppers, find recipes that utilize both of those ingredients so they don't go to waste.

Once your grocery list is made, figure out when you're going to shop and when you're going to cook. Many people like to plan a whole day to get both the shopping and cooking done. This way you can shop and immediately use up your unloaded groceries, instead of putting them all away and then having to take them all back out later when you're cooking. Plan to spend at least a few hours in the kitchen on cooking days.

When the time comes to cook, try to multitask as much as possible. You don't have to go through one recipe from start to finish before moving on to the next one. Instead, get a few things going at once. For example, if you're simmering something on the stove, chop vegetables for the next recipe while you wait. If a recipe requires oven time, get to it first so you can spend time working on something else while it cooks. If you need a total of three chopped onions for all of your recipes, chop them all at once and then divide them up as you go.

ALERT

Storage and Reheating

Properly storing and reheating your food is just as important as cooking it well. When you're meal prepping, you want the food to last as long as possible in the refrigerator or the freezer and you also want it to taste good when the time comes to eat it. No one likes soggy leftovers!

The best way to store your food is in airtight stainless steel or glass containers. These containers are a little heavier and slightly costlier than plastic, but they're nontoxic and they last longer. They also don't absorb smells and colors like plastic does. You can purchase meal prep containers that have separate compartments inside so that you can separate your sides from your main dish, or separate dressings and sauces from the other food so that things stay fresh and crisp and don't get soggy. Glass Mason jars also make excellent meal prep containers, especially for soups and salads.

When you put the prepped items in their containers, label them with the date they were made and what meal they are. For example, write "Monday breakfast, prepared on July 15." This will help you keep track of when you need to use them by, and it will help save time since you won't have to open the containers to see what's inside them every time. Rotate stored food and make sure the older items are in the front and the newer prepped meals go in the back.

Although it might not always be possible, the oven and the stovetop are the best way to reheat food. The microwave will heat your food, but you're more likely to end up with mushy, unappealing vegetables and rubbery meats if you do it that way.

When reheating in the oven, use low temperatures around 300°F and let things come up to temperature slowly. If you need to add some crispiness back into your food, broil it for a few minutes after reheating. When reheating on the stovetop, use a little bit of coconut oil or grass-fed butter in a skillet or saucepan over low heat and allow your food to slowly heat up. If the microwave is your only option, turn the microwave down to 50 percent power and heat in intervals of one minute at a time, checking and stirring between each minute to see if the food is hot enough. It's easier to overcook food in the microwave and when you do, the food becomes less appealing, so keep an eye on it!

Food Quality

When meal prepping, the quality of your food is just as important as the macronutrient breakdown. You want to meal prep with the highest quality foods that your budget allows. This will ensure that your food stays fresh as long as possible and that you're not taking in any unnecessary food additives. More than 2,500 different chemicals are purposely added to foods to transform their color, flavor, texture, ability to withstand the elements (temperature changes, bugs and other predators), and cost. Another 12,000 are used in a way that they may be unintentionally added to foods. These chemicals may be used during food packaging or processing, to feed livestock, or during crop growth. The National Academy of Sciences reports that of these almost 15,000 chemicals, 90 percent of them have never been tested for safety. That's not to say that all of these chemicals are bad. Some may have no effect at all, but some may be harmful and cause chronic health problems. Unfortunately, there's no way to know without longitudinal scientific studies, which take a long time and can cost a lot of money.

When there's limited information on how a certain substance or chemical will affect you long-term, many health advocates follow what's called "the precautionary principle." Basically, the precautionary principle states that if you're unsure about the ultimate or long-term health effects of something or if the effects have been disputed or there's not enough information to make definitive statements about its safety, then you avoid it completely.

ESSENTIAL

The official wording of the precautionary principle from the 1998 Wingspread Statement is that "when an activity raises threats of harm to human health or the environment, precautionary measures should be taken even if some cause and effect relationships are not fully established scientifically."

The way to avoid unwanted chemicals and additives is to prioritize food quality and choose high-quality, humanely sourced meats and organic produce whenever possible.

Meat and Dairy

A large majority of the pesticides that humans consume—around 90 percent, according to the Environmental Protection Agency—come from meat, poultry, fish, eggs, and dairy products. Because low-carb diets tend to contain a decent amount of meat and dairy (if you're okay with dairy products), it is especially important to prioritize the food quality of these foods.

Look for beef that's organic and grass-fed. Purchase pork, chicken, and eggs that are organic and pasture raised. Choose dairy products that come from cows that are grass-fed. If you have a farm nearby, develop a relationship with your local farmer. Get to know the farm's practices for raising and butchering its animals, and if the farm is humane and sustainable, support your local farmer instead of big supermarket chains.

A2 Milk

Cow's milk has two major proteins—whey and casein—but the large majority, or about 80 percent, is casein. But not all casein is the same. Regular cow's milk contains different types of casein, called A1 beta-casein and A2 beta-casein. When you drink cow's milk (or eat anything made with cow's milk, like cheese, sour cream, or yogurt) the A1 beta-casein is broken down into a compound called beta-casomorphin-7, or BCM-7 for short.

BCM-7 has been associated with gastrointestinal inflammation, gas, bloating, and diarrhea after consuming dairy; eczema, acne, and cognitive impairment (or problems with thinking and memory). BCM-7 has also been linked to an increased risk of Type 1 diabetes in children, autoimmune diseases, and an increased risk of heart disease. A1 casein also forms casomorphins, which are addictive, opioid-like peptides that can cause negative behavioral symptoms, especially in those with ADHD and autism.

On the other hand, A2 casein has not been shown to cause any of these ill effects. The problem is that modern, commercially farmed cows have been bred to produce milk that contains higher amounts of A1 casein. So, what's a dairy-loving person to do?

The first solution is to find milk and milk products that come from A2 cows. These cows produce milk that contains only A2 casein and no A1 casein. Manufacturers are starting to listen to consumer demands and companies that offer only A2 milk products are starting to pop up.

The second solution is to switch to goat's milk products. Goat's milk naturally contains only A2 casein and is not inflammatory. It also contains high levels of medium-chain triglycerides, or MCTs, which are healthy fats that help improve brain function and metabolism, and vitamin A, which keeps your skin healthy.

If you can't find A2 milk products, always choose organic, grass-fed dairy products. They not only have a richer nutrient profile, they contain fewer pesticides and toxic residues—and they tend to taste better too.

Produce

When shopping for fruits and vegetables, buy organic whenever possible. If your budget doesn't allow for a diet that's 100 percent organic, prioritize purchasing organic varieties of what the Environmental Working Group calls the "Dirty Dozen Plus." The "Dirty Dozen Plus" is a list of fruits and vegetables that, when tested, have been shown to have the highest amounts of pesticide residue on them. These fruits and vegetables include:

- Strawberries
- Spinach

- Nectarines
- Apples
- Peaches
- Pears
- Cherries
- Grapes
- Celery
- Tomatoes
- Bell peppers
- Potatoes
- Hot peppers

Another budget-friendly tip is to purchase organic frozen produce over its fresh counterparts. Unlike fresh produce, bags of frozen produce often go on sale and you may even be able to find some coupons for them. Check your supermarket flyers and keep an eye out for the best prices. When you find a deal that's too good to pass up, buy several bags at a time and keep them stored away in your freezer. In addition to saving money up front, this will also eliminate waste because frozen produce keeps significantly longer than fresh produce.

Oils

When selecting oils, opt for cold-pressed, unrefined varieties, if possible. The fats in oil go rancid if exposed to too much heat, light, and air, so choose oils that come in dark glass bottles. This protects them from the elements and makes them last longer. Store your oils away from your stove in a cool, dark place; and always pay attention to the smoke point. Different oils should be used for different things. For example, avocado oil and butter are good for high-heat cooking, while olive oil is more suitable for low-heat cooking, and sesame and flaxseed oils are best added to a food after cooking and shouldn't be heated at all.

Figure Out Your Routine

While these tips, tricks, and shortcuts can provide a good baseline to start with, there's no right or wrong way to meal prep. It's a learning process that you can adjust to suit your lifestyle as you go. The point is to help simplify your life and your routine so that nutrition doesn't become a major source of frustration. If you're able to figure out something that helps you stick to your plan, while providing some or all of the major benefits of meal prep, then you can consider it a success.

CHAPTER 3

Breakfast

Banana Nut Muffins

The banana flavor in these muffins comes from real banana extract, which gives you all the flavor without any of the carbs. Toast the muffins and spread some butter-flavored coconut oil on them for some added decadence and an extra serving of fat.

INGREDIENTS | SERVES 5 (MAKES 10 MUFFINS)

1¼ cups almond flour

½ cup powdered erythritol

2 teaspoons baking powder

½ teaspoon ground cinnamon

¼ teaspoon ground nutmeg

5 tablespoons butter-flavored coconut oil, melted

2 teaspoons banana extract

1 teaspoon vanilla extract

¼ cup unsweetened almond milk

¼ cup whole plain Greek yogurt

2 large eggs

¾ cup chopped walnuts

Can I Use Real Banana?

Bananas are considered a high-carbohydrate fruit, but that doesn't mean they're expressly forbidden on a ketogenic diet; you just have to make sure you can fit them into your macronutrient allotment or eat them on higher carb days. A small banana contains 23 grams of carbohydrates, but 3 of those grams are from fiber and more come from starch, a slow-digesting carbohydrate. If you add a small banana to this recipe, it adds only 2 grams of carbohydrates per muffin.

1. Preheat oven to 350°F. Line a muffin tray with ten paper liners and set aside.

2. Combine almond flour, erythritol, baking powder, cinnamon, and nutmeg in a large bowl.

3. Stir in melted coconut oil, banana extract, vanilla extract, almond milk, and Greek yogurt. Mix until combined.

4. Fold in 1 egg at a time and mix until just incorporated. Fold in chopped walnuts.

5. Fill each of ten muffin tin wells with equal parts of the muffin batter.

6. Bake 20 minutes or until muffins start to brown and a toothpick inserted in the center comes out clean.

7. Allow to cool and then transfer two muffins to each of five sealable sandwich bags or airtight containers. Store at room temperature until ready to eat, up to one week.

PER SERVING Calories: 269 | Fat: 14 g | Protein: 9 g | Sodium: 230 mg | Fiber: 2 g | Carbohydrates: 9 g | Sugar: 1 g | Net Carbohydrates: 7 g

Breakfast BLT

It may seem strange to have salad for breakfast, but starting your day with a bunch of veggies makes it easier for you to meet your micronutrient (vitamin and mineral) needs for the day.

INGREDIENTS | SERVES 4

2 teaspoons apple cider vinegar
2 tablespoons olive oil
¼ teaspoon salt
⅛ teaspoon freshly ground black pepper
8 large hard-boiled eggs, chopped
4 slices no-sugar-added bacon, cooked and roughly chopped
1 cup halved grape tomatoes
4 cups baby kale

1. Whisk vinegar, olive oil, salt, and black pepper together in a mixing bowl. Transfer mixture to four Mason jars.

2. In each Mason jar, layer ¼ chopped eggs, ¼ chopped bacon, ¼ cup tomatoes, and 1 cup baby kale (in that order) on top of dressing.

3. Cover Mason jar with lid and store in the refrigerator until ready to eat, up to four days.

4. When ready to eat, shake Mason jar vigorously until ingredients are thoroughly combined.

PER SERVING Calories: 336 | Fat: 27 g | Protein: 17 g | Sodium: 481 mg | Fiber: 1 g | Carbohydrates: 4 g | Sugar: 2 g | Net Carbohydrates: 3 g

Broccoli Cheese Muffins

These muffins are divine warm and toasty. For extra satisfaction (and extra fat), cut them in half, toast them for a few minutes, and spread some ghee or butter-flavored coconut oil on top before devouring them.

INGREDIENTS | SERVES 6 (MAKES 6 MUFFINS)

2 teaspoons ghee
1 cup chopped broccoli florets
2 cups almond flour
2 large eggs
1 cup unsweetened full-fat coconut milk
¼ cup shredded Cheddar cheese
1 teaspoon baking powder
½ teaspoon sea salt

1. Preheat oven to 350°F. Line six wells of a muffin tin with cupcake liners or parchment paper.

2. Combine all ingredients in a mixing bowl and stir well.

3. Scoop the mixture evenly into each prepared well.

4. Bake 30 minutes or until a toothpick inserted into the center of the muffin comes out clean.

5. Allow to cool, then transfer to an airtight container. Store at room temperature until ready to eat, up to one week.

PER SERVING Calories: 290 | Fat: 13 g | Protein: 9 g | Sodium: 344 mg | Fiber: 2 g | Carbohydrates: 8 g | Sugar: 0 g | Net Carbohydrates: 6 g

Beef and Egg Skillet

The sunflower seed butter in this recipe may seem out of place, but don't omit it!
It gives the skillet a creamy rich texture and some added nutty flavor.

INGREDIENTS | SERVES 6

2 tablespoons butter-flavored coconut oil

½ medium yellow onion, peeled and diced

2 cloves garlic, minced

1 pound 85/15 ground beef

2 teaspoons sea salt, divided

1 teaspoon freshly ground black pepper, divided

1 teaspoon onion powder

1 small head cauliflower, grated

½ cup avocado oil mayonnaise

½ cup water

¼ cup sunflower seed butter

1 tablespoon coconut aminos

1 teaspoon ground cumin

6 large eggs

1 jalapeño pepper, seeded and minced (optional)

Making Your Mayonnaise

Several companies have responded to the rise in popularity of keto and Paleo-style diets by making mayonnaise with only high-quality ingredients. You can find keto-approved avocado oil mayonnaise from Primal Kitchen in many grocery stores and online specialty stores. If you prefer, you can also make your own. Make sure to use avocado oil or extra-light olive oil. Extra virgin olive oil has a distinct taste that can be off-putting when incorporated into some recipes.

1. Melt coconut oil in an oven-safe skillet over medium-high heat. Add onion and garlic and cook until fragrant and softened, about 3 minutes.

2. Add ground beef, 1 teaspoon salt, ½ teaspoon ground pepper, and onion powder and cook until beef is no longer pink, about 7 minutes.

3. Reduce heat to medium-low and add grated cauliflower. Stir and cook until cauliflower starts to soften, about 3 minutes.

4. While cauliflower is softening, whisk together mayonnaise, water, sunflower seed butter, coconut aminos, and cumin.

5. Pour mayonnaise mixture over beef and stir until fully incorporated. Cook until liquid has been reduced, about 4 minutes.

6. Spread mixture out in an even layer and make six wells. Crack an egg into each well and sprinkle with remaining salt, pepper, and jalapeño if using.

7. Turn oven on broil and place skillet under broiler until eggs are cooked, about 7 minutes. Remove from oven, break yolks on each egg, and allow to ooze out over skillet.

8. Allow to cool and then divide into six equal portions. Transfer each portion to an airtight container and store in the refrigerator until ready to eat, up to four days.

PER SERVING Calories: 442 | Fat: 34 g | Protein: 24 g | Sodium: 932 mg | Fiber: 3 g | Carbohydrates: 9 g | Sugar: 3 g | Net Carbohydrates: 6 g

Baked Eggs

When it comes to meal prep, easiest is best. These eggs are cooked on a baking pan, so you can cook a whole dozen at once and preparation and cleanup are a breeze.

INGREDIENTS | SERVES 6

12 large eggs
1 teaspoon sea salt
½ teaspoon freshly ground black pepper
¼ cup diced red bell peppers
¼ cup diced green bell peppers
¼ cup chopped fresh chives

Eat the Yolks

Egg yolks were blacklisted for a long time, but in the past few years, science has shown that they can be an essential part of a healthy diet. Egg yolks are rich in fat-soluble vitamins, essential fatty acids, and choline, which keeps your metabolism running efficiently.

1. Preheat oven to 350°F. Grease a 12" × 17" rimmed baking sheet with butter-flavored coconut oil.

2. Crack eggs into a large bowl and add salt and pepper. Whisk until frothy. Add remaining ingredients and whisk until combined.

3. Pour egg mixture into prepared pan and bake until eggs are set, about 15 minutes.

4. Remove from oven and allow to cool. Cut into six equal-sized squares and transfer each square to an airtight container. Store in the refrigerator, up to one week.

PER SERVING Calories: 151 | Fat: 9 g | Protein: 13 g | Sodium: 530 mg | Fiber: 1 g | Carbohydrates: 2 g | Sugar: 1 g | Net Carbohydrates: 1 g

Zucchini Hash

When you're ready to eat this Zucchini Hash, top it with a fried egg and half an avocado for a complete, satisfying meal.

INGREDIENTS | SERVES 4

4 slices no-sugar-added bacon, roughly chopped
1 tablespoon butter-flavored coconut oil
½ small white onion, peeled and diced
2 cloves garlic, minced
2 large zucchini, shredded
1 tablespoon chopped fresh chives
½ teaspoon sea salt

1. Add bacon to a medium skillet and cook over medium-high heat until almost crispy, about 5 minutes. Add coconut oil.

2. Once coconut oil is melted, add onion and garlic and cook until fragrant and softened, about 4 minutes.

3. Add zucchini and cook until softened, about 5 minutes. Remove from heat and stir in chives and sea salt.

4. Allow to cool and transfer equal portions to four airtight containers. Store in the refrigerator, up to four days.

PER SERVING Calories: 181 | Fat: 15 g | Protein: 6 g | Sodium: 489 mg | Fiber: 2 g | Carbohydrates: 7 g | Sugar: 5 g | Net Carbohydrates: 5 g

Paleo Porridge

This Paleo Porridge will thicken as it sits in the fridge. If you want to thin it out before eating, add a little more almond milk or water after heating.

INGREDIENTS | SERVES 4

2 cups water

1 cup unsweetened almond milk

¼ cup full-fat coconut milk

½ cup coconut flour

½ cup golden flaxseed meal

4 large eggs, beaten

½ cup ghee or butter-flavored coconut oil

¼ cup powdered erythritol

Grind As You Go

Your body can't absorb the nutrients from whole flaxseed; it must be ground first. However, ground flaxseed goes rancid faster than whole and loses its nutritional value as it sits. It's best to buy whole flaxseed, store in a cool, dark, dry place, and grind it as you need it.

1. Combine water, almond milk, and coconut milk in a medium saucepan over medium heat. When mixture starts to simmer, stir in coconut flour and flaxseed meal. Turn heat down to low and allow to simmer until mixture starts to thicken, about 4 minutes.

2. Remove from heat and slowly stir in beaten eggs until fully incorporated.

3. Stir in remaining ingredients and whisk until mixture thickens, about 30 seconds.

4. Divide into four equal-sized portions and transfer each portion to a separate airtight container. Store in the refrigerator until ready to eat, up to four days.

PER SERVING Calories: 453 | Fat: 42 g | Protein: 13 g | Sodium: 98 mg | Fiber: 13 g | Carbohydrates: 16 g | Sugar: 0 g | Net Carbohydrates: 3 g

Cheesy Cauliflower Grits

To make this a complete savory meal, top with a fried egg and crumbled bacon. If you want an oatmeal-like breakfast, stir in a small handful of wild blueberries and a keto-friendly sweetener of your choice.

INGREDIENTS | SERVES 4

2 teaspoons coconut oil
6 cups riced cauliflower
¼ cup chicken bone broth
½ cup shredded sharp Cheddar cheese
2 tablespoons heavy cream
1 teaspoon sea salt
½ teaspoon freshly ground black pepper

1. Heat coconut oil in a medium skillet over medium heat. Add riced cauliflower and cook until it starts to soften, about 5 minutes.

2. Stir in chicken bone broth and cover. Cook another 5 minutes.

3. Use an immersion blender to purée cooked cauliflower until it reaches a creamy consistency. Remove from heat and stir in remaining ingredients until combined.

4. Allow to cool and transfer equal portions to four separate airtight containers. Store in the refrigerator until ready to eat, up to four days.

PER SERVING Calories: 154 | Fat: 11 g | Protein: 7 g | Sodium: 794 mg | Fiber: 3 g | Carbohydrates: 8.5 g | Sugar: 3 g | Net Carbohydrates: 5.5 g

Sage Breakfast Sausage

Most ready-to-eat breakfast sausage that you find in the store has added sugar that makes it unacceptable for a keto diet. This version has all the flavor of the big-name brands, but with only whole, unprocessed ingredients.

INGREDIENTS | SERVES 4

1 teaspoon fennel seed
½ teaspoon garlic powder
½ teaspoon freshly ground black pepper
1 teaspoon dried sage
¾ teaspoon sea salt
¼ teaspoon onion powder
¼ teaspoon coriander
1 pound ground pork
2 tablespoons coconut oil

1. Combine all spices in a small bowl.

2. Place the pork into a medium bowl and add spice mixture to pork and mix to thoroughly combine.

3. Divide pork into eight equal-sized portions and shape into sausage patties.

4. Heat coconut oil in a medium skillet over medium heat. Add prepared patties to the pan and cook 4 minutes. Flip each patty over and continue to cook until no longer pink in the middle, about 3 more minutes.

5. Remove from heat and allow to cool. Transfer two patties to each of four airtight containers.

6. Store in the refrigerator up to one week or the freezer up to three months.

PER SERVING Calories: 359 | Fat: 30 g | Protein: 19 g | Sodium: 499 mg | Fiber: 0.5 g | Carbohydrates: 1 g | Sugar: 0 g | Net Carbohydrates: 0.5 g

Bacon Cauliflower Hash

This Bacon Cauliflower Hash pairs perfectly with fried or scrambled eggs. For even easier meal prep, hard-boil some eggs and take it all with you on the go.

INGREDIENTS | SERVES 4

6 slices no-sugar-added bacon

2 cloves garlic, minced

1 medium yellow onion, peeled and diced

1 large head cauliflower, chopped into small florets

½ teaspoon paprika

1 teaspoon sea salt

½ teaspoon freshly ground black pepper

3 tablespoons chicken bone broth

1 tablespoon chopped fresh parsley

Tracking Down Bacon

Most bacon has sugar in some form added to it. It may be brown sugar, maple syrup, or honey—all of which are out on a keto diet. If you can't find no-sugar-added bacon at your local supermarket, you can often request it be specially made from your local meat farmer or butcher shop.

1. Cook bacon in a large skillet over medium-high heat until crispy, about 4 minutes each side. Remove bacon from pan and set on a paper towel–lined plate. Leave bacon fat in skillet and reduce heat to medium.

2. Add garlic and onion and cook until slightly softened, about 4 minutes. Add cauliflower and continue cooking 3 minutes. Add paprika, salt, and pepper and stir to combine.

3. Pour in bone broth, reduce heat to low, and cover. Cook 5 minutes, covered, until cauliflower is softened.

4. While cauliflower is cooking, roughly chop cooked bacon. Remove skillet from heat and stir in chopped bacon. Sprinkle parsley on top.

5. Divide into four equal-sized portions and transfer each portion to an airtight container. Store in the refrigerator until ready to eat, up to four days.

PER SERVING Calories: 246 | Fat: 18 g | Protein: 10 g | Sodium: 905 mg | Fiber: 3.5 g | Carbohydrates: 11 g | Sugar: 4 g | Net Carbohydrates: 7.5 g

Bacon Cheddar Muffins

These savory muffins are a nice break from eggs and sweet muffins. You can double the batch and store them in the freezer up to two months for easier meal prep down the road.

INGREDIENTS | SERVES 6 (MAKES 12 MUFFINS)

2½ cups almond flour

¼ teaspoon baking powder

½ teaspoon baking soda

¼ teaspoon sea salt

¼ cup unsalted grass-fed butter, melted

¾ cup heavy cream

1 large egg

4 slices no-sugar-added bacon, cooked and roughly chopped

⅓ cup shredded sharp Cheddar cheese

¼ cup chopped fresh chives

1. Preheat oven to 375°F. Line a muffin pan with paper cupcake liners. Set aside.

2. Combine almond flour, baking powder, baking soda, and salt in a bowl and mix well.

3. In a separate bowl, whisk butter, heavy cream, and egg together. Add bacon, cheese, and chives and continue to whisk until combined. Fold in almond flour mixture.

4. Scoop mixture into prepared muffin tin and bake until toothpick inserted in center comes out clean, about 15 minutes.

5. Allow to cool and transfer two muffins to each of six airtight containers. Store in the refrigerator until ready to eat, up to five days.

PER SERVING Calories: 486 | Fat: 30 g | Protein: 12 g | Sodium: 418 mg | Fiber: 3.5 g | Carbohydrates: 8 g | Sugar: 1.5 g | Net Carbohydrates: 4.5 g

Double Chocolate Muffins

Spread some grass-fed butter or ghee on these Double Chocolate Muffins and they're perfectly macro-balanced to start your day. Even though they're a suitable breakfast, they're so delicious, they double as the perfect dessert too.

INGREDIENTS | SERVES 6 (MAKES 12 MUFFINS)

2 cups almond flour

¾ cup unsweetened raw cacao powder

1½ teaspoons baking powder

¼ cup powdered erythritol

1 cup unsalted grass-fed butter, melted

3 large eggs

1½ teaspoons vanilla extract

1 cup stevia-sweetened chocolate chips

Stocking Up on Specialized Ingredients

Stevia-sweetened chocolate chips are a somewhat specialized ingredient that are regularly available for sale on Vitacost.com. Keep your pantry keto-ready by buying a few packages at a time when they're on sale and storing them away until you're ready to use them. That way, you'll always have the ingredients you need that aren't as easily accessible at the grocery store.

1. Preheat oven to 350°F. Line a muffin pan with paper liners and set aside.

2. Combine almond flour, cacao powder, baking powder, and erythritol into a bowl and stir until mixed well. Add remaining ingredients, except chocolate chips, and combine.

3. Fold in chocolate chips and mix until incorporated. Scoop equal parts of batter into each prepared muffin well.

4. Bake 11 minutes, or until toothpick inserted in center comes out clean.

5. Remove muffins from pan and allow to cool. Transfer two muffins to six separate sealable bags. Store at room temperature until ready to eat, up to one week.

PER SERVING Calories: 483 | Fat: 39 g | Protein: 10 g | Sodium: 165 mg | Fiber: 6.5 g | Carbohydrates: 12 g | Sugar: 5 g | Net Carbohydrates: 5.5 g

Southwest Egg and Cheese Muffins

These Southwest muffins have the perfect amount of kick to get those taste buds going. If you want to make them a little milder, use Cheddar in place of pepper jack cheese. If you want to spice them up even more, add some jalapeños.

INGREDIENTS | SERVES 6 (MAKES 12 MUFFINS)

12 large eggs

½ cup unsweetened full-fat coconut milk

1 (4-ounce) can chopped green chili peppers

1 cup shredded pepper jack cheese

½ teaspoon smoked paprika

1 teaspoon salt

½ cup salsa

1. Preheat oven to 350°F. Line a muffin tin with paper liners. Set aside.

2. Combine eggs and coconut milk in a bowl and whisk until frothy. Whisk in remaining ingredients, except salsa.

3. Pour equal amounts of egg mixture into each prepared muffin tin. Bake 20 minutes. Scoop equal amounts of salsa on top of each egg cup and return to oven for 5 minutes or until eggs are set.

4. Allow to cool slightly. Remove from muffin pan and transfer two muffins to each of six separate airtight containers. Store in the refrigerator until ready to eat, up to one week.

PER SERVING Calories: 284 | Fat: 21 g | Protein: 18 g | Sodium: 844 mg | Fiber: 1 g | Carbohydrates: 5 g | Sugar: 2 g | Net Carbohydrates: 4 g

Bacon and Egg Cups

You can make these Bacon and Egg Cups your own (and more micronutrient-rich) by adding whatever low-carb veggies you want (or have on hand).

INGREDIENTS | SERVES 6 (MAKES 12 EGG CUPS)

12 slices no-sugar-added bacon, cooked and roughly chopped

12 large eggs

¼ cup chopped scallions

1 teaspoon sea salt

½ teaspoon freshly ground black pepper

Easy Salad Toppings

Eggs cups are ideal for quickly adding some protein (and vitamins) to any of the Mason jar salads. If you want to add them to your salads, just chop them up after they cool and layer them in the bottom of your Mason jar before layering in the rest of the ingredients.

1. Preheat oven to 350°F.

2. Grease a muffin tin with coconut oil.

3. Whisk together all ingredients in a large bowl. And pour equal parts of mixture into each muffin well.

4. Bake 25 minutes or until eggs are set.

5. Remove from oven and allow to cool. Transfer two Bacon and Egg Cups to each of six airtight containers and store in the refrigerator until ready to eat, up to one week.

PER SERVING Calories: 378 | Fat: 31 g | Protein: 19 g | Sodium: 900 mg | Fiber: 0 g | Carbohydrates: 2 g | Sugar: 1 g | Net Carbohydrates: 2 g

Ham and Cheese Hash Brown Casserole

If you can't find ham without added sugar, you can swap it for no-sugar-added bacon or just omit the meat completely. This casserole will hit the spot either way!

INGREDIENTS | SERVES 4

2 tablespoons butter-flavored coconut oil

6 cups riced cauliflower

½ cup diced green bell pepper

1 cup no-sugar-added diced ham

½ cup shredded pepper jack cheese

1 teaspoon sea salt

½ teaspoon freshly ground black pepper

1. Heat coconut oil in a large skillet over medium heat. When oil is hot, add cauliflower and green pepper. Mix and then allow to sit in oil without stirring for 5 minutes or until it starts to brown. Flip mixture over and cook 5 more minutes, or until cauliflower is golden brown.

2. Add ham, cheese, salt, and pepper and stir until cheese is melted.

3. Remove from heat and allow to cool slightly.

4. Divide into four equal portions and transfer each portion to an airtight container. Store in the refrigerator until ready to eat, up to one week.

PER SERVING Calories: 227 | Fat: 15 g | Protein: 13 g | Sodium: 1,183 mg | Fiber: 3.5 g | Carbohydrates: 10 g | Sugar: 3.5 g | Net Carbohydrates: 7.5 g

Oven Scrambled Eggs

These Oven Scrambled Eggs are ideal when you're meal prepping and using all the burners on your stove. Just put them in the oven and 20 minutes later, you have a whole tray of scrambled eggs ready to divide into your containers.

INGREDIENTS | SERVES 6

¼ cup grass-fed butter, melted
12 large eggs
1 teaspoon salt
1 cup heavy cream

1. Preheat oven to 350°F.

2. Pour melted butter into a 9" × 13" baking pan.

3. Whisk eggs, salt, and cream together in a large bowl until frothy.

4. Pour egg mixture into baking dish and bake uncovered for 10 minutes. Stir and return to oven. Bake 10 more minutes or until eggs are set.

5. Divide into six equal portions and transfer each portion to an airtight container. Store in the refrigerator until ready to eat, up to one week.

PER SERVING Calories: 348 | Fat: 31 g | Protein: 13 g | Sodium: 545 mg | Fiber: 0 g | Carbohydrates: 2 g | Sugar: 1 g | Net Carbohydrates: 2 g

Crustless Spinach Quiche

This recipe is written for six servings, but it's easy to double it if you need to stretch it a little further. Just double the ingredients and use a bigger pan and freeze whatever you're saving for later.

INGREDIENTS | SERVES 6

1 tablespoon avocado oil, plus extra for greasing

1 large yellow onion, peeled and diced

1 (10-ounce) package frozen chopped spinach, thawed and drained

6 large eggs, beaten

2½ cups shredded Muenster cheese

¼ teaspoon sea salt

¼ teaspoon garlic salt

¼ teaspoon freshly ground black pepper

⅛ teaspoon ground nutmeg

Paying Attention to Smoke Point

Olive oil is often the go-to cooking oil, but it's not appropriate for high heat. Olive oil has a smoke point (the point at which it goes from simmering to burning) of 325°F, making it appropriate for low to medium heat cooking; while avocado oil has a smoke point of 400°F, making it the better choice for high heat.

1. Preheat oven to 350°F. Grease a 9" pie pan with avocado oil. Set aside.

2. Heat 1 tablespoon avocado oil in a medium skillet over medium-high heat. Add onions and cook until onions soften, about 5 minutes Stir in spinach and cook 5 more minutes, until excess moisture evaporates. Remove from heat.

3. Combine eggs, cheese, and spices in a medium bowl and whisk until frothy. Add spinach mixture to eggs and stir to combine.

4. Pour into prepared pie plate and bake 30 minutes, or until eggs have set.

5. Remove from oven and allow to cool slightly. Cut into six equal portions and transfer each portion to an airtight container.

6. Store in the refrigerator until ready to eat, up to one week.

PER SERVING Calories: 336 | Fat: 25 g | Protein: 21 g | Sodium: 656 mg | Fiber: 2 g | Carbohydrates: 5 g | Sugar: 1.5 g | Net Carbohydrates: 3 g

Turnip Hash

When you try this Turnip Hash, you won't even miss potatoes. These root vegetables have a similar texture and taste to white potatoes, but with a lot fewer carbs, and the accompanying herbs bring out a delicious, earthy flavor that pairs well with eggs.

INGREDIENTS | SERVES 4

2 tablespoons butter-flavored coconut oil

1 small red onion, peeled and diced

2 cloves garlic, minced

2 teaspoons dried tarragon

2 teaspoons dried dill

½ teaspoon sea salt

¼ teaspoon freshly ground black pepper

3 large turnips, peeled and diced

½ cup vegetable broth

Turn Up with Turnips

Turnips are low-carb root vegetables that have a taste similar to that of white potatoes. As a general rule, the smaller the turnip, the sweeter the flavor, while the larger the turnip, the woodier the flavor. If you want a sweeter taste when using turnips, replace one large turnip in a recipe with two small ones.

1. Heat coconut oil in a medium skillet over medium heat. When oil is hot, add onion and garlic and cook until softened, about 4 minutes.

2. Add tarragon, dill, salt, and pepper to the onions and garlic and cook 1 more minute. Add turnips and cook until they start to soften, about 4 minutes.

3. Pour vegetable broth over turnips and reduce heat to low. Cover skillet and allow to cook until turnips are softened, about 8 minutes.

4. Remove cover from pan and cook 5 more minutes, allowing some of the liquid to evaporate and the turnips to brown.

5. Remove from heat and allow to cool slightly. Divide into four equal portions and transfer each portion to a separate airtight container.

6. Store in the refrigerator until ready to eat, up to one week.

PER SERVING Calories: 109 | Fat: 7 g | Protein: 2 g | Sodium: 384 mg | Fiber: 3 g | Carbohydrates: 11 g | Sugar: 6 g | Net Carbohydrates: 8 g

Spinach Squares

This recipe uses spinach because of its mild flavor, but you can replace it with any of your favorite low-carb greens. Kale, Swiss chard, and beet greens work well, too, but have a more distinctive flavor.

INGREDIENTS | SERVES 6

1 (10-ounce) package frozen chopped spinach, thawed and drained
½ cup water
½ cup Paleo flour
½ teaspoon salt
½ teaspoon baking powder
1 large egg
½ cup full-fat coconut milk
¼ cup grass-fed butter, melted
1 small yellow onion, peeled and diced
1 cup shredded mozzarella cheese

1. Preheat oven to 375°F. Grease a 9" × 9" baking dish and set aside.

2. Place spinach in a medium saucepan and add water. Bring to a boil over high heat and then reduce heat to low. Allow spinach to simmer 4 minutes. Remove from heat and drain.

3. Combine flour, salt, and baking powder in a mixing bowl. Add egg, milk, and butter and whisk to mix well.

4. Add spinach, onion, and mozzarella and whisk until combined.

5. Pour mixture into baking dish and bake 30 minutes or until set.

6. Cut into six equal-sized squares and transfer each square to an airtight container. Store in the refrigerator until ready to eat, up to one week.

PER SERVING Calories: 209 | Fat: 18 g | Protein: 8 g | Sodium: 533 mg | Fiber: 7 g | Carbohydrates: 10 g | Sugar: 1 g | Net Carbohydrates: 3 g

Keto Bread

Bread is one of the most commonly missed items on the keto diet, but you can satisfy that bread craving with this low-carbohydrate version. Eat it toasted with butter, use it to make sandwiches, or dip it in your soup.

INGREDIENTS | SERVES 6

6 large eggs

1½ cups extra-fine blanched almond flour

½ teaspoon fine sea salt

2 teaspoons baking powder

¼ cup grass-fed butter, melted

⅛ teaspoon cream of tartar

Stabilizing Egg Whites

Cream of tartar acts as a stabilizer in recipes that call for whipped egg whites. It helps cakes, breads, and soufflés hold their shape. If you're in a pinch and you don't have any cream of tartar handy, you can substitute fresh lemon juice or white vinegar in its place. Replace every ½ teaspoon cream of tartar with 1 teaspoon lemon juice or white vinegar.

1. Preheat oven to 375°F. Grease a 9" × 5" loaf pan and set aside.

2. Separate egg yolks from egg whites, placing egg yolks in one medium bowl and egg whites in another.

3. Combine almond flour, salt, egg yolks, baking powder, and butter in a food processor. Pulse until mixture starts to form a dough, scraping down sides of food processor when necessary.

4. Add cream of tartar to egg whites and whisk until soft peaks form.

5. Add ⅓ of the egg whites to the food processor and pulse until combined. Pour mixture into the remaining egg whites and fold until combined.

6. Pour mixture into prepared loaf pan and bake 30 minutes or until a toothpick inserted in the center comes out clean.

7. Allow to cool 15 minutes and then remove from loaf pan. Transfer to a wire rack and allow to cool completely.

8. Slice bread into twelve slices and store two slices in each of six sealable bags. Store at room temperature until ready to eat, up to one week, or freeze for later use, up to three months.

PER SERVING Calories: 254 | Fat: 12 g | Protein: 9 g | Sodium: 325 mg | Fiber: 1 g | Carbohydrates: 5 g | Sugar: 0 g | Net Carbohydrates: 4 g

CHAPTER 4

Poultry

Feta Cheese Turkey Burgers

You can make these burgers right on the stovetop, but if you prefer, heat up the grill and cook them that way. Serve with a side of Greek Spinach or Spanakorizo (see recipes in Chapter 10) for a completely satisfying low-carb, micronutrient-rich meal.

INGREDIENTS | SERVES 6

1½ pounds ground turkey

1½ cups crumbled feta cheese

1 clove garlic, minced

¼ cup chicken bone broth

½ cup Kalamata olives, pitted and minced

2 teaspoons Greek seasoning

½ teaspoon freshly ground black pepper

2 tablespoons avocado oil

1. Combine all ingredients, except oil, in a medium bowl. Use your hands to mix until incorporated. Form into six patties.

2. Heat oil in a medium skillet over medium heat. Transfer patties to hot pan and cook 5 minutes on each side, or until turkey is cooked through.

3. Remove from heat and allow to cool slightly. Transfer each burger to a separate airtight container and store in the refrigerator until ready to eat, up to one week.

PER SERVING Calories: 318 | Fat: 21 g | Protein: 27 g | Sodium: 412 mg | Fiber: 0 g | Carbohydrates: 5 g | Sugar: 1 g | Net Carbohydrates: 5 g

Curry Chicken Salad

If you want to whip this Curry Chicken Salad up even faster, use canned chicken breast instead of cooking your own.

INGREDIENTS | SERVES 6

1½ pounds boneless, skinless chicken breasts, cooked and diced

2 medium stalks celery, finely chopped

½ medium white onion, peeled and minced

½ cup toasted walnuts

¼ teaspoon freshly ground black pepper

½ teaspoon curry powder

¾ cup coconut oil mayonnaise

1. Combine all ingredients in a medium bowl and stir until evenly incorporated.

2. Divide into six equal portions and transfer each portion to a separate airtight container. Store in the refrigerator until ready to eat, up to one week.

PER SERVING Calories: 206 | Fat: 9 g | Protein: 26 g | Sodium: 68 mg | Fiber: 1 g | Carbohydrates: 3 g | Sugar: 1 g | Net Carbohydrates: 2 g

Rolled Pesto Chicken

This Rolled Pesto Chicken calls for basic basil pesto and provolone cheese, but you can add some variety to your meal prep rotation by switching up the ingredients. Use some spinach in place of the basil or spice it up with some pepper jack cheese instead of provolone.

INGREDIENTS | SERVES 6

2 cups fresh basil

3 cloves garlic

1 tablespoon pine nuts

¼ cup whole milk ricotta cheese

¼ cup grated Parmesan cheese

2½ tablespoons olive oil

½ teaspoon sea salt

¼ teaspoon freshly ground black pepper

6 (4-ounce) boneless, skinless chicken breasts

6 slices provolone cheese

1. Preheat oven to 350°F.

2. Combine basil, garlic, and pine nuts in a food processor and process until chopped. Add ricotta cheese and process until incorporated. Add Parmesan cheese, olive oil, salt, and pepper and process until smooth.

3. Butterfly each chicken breast and pound to ¼" thickness.

4. Spread 3 tablespoons of prepared pesto onto each flattened chicken breast and place 1 slice of cheese on top of pesto.

5. Roll chicken breast tightly and secure in place with toothpicks. Transfer each chicken breast to a 9" × 13" baking dish.

6. Bake 45 minutes or until chicken is cooked through. Allow to cool and transfer each chicken breast to a separate airtight container. Store in the refrigerator until ready to eat, up to one week.

PER SERVING Calories: 338 | Fat: 20 g | Protein: 35 g | Sodium: 575 mg | Fiber: 0.5 g | Carbohydrates: 3 g | Sugar: 0 g | Net Carbohydrates: 3 g

Chicken Divan Casserole

This creamy chicken casserole is the ultimate comfort food, but unlike other recipes of its kind, it doesn't use any canned cream soups—only fresh, whole foods without any of the artificial ingredients!

INGREDIENTS | SERVES 6

3 tablespoons grass-fed butter

1 small yellow onion, peeled and diced

2 teaspoons minced garlic

½ teaspoon garlic salt

¼ teaspoon dried parsley

¼ teaspoon sea salt

¼ teaspoon freshly ground black pepper

2 cups cauliflower rice

1 cup chicken bone broth

1 cup heavy cream

1 teaspoon lemon juice

½ cup mayonnaise

1½ pounds boneless, skinless chicken breasts, cooked and shredded

4 cups broccoli florets, steamed and chopped

1 cup shredded Cheddar cheese

1 cup shredded mozzarella cheese

Freezer Meals

Casseroles are a meal prep favorite for several reasons. They're easy to put together, they make a lot of servings, and you can freeze them and cook them later. Stock your freezer by preparing two casseroles at a time, cooking one, and freezing one. When you're ready to cook it, you can put it in the oven right out of the freezer; just increase the cooking time. If you do this every time you make a casserole, you'll build up a freezer full of meals you'll have ready to go when you don't have time to spend cooking.

1. Preheat oven to 350°F.

2. Melt butter in a medium saucepan over medium heat. Add onion and garlic and cook until softened, about 6 minutes. Stir in garlic salt, parsley, sea salt, and pepper.

3. Add cauliflower rice and chicken bone broth and cook until most of the broth has been absorbed into the cauliflower, about 10 minutes.

4. Stir in heavy cream and lemon juice and reduce heat to low. Simmer 10 minutes. Remove from heat and stir in mayonnaise.

5. Spread cooked chicken in the bottom of a 9" × 13" pan and pour half of the sauce on top. Stir to combine and then spread out again. Layer chopped broccoli on top and pour remaining sauce over broccoli.

6. Sprinkle cheeses on top. Cover and bake 30 minutes. Remove cover and bake 10 more minutes or until cheese starts to brown on edges.

7. Allow to cool and then cut into six equal portions. Transfer each portion to a separate airtight container and store in the refrigerator until ready to eat, up to one week.

PER SERVING Calories: 642 | Fat: 50 g | Protein: 38 g | Sodium: 816 mg | Fiber: 2.5 g | Carbohydrates: 9 g | Sugar: 3.5 g | Net Carbohydrates: 6.5 g

Bacon and Onion Chicken Breasts

The saltiness of the bacon and sweetness of the caramelized onions complement each other perfectly in this simple, yet decadent, recipe.

INGREDIENTS | SERVES 6

1 pound no-sugar-added bacon
1 large yellow onion, peeled and sliced
¼ cup granulated erythritol
2 teaspoons coconut aminos
¼ teaspoon sea salt
½ teaspoon lemon pepper seasoning
6 (4-ounce) boneless, skinless chicken
 breasts
2 tablespoons avocado oil
1 cup shredded Monterey jack cheese

1. Preheat oven to 350°F.

2. Cook bacon in a large skillet over medium-high heat. Transfer to a paper towel–lined plate and reserve bacon grease.

3. Add onion, erythritol, and coconut aminos to the hot pan and cook until onions are caramelized, about 10 minutes.

4. Chop bacon and stir into onion mixture.

5. Sprinkle salt and lemon pepper over chicken breasts and add avocado oil to a clean medium skillet over medium heat.

6. When oil is hot, add chicken to pan. Cook 7 minutes, flip over, and cook another 8 minutes or until chicken is cooked through.

7. Top each chicken breast with equal parts of onion and bacon mixture. Sprinkle cheese on top of each breast and cover skillet until cheese melts, about 3 minutes.

8. Remove chicken from pan and allow to cool. Transfer each breast to an airtight container and store in the refrigerator until ready to eat, up to one week.

PER SERVING Calories: 585 | Fat: 44 g | Protein: 40 g | Sodium: 748 mg | Fiber: 0.5 g | Carbohydrates: 11 g | Sugar: 1.5 g | Net Carbohydrates: 10.5 g

Pizza Chicken

This Pizza Chicken is perfect for when you need to satisfy that pizza craving without getting kicked out of ketosis. You can add your favorite low-carb pizza toppings in place of the pepperoni—green peppers and mushrooms work nicely.

INGREDIENTS | SERVES 6

1 cup crushed pork rinds

1 teaspoon Italian seasoning

¾ cup grated Parmesan cheese

1 teaspoon sea salt

1 teaspoon freshly ground black pepper

1 cup almond flour

1 teaspoon granulated garlic

1 teaspoon granulated onion

3 large eggs

3 tablespoons lemon juice

6 (4-ounce) boneless, skinless chicken breasts

1½ cups no-sugar-added pizza sauce

18 slices pepperoni

1½ cups shredded mozzarella cheese

1. Preheat oven to 400°F.

2. Combine pork rinds, Italian seasoning, Parmesan cheese, salt, and pepper in a medium bowl. Combine almond flour, granulated garlic, and granulated onion in a separate medium bowl. Whisk together eggs and lemon juice in a third medium bowl.

3. Dip each chicken breast in egg mixture, then cover with almond flour mixture. Dip in egg mixture a second time and then coat with pork rinds.

4. Place coated chicken breasts in a 9" × 13" baking dish and bake 20 minutes, or until chicken is cooked through and coating starts to turn golden brown.

5. Spoon equal amounts of pizza sauce onto each chicken breast. Place 3 pieces of pepperoni on top of pizza sauce, and sprinkle mozzarella cheese on top.

6. Bake 10 more minutes. Remove from oven and allow to cool.

7. Transfer each chicken breast to a separate airtight container and store in the refrigerator until ready to eat, up to one week.

PER SERVING Calories: 437 | Fat: 18 g | Protein: 42 g | Sodium: 1,196 mg | Fiber: 2 g | Carbohydrates: 8 g | Sugar: 3 g | Net Carbohydrates: 6 g

Jerk Chicken

Habanero peppers are no joke, so remember to use gloves when slicing them up for this recipe. If you want the flavors of the Jerk Chicken but with a little less kick, you can use half the habanero pepper or substitute with a jalapeño.

INGREDIENTS | SERVES 6

2 teaspoons finely minced white onion

¼ cup granulated erythritol

¼ cup coconut aminos

¼ cup red wine vinegar

1 teaspoon dried thyme

2 teaspoons sesame oil

4 cloves garlic, minced

¾ teaspoon ground allspice

1 habanero pepper, sliced

1½ pounds boneless, skinless chicken thighs, cut into strips

Metabolism-Boosting Capsaicin

The compound in peppers that's responsible for their heat is called capsaicin. Studies have shown that consuming capsaicin may help temporarily increase metabolism by about 8 percent. If weight loss is one of your goals, add a little spice to your meals.

1. Combine onion, erythritol, coconut aminos, red wine vinegar, thyme, sesame oil, garlic, allspice, and habanero in a food processor and process until smooth. Transfer ¾ of the mixture to a sealable bag and add chicken strips. Massage to coat and refrigerate 1 hour.

2. Turn your oven on broil. While oven is preheating, transfer chicken to a baking sheet. Broil 7 minutes, flip chicken over, and broil an additional 8 minutes.

3. Remove chicken from oven and pour reserved jerk sauce on top. Allow to cool, then transfer equal portions to six separate airtight containers. Store in the refrigerator until ready to eat, up to one week.

PER SERVING Calories: 155 | Fat: 6 g | Protein: 22 g | Sodium: 157 mg | Fiber: 0 g | Carbohydrates: 9 g | Sugar: 0 g | Net Carbohydrates: 9 g

Italian Herb Chicken

If you want to make this Italian Herb Chicken dairy-free, simply omit the feta cheese and dress it up a little bit with some fresh basil.

INGREDIENTS | SERVES 6

6 (4-ounce) boneless, skinless chicken breasts
3 tablespoons Italian seasoning
1 teaspoon sea salt
¾ teaspoon crushed red pepper
6 cloves garlic, minced
3 Roma tomatoes, sliced thinly
½ cup crumbled feta cheese

1. Preheat oven to 350°F. Coat a 9" × 13" baking dish with cooking spray.

2. Place chicken breasts in prepared baking dish and sprinkle Italian seasoning, salt, and red pepper over them.

3. Top chicken with minced garlic and sliced tomato and cover. Bake 25 minutes. Remove cover, sprinkle feta on top of each chicken breast, and bake another 15 minutes or until chicken is cooked through.

4. Allow to cool and then transfer each chicken breast to a separate airtight container. Store in the refrigerator until ready to eat, up to one week.

PER SERVING Calories: 178 | Fat: 6 g | Protein: 27 g | Sodium: 554 mg | Fiber: 0.5 g | Carbohydrates: 3 g | Sugar: 1 g | Net Carbohydrates: 2.5 g

Buffalo Bleu Cheese Chicken Burgers

If you're not a fan of the distinct flavor of blue cheese, you can swap it for feta cheese.

INGREDIENTS | SERVES 6

1½ pounds ground chicken
1½ cups almond meal
¾ cup crumbled blue cheese
1 large egg
2 tablespoons dried minced onion
½ cup Frank's RedHot sauce

1. Combine all ingredients in a medium bowl and mix with your hands until incorporated. Refrigerate 1 hour.

2. Preheat oven to 350°F. Line a baking sheet with parchment paper.

3. Form mixture into six patties and transfer to prepared baking sheet. Bake 20 minutes, or until chicken reaches an internal temperature of 165°F, flipping once during cooking.

4. Allow to cool and transfer each patty to a separate airtight container. Store in the refrigerator until ready to eat, up to one week.

PER SERVING Calories: 436 | Fat: 24 g | Protein: 26 g | Sodium: 296 mg | Fiber: 1 g | Carbohydrates: 6 g | Sugar: 0.5 g | Net Carbohydrates: 5 g

Thai Peanut Chicken and "Rice"

If you're allergic to peanuts or prefer to avoid them, you can replace the peanut butter with almond butter, the peanut oil with avocado oil, and the roasted peanuts with roasted almonds.

INGREDIENTS | SERVES 6

6 tablespoons coconut aminos

4 tablespoons no-sugar-added creamy peanut butter

4 teaspoons white wine vinegar

¼ teaspoon cayenne pepper

3 tablespoons peanut oil

1½ pounds boneless, skinless chicken breasts, cut into thin strips

2 tablespoons minced garlic

1 tablespoon minced fresh ginger

½ cup chopped green onion

2½ cups broccoli florets

⅓ cup roasted peanuts

2 cups cauliflower rice

½ cup fresh chopped cilantro

Get Down with Ginger

One of the major benefits of the ketogenic diet is that as your body gets used to it, your blood sugar levels stabilize. Fresh ginger also helps stabilize blood sugar and can even lower blood sugar levels in diabetics. Incorporating ginger into your diet, especially in the beginning stages of keto, can help make the transition easier.

1. Combine coconut aminos, peanut butter, white wine vinegar, and cayenne pepper in a small bowl and stir until mixed. Set aside.

2. Heat peanut oil in a medium skillet or wok over high heat. Add chicken, garlic, and ginger and cook until chicken starts to brown, about 5 minutes.

3. Reduce heat to medium and add green onion, broccoli, peanuts, and peanut butter sauce. Cook 5 minutes, stirring constantly. Add cauliflower rice and cook another 4 minutes, or until cauliflower and broccoli are tender and chicken is cooked through. Stir in cilantro and remove from heat.

4. Divide into six equal portions and transfer each portion to a separate airtight container. Store in the refrigerator until ready to eat, up to one week.

PER SERVING Calories: 342 | Fat: 20 g | Protein: 31 g | Sodium: 260 mg | Fiber: 3 g | Carbohydrates: 10 g | Sugar: 3 g | Net Carbohydrates: 7 g

Chicken Tandoori

This recipe requires you to marinate the chicken at least 8 hours, so keep that in mind when planning your prep and cooking days.

INGREDIENTS | SERVES 6

1¼ cups plain Greek yogurt

1½ teaspoons sea salt

1 teaspoon freshly ground black pepper

½ teaspoon ground cloves

½ teaspoon ground ginger

3 teaspoons paprika

2 teaspoons ground cumin

2 teaspoons ground coriander

2 teaspoons ground cinnamon

4 cloves garlic, minced

1½ pounds boneless, skinless chicken thighs

1. Combine yogurt, spices, and garlic in a small bowl and mix well. Transfer to a sealable bag and add chicken. Squeeze excess air out of bag, seal tightly, and massage marinade and chicken together. Refrigerate overnight (or at least 8 hours).

2. Preheat oven to 350°F.

3. Set a wire cake rack inside a rimmed baking sheet. Remove chicken from bag and wipe off most of the yogurt marinade, leaving a thin layer on chicken.

4. Arrange chicken on top of wire rack. Bake 25 minutes, turn oven to broil, and bake 5 more minutes or until chicken is cooked through and crispy on the outside.

5. Remove from oven and allow to cool. Divide into six equal portions and transfer each portion to a separate airtight container. Store in the refrigerator until ready to eat, up to one week.

PER SERVING Calories: 181 | Fat: 6 g | Protein: 24 g | Sodium: 714 mg | Fiber: 2 g | Carbohydrates: 5 g | Sugar: 2.5 g | Net Carbohydrates: 3 g

Baked Garlic Chicken

Make sure to pour any extra butter mixture that falls into the pan on top of the chicken when you're transferring it to your meal prep containers. It gives it a rich flavor and adds some healthy fats to your finished meal.

INGREDIENTS | SERVES 6

½ cup grass-fed butter

3 tablespoons coconut aminos

3 tablespoons minced garlic

¼ teaspoon freshly ground black pepper

1 tablespoon dried rosemary

6 (4-ounce) boneless chicken thighs, skin on

What Is Coconut Aminos?

Coconut aminos is the sauce made from coconut sap. The sap is fermented and then blended with sea salt to create a salty-sweet flavor that's reminiscent of soy sauce, but without the soy (and with 73 percent less sodium). Although the flavor is a little sweeter, you can use it to replace soy sauce tablespoon for tablespoon in any recipe.

1. Preheat oven to 375°F.

2. Combine butter, coconut aminos, garlic, pepper, and rosemary in a small saucepan over low heat. Cook until butter is melted, about 3 minutes, stirring occasionally.

3. Place chicken in a medium baking pan and pour butter mixture on top.

4. Bake 45 minutes, flipping once during cooking, or until chicken is cooked through. Allow to cool.

5. Transfer each chicken thigh to a separate airtight container and store in the refrigerator until ready to eat, up to one week.

PER SERVING Calories: 279 | Fat: 20 g | Protein: 22 g | Sodium: 314 mg | Fiber: 0.5 g | Carbohydrates: 1 g | Sugar: 0 g | Net Carbohydrates: 0.5 g

Chicken Makhani

Chicken Makhani, also called Murgh Makhani or butter chicken, combines a rich, buttery flavor with perfectly spiced tomato sauce. Soak up the extra sauce by meal prepping this chicken with some basic cauliflower rice.

INGREDIENTS | SERVES 6

2 tablespoons butter-flavored coconut oil, divided

1 medium shallot, minced

½ medium white onion, peeled and diced

2 tablespoons grass-fed butter

2 teaspoons lemon juice

1 tablespoon minced garlic

1 teaspoon minced fresh ginger

2 teaspoons garam masala, divided

1 teaspoon chili powder

1 teaspoon ground cumin

1 teaspoon ground coriander

1 bay leaf

1 cup tomato sauce

1 cup heavy cream

¼ cup plain Greek yogurt

¼ teaspoon cayenne pepper, divided

¼ teaspoon sea salt

¼ teaspoon freshly ground black pepper

1½ pounds boneless, skinless chicken breasts, cubed

¼ cup finely ground cashews

1. Heat 1 tablespoon coconut oil in a large saucepan over medium-high heat. Add shallot and onion and cook until softened, about 5 minutes. Stir in butter, lemon juice, garlic, ginger, 1 teaspoon garam masala, chili powder, cumin, coriander, and bay leaf.

2. Cook 1 minute then add tomato sauce, cooking another 3 minutes while stirring constantly.

3. Reduce heat to low and stir in cream, yogurt, ⅛ teaspoon cayenne pepper, sea salt, and black pepper. Simmer 10 minutes, stirring frequently. Remove from heat and set aside.

4. Heat remaining coconut oil in a medium skillet over medium heat. Sprinkle 1 teaspoon garam masala and ⅛ teaspoon cayenne pepper on chicken cubes and add them to hot pan. Cook 8 minutes, or until chicken is cooked through.

5. Stir tomato sauce into chicken. Add cashews and stir again. Reduce heat to low and allow to simmer 8 minutes, or until sauce thickens.

6. Remove from heat and allow to cool. Divide into six equal portions and transfer each portion to a separate airtight container. Store in the refrigerator until ready to eat, up to one week.

PER SERVING Calories: 408 | Fat: 29 g | Protein: 28 g | Sodium: 376 mg | Fiber: 2 g | Carbohydrates: 7.5 g | Sugar: 4 g | Net Carbohydrates: 5.5 g

Bacon-Roasted Chicken

Chicken thighs are darker than chicken breasts, so they tend to offer more flavor and a juicier result, but if you have chicken breasts on hand, feel free to use them in place of the thighs.

INGREDIENTS | SERVES 6

1 teaspoon sea salt

½ teaspoon freshly ground black pepper

1½ pounds boneless, skinless chicken thighs

12 slices no-sugar-added bacon

1 medium yellow onion, peeled and roughly chopped

Saving Some Money

In addition to offering a juicier end result in recipes, chicken thighs also tend to be cheaper than chicken breasts and they're often on sale. If you see a great deal, grab a few packages and freeze the chicken to use during your meal prep down the road. You can use the thighs instead of breasts in any recipe that calls for chicken.

1. Preheat oven to 400°F.

2. Sprinkle salt and pepper all over chicken thighs. Wrap each thigh in bacon, covering as much of the chicken as possible. Secure in place with toothpicks.

3. Transfer chicken to a 9" × 13" baking dish and sprinkle onions on top.

4. Bake 40 minutes, turning once during cooking. Switch oven to broil and bake an additional 3 minutes on each side, or until bacon is crispy and chicken is cooked through.

5. Remove from heat and allow to cool slightly. Divide into six equal portions and transfer each portion to a separate airtight container. Store in the refrigerator until ready to eat, up to one week.

PER SERVING Calories: 376 | Fat: 26 g | Protein: 29 g | Sodium: 803 mg | Fiber: 0.5 g | Carbohydrates: 2.5 g | Sugar: 1 g | Net Carbohydrates: 2 g

Prosciutto-Wrapped Mushroom Chicken

*For alternative options, or to use what you have on hand, you can swap
the prosciutto in this recipe with no-sugar-added bacon.*

INGREDIENTS | SERVES 6

2 tablespoons grass-fed butter

1 cup sliced baby bella mushrooms

1 medium yellow onion, peeled and chopped

½ teaspoon sea salt

¼ teaspoon freshly ground black pepper

2 tablespoons minced garlic

6 (4-ounce) boneless, skinless chicken breasts

6 slices prosciutto, thinly sliced

1 cup full-fat sour cream

¼ cup grated Asiago cheese

1. Preheat oven to 350°F.

2. Melt butter and drizzle into the bottom of a 9" × 13" baking dish.

3. Spread mushrooms and onion out on the bottom of buttered baking dish.

4. Combine sea salt, black pepper, and minced garlic in a small bowl and then spread over chicken. Wrap each chicken breast with a slice of prosciutto and secure with a toothpick.

5. Bake 1 hour or until chicken is cooked through. Remove from oven and allow to cool. Transfer equal portions of chicken, mushrooms, and onion to each of six separate airtight containers.

6. Spoon pan juices into a small saucepan over low heat. Stir in sour cream and Asiago cheese and continue stirring until melted and combined. Pour sauce over each portion of chicken.

7. Store in the refrigerator until ready to eat, up to one week.

PER SERVING Calories: 386 | Fat: 25 g | Protein: 33 g | Sodium: 826 mg | Fiber: 0.5 g | Carbohydrates: 4.5 g | Sugar: 2.5 g | Net Carbohydrates: 4 g

Indian Chicken Thighs

If you like the kick that only ginger can provide, you can use a bigger piece than called for in this recipe. This 1" piece adds a mild bite.

INGREDIENTS | SERVES 6

1 large yellow onion, peeled and diced

4 cloves garlic

1 (1") piece fresh ginger

2 tablespoons butter-flavored coconut oil

2 teaspoons ground cumin

1 teaspoon ground turmeric

½ teaspoon ground cardamom

1 teaspoon ground cinnamon

¼ teaspoon ground cloves

1 teaspoon sea salt

1 teaspoon freshly ground black pepper

6 (4-ounce) boneless, skinless chicken thighs

3 Roma tomatoes, diced and crushed

Fighting Inflammation with Turmeric

Turmeric is one of the most well-studied herbs in holistic (and even allopathic) medicine and that's because it's seriously powerful. On its own, turmeric is as effective as prednisone in reducing inflammation. When combined with the keto diet, the anti-inflammatory properties of turmeric are boosted even more. To effectively absorb turmeric, it must be combined with black pepper, so make sure to always have the two together!

1. Combine onion, garlic, and ginger in a food processor and process until a paste forms.

2. Heat coconut oil in a medium skillet over medium heat. Add onion mixture and sauté until softened, stirring frequently, for 5 minutes.

3. Stir in spices and cook another 2 minutes.

4. Place chicken thighs in skillet and spoon onion mixture over them until coated. Cook 5 minutes and then pour in tomatoes and any juices released from crushing.

5. Reduce heat to low and simmer 45 minutes covered, and other 45 minutes uncovered, or until chicken is cooked through and sauce has thickened.

6. Remove from heat and allow to cool. Transfer chicken thighs to each of six separate airtight containers. Store in the refrigerator until ready to eat, up to one week.

PER SERVING Calories: 200 | Fat: 9.5 g | Protein: 22 g | Sodium: 498 mg | Fiber: 1.5 g | Carbohydrates: 5.5 g | Sugar: 2 g | Net Carbohydrates: 4 g

Rosemary-Roasted Turkey

Many people roast turkey once a year on Thanksgiving, but the white meat deserves a spot in your regular meal prep rotation. Don't be intimidated! You can make a deliciously moist turkey with just a handful of simple ingredients.

INGREDIENTS | SERVES 6

½ cup olive oil

2 tablespoons minced garlic

2 tablespoons chopped fresh rosemary, plus 2 rosemary sprigs

1 tablespoon chopped fresh basil

1 tablespoon dried Italian seasoning

1 teaspoon sea salt

1 teaspoon freshly ground black pepper

1 (6-pound) whole turkey

1 medium yellow onion, peeled and quartered

2 cups chicken bone broth

1. Preheat oven to 325°F.

2. Combine olive oil, garlic, chopped rosemary, basil, Italian seasoning, salt, and pepper in a bowl and mix well.

3. Rub herbed oil mixture all over turkey, covering as much as you can.

4. Place onion and rosemary sprigs in turkey cavity.

5. Place turkey on a rack in a roast pan and add chicken broth to the bottom of the pan.

6. Roast for 2½ hours or until internal temperature reaches 165°F. Allow to cool and remove meat from bones.

7. Divide into six equal portions and transfer each portion to a separate airtight container. Store in the refrigerator until ready to eat, up to one week.

PER SERVING Calories: 185 | Fat: 18 g | Protein: 2 g | Sodium: 413 mg | Fiber: 0.5 g | Carbohydrates: 4 g | Sugar: 1 g | Net Carbohydrates: 3.5 g

Spinach and Cheese Turkey Pinwheels

This Italian-style turkey pinwheel combines several cheeses, but you can change the flavor by using crumbled feta in place of the cheese mixture.

INGREDIENTS | SERVES 6

1½ pounds ground turkey

¾ cup almond meal

1 large egg

1¼ teaspoons sea salt, divided

½ teaspoon freshly ground black pepper

1 (10-ounce) package frozen chopped spinach, thawed and drained

¾ cup shredded mozzarella cheese, divided

½ cup shredded provolone cheese

2 tablespoons grated Parmesan cheese

1 teaspoon Italian seasoning

¼ teaspoon dried basil

¼ teaspoon granulated garlic

¼ cup no-sugar-added ketchup

Fresh or Frozen?

Frozen veggies aren't just more convenient, they're often richer in nutrients too. When veggies are picked at the height of their ripeness and then immediately frozen, they retain more nutrients than when they're picked and sit in a transportation truck or sit at the store for weeks at a time. The longer produce sits, the less nutrient rich it becomes, as heat, light, and air can destroy some of the vitamins and minerals.

1. Preheat oven to 350°F. Line a baking sheet with parchment paper and set aside.

2. Combine ground turkey, almond meal, egg, 1 teaspoon salt, and pepper in a medium bowl and mix with hands until incorporated.

3. Place turkey mixture on prepared baking sheet and flatten into a 10" × 14" rectangle.

4. Combine spinach, ½ cup mozzarella cheese, provolone cheese, Parmesan cheese, and remaining spices in a separate medium bowl. Stir to mix.

5. Spread spinach mixture over turkey leaving ½" of empty space around the edges. Pick up one short edge of the parchment paper and roll into a pinwheel, peeling back the parchment paper as you go. Pinch seam closed.

6. Place a wire rack in the baking sheet and place turkey pinwheel, seam side down, onto rack. Bake 50 minutes.

7. Remove from oven, spread ketchup evenly over the top of the roll, and sprinkle with remaining mozzarella cheese. Return to oven and bake 10 more minutes or until cooked through and turkey reaches an internal temperature of 165°F.

8. Allow to cool and cut into six equal-sized slices. Transfer each slice to a separate airtight container and store in the refrigerator until ready to eat, up to one week.

PER SERVING Calories: 349 | Fat: 16 g | Protein: 32 g | Sodium: 934 mg | Fiber: 1.5 g | Carbohydrates: 9 g | Sugar: 1 g | Net Carbohydrates: 7.5 g

Mozzarella-Stuffed Turkey Meatballs

You can eat these meatballs plain or add them to your favorite marinara sauce recipe when they're done cooking and pour them over a serving of zoodles (zucchini noodles) or spaghetti squash.

INGREDIENTS | SERVES 6 (MAKES 18 MEATBALLS)

1½ pounds ground turkey

½ cup minced yellow onion

2 cloves garlic, minced

1 large egg

½ cup almond meal

½ teaspoon Italian seasoning

¼ cup grated Parmesan-Reggiano cheese

¼ cup chopped fresh parsley

1 teaspoon dried basil

2 tablespoons chicken bone broth

1½ teaspoons sea salt

1 teaspoon freshly ground black pepper

½ pound fresh mozzarella, cut into 18 small cubes

1. Preheat oven to 375°F. Line a baking sheet with parchment paper.

2. Combine all ingredients, except mozzarella, in a bowl and mix with hands until incorporated.

3. Divide mixture into eighteen equal portions and form each portion into a ball. Poke a hole in each meatball with your finger and stick a cheese cube inside the hole. Cover the hole by rerolling the meatball and arrange on prepared pan.

4. Bake 30 minutes or until meatballs are cooked through and starting to brown. Remove from oven and allow to cool.

5. Transfer three meatballs to each of six separate airtight containers. Store in the refrigerator until ready to eat, up to one week.

PER SERVING Calories: 336 | Fat: 17 g | Protein: 32 g | Sodium: 894 mg | Fiber: 0.5 g | Carbohydrates: 10 g | Sugar: 1 g | Net Carbohydrates: 9.5 g

Turkey Bacon Cheeseburger Meatloaf

This recipe calls for ground turkey, which is leaner than ground beef, but tends to be a little drier. You can replace the ground turkey with ground beef, or just a 50/50 mixture, for added moisture.

INGREDIENTS | SERVES 6

6 slices no-sugar-added bacon, cooked and crumbled

1½ pounds ground turkey

1 cup shredded Cheddar cheese

1 large egg

1 small yellow onion, peeled and diced

2 tablespoons coconut aminos

2 teaspoons granulated garlic

1 teaspoon dry mustard

¼ teaspoon freshly ground black pepper

½ cup no-sugar-added ketchup, divided

Making Your Ketchup

Although food manufacturers are responding to the increasing popularity of keto diets by offering more low-carb options made with whole ingredients, finding ketchup without sugar added at your local supermarket may be difficult. If you forgot to plan ahead and order some online, you can quickly make your own by combining 1 can tomato paste, 1 cup water, ¼ cup powdered erythritol, 3 tablespoons apple cider vinegar, 1 teaspoon sea salt, ¾ teaspoon onion powder, ½ teaspoon garlic powder, ¼ teaspoon paprika, ⅛ teaspoon ground cloves, and ⅛ teaspoon dry mustard in a small saucepan, simmering for 30 minutes over low heat, then puréeing with an immersion blender.

1. Preheat oven to 350°F.

2. Combine all ingredients, except ¼ cup ketchup, in a medium bowl and mix with your hands until fully incorporated.

3. Transfer mixture to a 9" × 5" loaf pan and spread remaining ketchup on top.

4. Bake 1 hour, or until internal temperature reaches 165°F. Remove from oven and allow to cool.

5. Cut into six equal portions and transfer each portion to a separate airtight container. Store in the refrigerator until ready to eat, up to one week.

PER SERVING Calories: 415 | Fat: 27 g | Protein: 32 g | Sodium: 619 mg | Fiber: 0.5 g | Carbohydrates: 9 g | Sugar: 5 g | Net Carbohydrates: 8.5 g

CHAPTER 5

Beef

Salisbury Steak with Mushrooms

The best way to heat up Salisbury Steak is low and slow on the stovetop; but it's also delicious cold right out of the refrigerator by itself or on top of a salad.

INGREDIENTS | SERVES 6

1½ pounds 85/15 ground beef

½ cup almond meal

1 small yellow onion, peeled and diced

1 large egg, lightly beaten

1 teaspoon salt

½ teaspoon freshly ground black pepper

2 tablespoons butter-flavored coconut oil

1 (14.5-ounce) can beef broth

1 tablespoon Worcestershire sauce

1 large yellow onion, peeled and sliced into thin strips

1½ cups sliced baby bella mushrooms

2 teaspoons arrowroot starch

¼ cup water

A Buttery Boost

Coconut oil is one of the best oils available for cooking, but its strong flavor can be off-putting in some recipes, especially if you're not a fan of coconut oil. Enter buttery flavor coconut oil, manufactured by Nutiva. It combines a vegan butter, made from non-GMO sunflower, mint, and coconut, with coconut oil and tastes like butter instead of coconut.

1. Combine ground beef, almond meal, diced onion, egg, salt, and pepper in a medium bowl and mix with your hands until fully incorporated. Shape into six equal-sized patties.

2. Heat coconut oil in a medium skillet over medium heat. Place patties in the pan and cook 5 minutes on each side.

3. Add beef broth, Worcestershire sauce, sliced onions, and mushrooms and bring mixture to a boil. Reduce heat to low, cover, and simmer until patties are cooked through, about 10 more minutes. Remove patties from broth mixture and set each patty in a separate airtight container.

4. Increase heat to medium-high and bring broth to a boil. Whisk together arrowroot starch and water in a small bowl. Pour into beef mixture. Cook, whisking constantly, until thickened, about 5 minutes.

5. Pour equal amounts of onion and mushroom mixture over each patty and cover. Allow to cool. Store in the refrigerator until ready to eat, up to one week.

PER SERVING Calories: 316 | Fat: 16 g | Protein: 26 g | Sodium: 756 mg | Fiber: 1 g | Carbohydrates: 13 g | Sugar: 2.5 g | Net Carbohydrates: 12 g

Pizza Casserole

This Pizza Casserole gives you all the pizza taste with hardly any of the carbs. You can add your favorite pizza toppings into the beef mixture to give it that true comfort food feel.

INGREDIENTS | SERVES 6

2 tablespoons butter-flavored coconut oil

1 medium yellow onion, peeled and diced

2 cloves garlic, minced

1 medium green bell pepper, seeded and diced

1 pound 85/15 ground beef

⅔ cup chopped pepperoni

2 cups no-sugar-added pizza sauce

2 cups cooked spaghetti squash

1 cup shredded mozzarella cheese

¼ cup grated Parmesan cheese

1. Preheat oven to 350°F.

2. Heat coconut oil in a medium skillet over medium heat. Add onions and garlic and cook until starting to soften, about 2 minutes. Add green pepper and continue cooking 4 more minutes.

3. Crumble beef into onion mixture and cook until no longer pink, about 7 minutes.

4. Stir in pepperoni and pizza sauce.

5. Arrange cooked spaghetti squash in a 9" × 13" baking dish. Pour sauce mixture over cooked squash and stir until fully combined. Sprinkle cheeses on top.

6. Bake 25 minutes or until hot and bubbly and cheese starts to turn golden. Remove from oven and allow to cool.

7. Divide into six equal portions and transfer each portion to a separate airtight container. Store in the refrigerator until ready to eat, up to one week.

PER SERVING Calories: 410 | Fat: 29 g | Protein: 23 g | Sodium: 862 mg | Fiber: 4 g | Carbohydrates: 14 g | Sugar: 6.5 g | Net Carbohydrates: 10 g

Beef and Veggie Spaghetti Squash Casserole

Casseroles are one of the best ways to use up any veggies that you have in your refrigerator. This recipe calls for bell peppers and tomatoes, but you can make it your own by adding whatever veggies you want to use before you stock your fridge for your next meal prep cooking day.

INGREDIENTS | SERVES 6

2 tablespoons butter-flavored coconut oil

¼ cup diced red onion

2 cloves garlic, minced

½ cup diced orange bell pepper

½ cup diced red bell pepper

¾ pound 85/15 ground beef

½ pound hot Italian sausage

1 (14.5-ounce) can fire-roasted diced tomatoes, drained

1 teaspoon Italian seasoning

1 teaspoon sea salt

½ teaspoon freshly ground black pepper

1 medium spaghetti squash, cooked

1 cup shredded sharp Cheddar cheese

1 cup shredded mozzarella cheese

Preparing Your "Spaghetti"

Most people cut spaghetti squash in half lengthwise, scoop out the seeds, and cook. But the strands of "spaghetti" in the squash actually grow concentrically—or in circles around the middle of the squash. To get longer strands, instead of cutting the squash lengthwise, cut the squash into fourths crosswise then scoop out the seeds. Before cooking the squash, sprinkle sea salt all over the cut pieces and let it sit for 15 minutes. This will pull excess water out of the squash and prevent soggy "noodles." Once you've done this, wipe the water and salt away with a paper towel and cook the squash in a 400°F oven about 30 minutes, allow it to cool, and then peel the strands away from the skin or cut them out.

1. Preheat oven to 375°F.

2. Heat coconut oil in a large pot over medium heat. Add onion and garlic and cook 2 minutes. Add bell peppers and cook another 5 minutes, or until softened.

3. Crumble beef and sausage in pepper mixture and cook until no longer pink, about 7 minutes.

4. Add tomatoes, Italian seasoning, salt, and pepper and stir to combine. Remove from heat.

5. Place spaghetti squash in a 9" × 13" baking dish and top with beef mixture. Sprinkle cheeses on top and bake 30 minutes or until casserole is hot and bubbly and cheese starts to brown.

6. Remove from oven and cool. Divide into six equal-sized portions and transfer each portion to a separate airtight container. Store in the refrigerator until ready to eat, up to one week.

PER SERVING Calories: 443 | Fat: 33 g | Protein: 26 g | Sodium: 941 mg | Fiber: 2 g | Carbohydrates: 10 g | Sugar: 4 g | Net Carbohydrates: 8 g

Deconstructed Cabbage Roll Casserole

Cabbage rolls are delicious, but they can be time-consuming to make. This Deconstructed Cabbage Roll Casserole gives you all of the same flavors, but without the added work of boiling the cabbage and stuffing it and forming it into rolls.

INGREDIENTS | SERVES 6

1 pound 85/15 ground beef
½ cup chopped yellow onion
1 teaspoon granulated garlic
1 teaspoon granulated onion
½ teaspoon red pepper flakes
1 (14.5-ounce) can tomato sauce
1 large head cabbage, chopped
1 cup riced cauliflower
½ teaspoon sea salt
¼ teaspoon freshly ground black pepper
1 (14-ounce) can beef broth

1. Preheat oven to 350°F.

2. Brown beef in a medium skillet over medium-high heat, about 8 minutes. Add onion, granulated garlic, granulated onion, and red pepper flakes and cook until softened, about 4 minutes. Remove from heat.

3. Add tomato sauce, cabbage, cauliflower, salt, and pepper to skillet and stir to combine. Transfer mixture to a 9" × 13" baking dish.

4. Pour beef broth over mixture and bake 1 hour, stirring once halfway through cooking. Remove from heat and allow to cool.

5. Divide into six equal portions and transfer each portion to a separate airtight container. Store in the refrigerator until ready to eat, up to one week.

PER SERVING Calories: 246 | Fat: 14 g | Protein: 17 g | Sodium: 837 mg | Fiber: 5.5 g | Carbohydrates: 15 g | Sugar: 8 g | Net Carbohydrates: 9.5 g

Spanish Cauliflower Rice Bake

If you like your food spicy, douse this bake in hot sauce right before eating it. It may make you sweat, but it's oh-so-good!

INGREDIENTS | SERVES 6

1 pound 85/15 ground beef
1 teaspoon granulated garlic
1 teaspoon granulated onion
1 teaspoon sea salt, divided
½ teaspoon freshly ground black pepper, divided
½ cup minced yellow onion
¼ cup chopped green bell pepper
1 (14.5-ounce) can fire-roasted diced tomatoes
1½ cups riced cauliflower
1 cup beef bone broth
½ cup red chili garlic sauce
½ teaspoon ground cumin
1 teaspoon Worcestershire sauce
½ cup shredded nacho cheese mix

Worcestershire Substitutions

Worcestershire sauce has a pretty unique flavor profile and there's no sauce out there that can totally take its place, but there are some substitutions you can make if you don't have any on hand. You can mix red wine vinegar with some fish sauce and salt or use coconut aminos instead, especially when substituting in marinades. You can also use oyster sauce, which is available in the Asian section of most supermarkets.

1. Preheat oven to 375°F.

2. Crumble ground beef in a medium skillet, add granulated garlic, granulated onion, ½ teaspoon salt, and ¼ teaspoon pepper, and cook over medium-high heat until no longer pink, about 8 minutes.

3. Add all remaining ingredients, except cheese, and stir to mix. Reduce heat to low and simmer 20 minutes or until most liquid is absorbed.

4. Transfer to a 9" × 13" baking dish and sprinkle cheese on top.

5. Bake 20 minutes or until casserole is bubbly and cheese starts to turn golden. Remove from oven and cool.

6. Divide into six equal portions and transfer each portion to a separate airtight container. Store in the refrigerator until ready to eat, up to one week.

PER SERVING Calories: 276 | Fat: 17 g | Protein: 18 g | Sodium: 880 mg | Fiber: 3 g | Carbohydrates: 11 g | Sugar: 5.5 g | Net Carbohydrates: 8 g

Cheeseburger Meatloaf

This Cheeseburger Meatloaf tastes just like a cheeseburger, but without the bun. Throw some Creamed Onions on top and Cauliflower Risotto (see recipes in Chapter 10) on the side and you have a complete, rich meal that satisfies all your comfort food cravings.

INGREDIENTS | SERVES 6

1½ pounds 85/15 ground beef

½ cup almond meal

1 small yellow onion, peeled and minced

1 large egg, lightly beaten

1 teaspoon Worcestershire sauce

¾ cup no-sugar-added ketchup, divided

1 teaspoon sea salt

1 teaspoon freshly ground black pepper

2 cups shredded Cheddar cheese

1. Preheat oven to 350°F.

2. Combine beef, almond meal, onion, egg, Worcestershire sauce, ¼ cup ketchup, salt, and pepper in a large bowl and use your hands to mix thoroughly.

3. Divide meat mixture into three equal portions. Press one portion in the bottom of a loaf pan and sprinkle 1 cup shredded cheese on top. Place another portion of meat on top of cheese and press to spread into pan. Sprinkle remaining cheese on top and repeat with remaining meat portion.

4. Spread remaining ketchup on top and bake 1 hour or until internal temperature reaches 160°F. Remove from oven and allow to cool.

5. Divide into six equal portions and transfer each portion to a separate airtight container. Store in the refrigerator until ready to eat, up to one week.

PER SERVING Calories: 531 | Fat: 36 g | Protein: 33 g | Sodium: 970 mg | Fiber: 0.5 g | Carbohydrates: 8 g | Sugar: 1 g | Net Carbohydrates: 7.5 g

Ranch Burgers

Ranch flavor is a real crowd-pleaser for most people. You can double up on the ranch goodness by dipping these burgers in some Jalapeño Ranch Dressing (Chapter 9).

INGREDIENTS | SERVES 6

1½ pounds 85/15 ground beef
1 teaspoon dried parsley
1 teaspoon garlic powder
1 teaspoon onion powder
½ teaspoon dried dill
¼ teaspoon dried chives
¼ teaspoon sea salt
¼ teaspoon freshly ground black pepper
1 small white onion, peeled and minced
¼ cup grass-fed butter, melted

1. Preheat grill to high.

2. Combine all ingredients, except butter, in a medium bowl and mix with your hands until fully incorporated. Divide into six equal-sized portions and form into patties.

3. Grease the grill grate with butter. Place patties on the grill and cook 4 minutes on each side or until burgers reach desired level of doneness. Remove from heat and allow to sit 10 minutes.

4. Transfer each burger to a separate airtight container. Store in the refrigerator until ready to eat, up to one week.

PER SERVING Calories: 338 | Fat: 28 g | Protein: 20 g | Sodium: 169 mg | Fiber: 0.5 g | Carbohydrates: 2 g | Sugar: 0.5 g | Net Carbohydrates: 1.5 g

Jalapeño Popper Burgers

If jalapeño poppers are your favorite appetizer, you're going to love these burgers as your main course. Heat them up slowly in a pan over low heat to get the cream cheese to re-melt after refrigerating.

INGREDIENTS | SERVES 6

1½ pounds 85/15 ground beef
3 slices no-sugar-added bacon, cooked and crumbled
1 cup minced fresh jalapeños
8 ounces cream cheese, softened
1 teaspoon Worcestershire sauce
½ teaspoon sea salt
¼ teaspoon freshly ground black pepper
¼ cup grass-fed butter, melted

1. Preheat grill to medium heat.

2. Combine all ingredients, except butter, in a medium bowl and mix with your hands until incorporated. Divide into six equal portions and form into patties.

3. Grease the grill grate with butter. Place patties on the grill and cook 4 minutes on each side or until burgers reach desired level of doneness. Remove from heat and allow to sit 10 minutes.

4. Transfer each burger to a separate airtight container. Store in the refrigerator until ready to eat, up to one week.

PER SERVING Calories: 521 | Fat: 46 g | Protein: 24 g | Sodium: 502 mg | Fiber: 0.5 g | Carbohydrates: 3 g | Sugar: 2 g | Net Carbohydrates: 2.5 g

Ricotta Meatballs

If you find it difficult to roll these into meatballs, refrigerate the meat mixture for an hour or two before shaping the balls.

INGREDIENTS | SERVES 6 (MAKES 24 MEATBALLS)

2 tablespoons olive oil

1 small yellow onion, peeled and minced

3 cloves garlic, minced

1 pound ground meatloaf mix

¾ cup whole milk ricotta cheese

¼ cup chopped Italian parsley

1 large egg, lightly beaten

1 teaspoon sea salt

½ teaspoon freshly ground black pepper

¼ cup almond meal

2 tablespoons Parmesan cheese

Meatloaf Mix Breakdown

Meatloaf mix, which combines ground beef, ground pork, and ground veal, is available near the ground beef in most grocery stores. Combining the three meats gives meatloaf and meatballs a better texture and a richer flavor. If you can't find it in your store, you can make your own by combining the three meats yourself or you can just use the ground meat of your choice.

1. Preheat oven to 425°F. Line a baking sheet with parchment paper and set aside.

2. Heat olive oil in a small skillet over medium heat. Add onion and garlic and sauté until softened, about 4 minutes.

3. Combine remaining ingredients and cooked onion mixture in a large bowl and mix with your hands to evenly incorporate.

4. Form into 1½" balls and arrange in a single layer on prepared baking sheet. Bake 20 minutes or until meatballs are cooked through. Remove from oven and allow to cool.

5. Transfer four meatballs to each of six separate airtight containers and store in the refrigerator until ready to eat, up to one week.

PER SERVING Calories: 316 | Fat: 23 g | Protein: 19 g | Sodium: 506 mg | Fiber: 0.5 g | Carbohydrates: 7 g | Sugar: 0.5 g | Net Carbohydrates: 6.5 g

Bolognese-Stuffed Peppers

Typically, Bolognese gets better with time, so these stuffed peppers will taste even better after they've been sitting in the refrigerator a day or two. You can heat them up by baking them on a low temperature for 20 minutes until heated through and then broiling them for a couple of minutes to crisp up the top.

INGREDIENTS | SERVES 6

6 medium red bell peppers, tops cut off and seeded

2 tablespoons olive oil

2 cloves garlic, minced

¼ cup minced celery

¼ cup minced white onion

¾ pound 85/15 ground beef

¼ pound pancetta, diced

2 cups no-sugar-added marinara sauce

¼ cup keto-friendly red wine

½ teaspoon red pepper flakes

½ teaspoon sea salt

¼ teaspoon onion powder

⅓ cup half-and-half

½ cup grated Parmesan cheese, divided

1 cup riced cauliflower

1. Preheat oven to 375°F.

2. Bring a large pot of water to a slow rolling boil. Fill a bowl of water with ice and water.

3. Place peppers in boiling water and boil for 3 minutes. Remove and immediately submerge in ice water. Arrange peppers in a 9" × 13" baking dish.

4. Heat olive oil in a medium skillet over medium heat. Add garlic, celery, and onion and cook until softened, about 4 minutes.

5. Add ground beef and pancetta and cook until no longer pink, about 8 minutes. Add marinara sauce, wine, red pepper flakes, salt, and onion powder and stir. Simmer 10 minutes.

6. Stir in half-and-half, ¼ cup Parmesan cheese, and riced cauliflower and simmer for another 7 minutes or until thickened.

7. Scoop equal portions of beef mixture into each pepper and sprinkle remaining Parmesan cheese on top. Bake 30 minutes or until hot and bubbly. Remove from oven and allow to cool.

8. Transfer each pepper to a separate airtight container and store in the refrigerator until ready to eat, up to one week.

PER SERVING Calories: 342 | Fat: 26 g | Protein: 19 g | Sodium: 996 mg | Fiber: 5 g | Carbohydrates: 12 g | Sugar: 5 g | Net Carbohydrates: 7 g

Beef, Pepper, and Cabbage Stir-Fry

Make sure to use coconut oil or another high-heat oil like avocado oil for this recipe as it requires you to cook over high heat. Olive oil will burn and smoke before the ingredients are able to properly cook.

INGREDIENTS | SERVES 6

2 tablespoons butter-flavored coconut oil

3 cloves garlic, minced

1 pound 85/15 ground beef

3 cups shredded cabbage

1 medium red bell pepper, seeded and cut into thin strips

1 medium yellow bell pepper, seeded and cut into thin strips

3 tablespoons coconut aminos

½ teaspoon arrowroot powder

¼ cup beef bone broth

1 teaspoon sea salt

½ teaspoon freshly ground black pepper

Arrow-what?

Arrowroot powder, also called arrowroot flour or arrowroot starch, comes from the root of a tropical plant known as *Maranta arundinacea*. It's gluten-free, grain-free, vegan, Paleo, and keto-friendly (in small amounts). The powder is extremely versatile and is often used as a thickener in recipes. It's also great for crisping things up. Arrowroot powder is more powerful than cornstarch, so when substituting, start with one-third to one-half of the amount and work up from there if you need to.

1. Heat coconut oil in a medium skillet over medium-high heat. Add garlic and cook 1 minute. Add beef and continue cooking until no longer pink, about 7 minutes.

2. Stir in cabbage and peppers and cook until vegetables are tender, but still crisp, another 6 minutes. Stir in coconut aminos.

3. In a small bowl, whisk together arrowroot powder, beef broth, salt, and pepper and then add to beef mixture. Continue stirring until mixture has thickened, about 5 minutes.

4. Remove from heat and allow to cool. Divide into six equal portions and transfer each portion to a separate airtight container. Store in the refrigerator until ready to eat, up to one week.

PER SERVING Calories: 239 | Fat: 18 g | Protein: 14 g | Sodium: 443 mg | Fiber: 2 g | Carbohydrates: 5.5 g | Sugar: 2.5 g | Net Carbohydrates: 3.5 g

Asian Fire Beef

This recipe gets its name because it's spicy! If you want the flavor without all of the heat, reduce the amount of crushed red pepper and/or omit the red chili paste.

INGREDIENTS | SERVES 6

½ cup coconut aminos

2 tablespoons sesame oil

4 cloves garlic, minced

1 large red onion, peeled and diced

¼ teaspoon freshly ground black pepper

2 teaspoons red pepper flakes

1 tablespoon red chili paste

3 leeks, chopped

1½ pounds flank steak, sliced thinly

2 tablespoons butter-flavored coconut oil

1. Combine all ingredients, except steak and coconut oil, in large sealable bag. Shake to combine. Add meat and massage to coat. Refrigerate 2 hours.

2. Heat coconut oil in a medium skillet over medium-high heat. Remove meat from marinade and cook until meat is cooked through, about 5 minutes. Remove from heat and allow to cool.

3. Divide meat into six equal portions and transfer each portion to a separate airtight container. Store in the refrigerator until ready to eat, up to one week.

PER SERVING Calories: 295 | Fat: 17 g | Protein: 25 g | Sodium: 71 mg | Fiber: 1.5 g | Carbohydrates: 10 g | Sugar: 3 g | Net Carbohydrates: 8.5 g

Beef and Cauliflower Rice

This Beef and Cauliflower Rice comes together in minutes and uses only ingredients that you likely already have on hand in a well-stocked keto kitchen. You can easily double the recipe if you're meal prepping for two and have lunch or dinner for the whole week done in minutes!

INGREDIENTS | SERVES 6

1½ pounds 85/15 ground beef

3 cups riced cauliflower

½ teaspoon onion powder

½ teaspoon garlic powder

½ teaspoon dried basil

¼ teaspoon dried thyme

½ teaspoon freshly ground black pepper

½ teaspoon white pepper

¼ teaspoon ground cayenne

1 teaspoon paprika

¾ teaspoon sea salt

1½ cups beef bone broth

1. Crumble beef in a large skillet over medium-high heat. Cook until no longer pink, about 7 minutes.

2. Stir in riced cauliflower and spices and cook 2 minutes. Add beef broth, reduce heat to low, and cover.

3. Simmer 20 minutes or until cauliflower is tender and almost all liquid is absorbed. Drain any excess liquid and allow to cool.

4. Divide into six equal portions and transfer each portion to a separate airtight container. Store in the refrigerator until ready to eat, up to one week.

PER SERVING Calories: 283 | Fat: 20 g | Protein: 21 g | Sodium: 600 mg | Fiber: 1.5 g | Carbohydrates: 3.5 g | Sugar: 1 g | Net Carbohydrates: 2 g

Rainbow Veggie Stir-Fry

The only color missing in this recipe is blue, but other than that, you've got all the colors covered! Put this stir-fry in your rotation regularly for a meal that's loaded with vitamins and minerals and low on the carbs.

INGREDIENTS | SERVES 6

1 large red bell pepper, seeded and sliced thinly

1 large orange bell pepper, seeded and sliced thinly

1 large yellow bell pepper, seeded and sliced thinly

1 small head broccoli, chopped

1 small head purple cauliflower, cut into bite-sized florets

1 small white onion, peeled and diced

2 tablespoons butter-flavored coconut oil

¾ pound boneless chuck roast, cut into 1" cubes

1 tablespoon orange zest

2 scallions, chopped

½ cup coconut aminos

1 tablespoon fish sauce

Eat the Rainbow

When nutritionists tell you to "eat the rainbow," they're not talking about Skittles. The more varied the color in your diet, the greater variety of micronutrients and antioxidants you'll take in. Make it one of your meal prep goals to include as many different colored veggies as you can.

1. Combine bell peppers, broccoli, cauliflower, and onion in a large pot with an inch of water at the bottom. Bring to a boil over medium-high heat, reduce heat to medium, cover, and steam for 8 minutes. Remove from pot and set aside.

2. Heat coconut oil in a large skillet over medium-high heat. Stir in chuck roast and cook until browned on all sides, about 5 minutes. Add remaining ingredients and cooked vegetables to pan and continue cooking until meat is cooked through, about 5 more minutes. Remove from heat and allow to cool.

3. Divide into six equal portions and transfer each portion to a separate airtight container. Store in the refrigerator until ready to eat, up to one week.

PER SERVING Calories: 195 | Fat: 8 g | Protein: 18 g | Sodium: 158 mg | Fiber: 5 g | Carbohydrates: 13 g | Sugar: 6 g | Net Carbohydrates: 8 g

Reduced Beef Stroganoff

Beef stroganoff is typically very creamy, but this version scales back on the amount of sauce, but still provides plenty of healthy fats to make it fit nicely into your keto meal plan.

INGREDIENTS | SERVES 6

2 tablespoons butter-flavored coconut oil

1½ pounds chuck roast, cut into thin strips

1 teaspoon sea salt

1 teaspoon freshly ground black pepper

1 small yellow onion, peeled and diced

8 ounces sliced baby bella mushrooms

3 cloves garlic, minced

½ teaspoon arrowroot powder

½ cup keto-friendly white wine

2 cups beef bone broth, divided

½ cup full-fat sour cream

¼ cup full-fat plain Greek yogurt

1. Heat coconut oil in a medium skillet over high heat. Season beef with salt and pepper and place into hot pan. Cook, stirring constantly, until meat browns, about 7 minutes. Remove meat from pan and set aside.

2. Add onion and mushrooms to the pan and cook until slightly softened, about 4 minutes. Add garlic and cook 1 more minute. Stir in arrowroot powder and mix until incorporated.

3. Stir in wine and 1 cup beef broth and bring to a simmer. Reduce heat to medium and simmer 5 minutes. Return meat to pan and stir in remaining broth. Simmer, covered, stirring occasionally, for 1 hour.

4. Remove from heat and stir in sour cream and yogurt. Allow to cool.

5. Divide into six equal portions and transfer each portion to a separate airtight container. Store in the refrigerator until ready to eat, up to one week.

PER SERVING Calories: 295 | Fat: 14 g | Protein: 31 g | Sodium: 784 mg | Fiber: 1 g | Carbohydrates: 5 g | Sugar: 2.5 g | Net Carbohydrates: 4 g

Deconstructed Beef Gyros

You can eat these Deconstructed Beef Gyros straight out of a bowl or throw everything onto a bed of lettuce and make it a fancy Greek-style salad!

INGREDIENTS | SERVES 6

2 cups full-fat plain Greek yogurt

3 tablespoons olive oil, divided

1 tablespoon chopped fresh dill

1 tablespoon lemon juice

3 cloves garlic

½ teaspoon sea salt

¼ teaspoon freshly ground black pepper

2 large cucumbers, peeled, seeded, shredded, and squeezed dry

1½ pounds sirloin, cut into thin strips

2 teaspoons steak seasoning

2 small Roma tomatoes, diced

1 small red onion, peeled and thinly sliced

1 cup shredded iceberg lettuce

2 tablespoons sliced black olives

½ cup crumbled feta cheese

1. Combine yogurt, 2 tablespoons olive oil, dill, lemon juice, garlic, salt, and pepper in a blender and blend until smooth. Stir in cucumbers. Set aside.

2. Heat remaining olive oil in a medium skillet over medium heat. Add sirloin and steak seasoning and cook until no longer pink, about 7 minutes. Remove from heat and allow to cool slightly.

3. Divide sirloin into six equal portions and transfer each portion to a separate airtight container. Top each portion with equal amounts of tomatoes, red onion, lettuce, olives, and feta cheese. Spoon equal amounts of tzatziki sauce over each gyro.

4. Store in the refrigerator until ready to eat, up to one week.

PER SERVING Calories: 315 | Fat: 17 g | Protein: 30 g | Sodium: 438 mg | Fiber: 1.5 g | Carbohydrates: 10 g | Sugar: 7 g | Net Carbohydrates: 8.5 g

Ginger Beef

It's best to use freshly grated ginger for this recipe since it has more zing than ground dried ginger, but if that's all you have on hand, you can substitute ¼ teaspoon of ground ginger for every tablespoon of fresh ginger.

INGREDIENTS | SERVES 6

2 medium white onions, peeled and chopped

3 cloves garlic, minced

2 tablespoons grated fresh ginger

1 teaspoon ground turmeric

¼ teaspoon crushed red pepper flakes

1 teaspoon sea salt

1½ pounds flank steak, cut into strips

1 tablespoon avocado oil

1 (14.5-ounce) can petite-diced tomatoes, drained

2 cups riced cauliflower

1. Combine onions, garlic, ginger, turmeric, red pepper flakes, and salt in a medium bowl and mix. Add steak to mixture and coat. Cover and refrigerate 1 hour.

2. Heat avocado oil in a medium skillet over medium-high heat. Add steak with seasonings and cook until browned, about 8 minutes. Stir in tomatoes and cauliflower and cook another 10 minutes.

3. Remove from heat and allow to cool. Divide into six equal portions and transfer each portion to a separate airtight container. Store in the refrigerator until ready to eat, up to one week.

PER SERVING Calories: 235 | Fat: 10 g | Protein: 25 g | Sodium: 464 mg | Fiber: 2.5 g | Carbohydrates: 9 g | Sugar: 4 g | Net Carbohydrates: 6.5 g

Settling Your Stomach

If you find you have lots of ginger left over after your meal prep, you can use it to create a ginger tea, which helps improve digestion, alleviates nausea, and reduces inflammation. To make it, combine 1 cup water with 1½ tablespoons freshly grated ginger, and 2 tablespoons lemon juice in a saucepan. Allow to simmer 20 minutes, then strain through a cheesecloth. If you like your tea sweet, you can add some erythritol, monk fruit, or another keto-friendly sweetener after straining.

Smothered Beef Tips

Beef stew meat tends to be one of the cheapest cuts because it's usually the odds and ends put together by the butcher from other cuts. If your budget allows, you can replace the stew meat with chuck roast, which is more consistently tender than stew meat.

INGREDIENTS | SERVES 6

3 tablespoons butter-flavored coconut oil

1 medium yellow onion, peeled and diced

1½ pounds cubed beef stew meat

2 cups beef bone broth

¼ cup coconut aminos

¼ cup Worcestershire sauce

1 teaspoon garlic powder

1 teaspoon sea salt

1 teaspoon freshly ground black pepper

1 teaspoon arrowroot powder

1. Heat coconut oil in a medium skillet over medium-high heat. Add onion and cook until softened, about 4 minutes. Add meat and continue cooking until browned on all sides, about 5 minutes.

2. Stir remaining ingredients into mixture and bring to a boil. Reduce heat to low, cover, and simmer 2 hours.

3. Remove from heat and allow to cool slightly. Divide into six equal portions, transfer each portion to an airtight container and store in the refrigerator until ready to eat, up to one week.

PER SERVING Calories: 255 | Fat: 14 g | Protein: 24 g | Sodium: 857 mg | Fiber: 0.5 g | Carbohydrates: 4 g | Sugar: 2 g | Net Carbohydrates: 3.5 g

Tarragon Beef Tenderloin

If you can't find fresh tarragon, you can substitute with fennel fronds or fennel seeds, which have the same licorice-y flavor. If you like a subtler flavor, you can use dill, basil, or marjoram instead.

INGREDIENTS | SERVES 6

¼ cup minced yellow onion

¼ cup chopped fresh tarragon

2 tablespoons dry mustard

2 teaspoons orange zest

1 teaspoon sea salt

4 cloves garlic, minced

1½ pounds beef tenderloin roast

1. Preheat oven to 325°F.

2. Combine onion, tarragon, dry mustard, orange zest, salt, and garlic in a small bowl. Rub mixture all over roast.

3. Place roast in a roasting pan and roast 45 minutes or until internal temperature reaches 130°F. Remove from oven and allow to rest for 15 minutes.

4. Cut into six equal portions and transfer each portion to a separate airtight container. Allow to cool slightly. Store in the refrigerator until ready to eat, up to one week.

PER SERVING Calories: 160 | Fat: 6 g | Protein: 25 g | Sodium: 490 mg | Fiber: 0.5 g | Carbohydrates: 1.5 g | Sugar: 0.5 g | Net Carbohydrates: 1 g

Beef Shish Kabobs

This recipe requires that you marinate the beef for at least 8 hours, so keep that in mind when scheduling your meal prep days.

INGREDIENTS | SERVES 6

½ cup avocado oil

¾ cup coconut aminos

¼ cup lemon juice

1 tablespoon yellow mustard

1 tablespoon Worcestershire sauce

2 cloves garlic, minced

1 teaspoon freshly ground black pepper

1½ teaspoons sea salt

1½ pounds sirloin, cut into 1" cubes

2 medium green bell peppers, seeded and cut into chunks

2 medium red bell peppers, seeded and cut into chunks

1 large onion, peeled and cut into chunks

1. Combine avocado oil, coconut aminos, lemon juice, mustard, Worcestershire sauce, garlic, pepper, and salt together in a large sealable bag and shake to mix. Add sirloin and massage to coat. Refrigerate 8 hours or overnight.

2. Preheat grill to high heat.

3. Remove meat from bag and thread equal amounts onto twelve metal skewers. Repeat with equal amounts of peppers and onion.

4. Cook skewers on heated grill for 15 minutes, or until meat is no longer pink in the center, turning as you cook.

5. Allow to cool. Transfer two skewers to each of six separate airtight containers and store in the refrigerator until ready to eat, up to one week.

PER SERVING Calories: 341 | Fat: 23 g | Protein: 25 g | Sodium: 708 mg | Fiber: 2 g | Carbohydrates: 8.5 g | Sugar: 4 g | Net Carbohydrates: 6.5 g

CHAPTER 6

Pork

Pork Carnitas

Who needs Chipotle Mexican Grill when you can make these keto-friendly Pork Carnitas right at home? Once cooked, this recipe freezes well, so double or triple up on it and keep some in the freezer for access to a quick protein source at the drop of a dime.

INGREDIENTS | SERVES 6

2 tablespoons olive oil

2 pounds pork shoulder, cut into pieces

1½ teaspoons sea salt

1 teaspoon garlic salt

1 small yellow onion, peeled and chopped

2 cloves garlic, minced

1 tablespoon lime juice

2 teaspoons chili powder

¼ teaspoon dried oregano

½ teaspoon ground cumin

2 (14.5-ounce) cans chicken broth

1. Heat olive oil in a Dutch oven over high heat. Season pork with sea salt and garlic salt and add to Dutch oven. Cook 10 minutes, browning on all sides.

2. Add onion, garlic, lime juice, chili powder, oregano, cumin, and chicken broth and stir. Bring to a boil.

3. Reduce heat to low, cover, and cook 2 hours or until pork is cooked through and tender.

4. Preheat oven to 400°F.

5. Transfer pork to a baking sheet. Cook 20 minutes, basting with cooking liquid a couple times during baking. Remove from oven and cool slightly. Use two forks to shred meat.

6. Transfer equal amounts of meat to six separate airtight containers. Store in the refrigerator until ready to eat, up to one week.

PER SERVING Calories: 292 | Fat: 16 g | Protein: 32 g | Sodium: 950 mg | Fiber: 0.5 g | Carbohydrates: 3.5 g | Sugar: 1 g | Net Carbohydrates: 3 g

Italian Sausage, Peppers, and Onions

This recipe uses basic ingredients, but the flavor truly delivers. When choosing an Italian sausage, double-check your labels to make sure there's no added sugar. If you can't find any premade, use ground pork and mix in some sausage seasonings before cooking.

INGREDIENTS | SERVES 6

2 tablespoons olive oil

1 large yellow onion, peeled and sliced

4 cloves garlic, minced

2 large red bell peppers, seeded and sliced

1 large yellow bell pepper, seeded and sliced

1 teaspoon dried basil

1 teaspoon dried oregano

1½ pounds Italian sausage, cut into coins

¼ cup keto-friendly white wine

1. Add olive oil to medium skillet and heat over medium heat. Stir in onion and garlic and cook 2 minutes. Stir in bell peppers, basil, oregano, and sausage. Cook until vegetables are tender and sausage is browned, about 7 minutes.

2. Add white wine, reduce heat to low, cover, and simmer 20 minutes. Remove from heat and allow to cool.

3. Divide into six equal portions and transfer each portion to a separate airtight container. Store in the refrigerator until ready to eat, up to one week.

PER SERVING Calories: 347 | Fat: 25 g | Protein: 18 g | Sodium: 720 mg | Fiber: 2 g | Carbohydrates: 9 g | Sugar: 4 g | Net Carbohydrates: 7 g

Herb-Rubbed Pork Loin

One of the best ways to enjoy pork is with a generous sprinkle of dried sage. It imparts a sweet, piney flavor that perfectly complements the saltiness of the pork. It may seem like a simple ingredient, but try not to omit it!

INGREDIENTS | SERVES 6

2 teaspoons dried sage

½ teaspoon garlic salt

½ teaspoon sea salt

¼ teaspoon freshly ground black pepper

2 cloves garlic, minced

1 (2-pound) boneless pork loin

1. Preheat oven to 325°F. Place a wire rack in a roasting pan.

2. Combine spices and garlic in a small bowl and mix well. Rub spice mixture over pork, covering as much as possible.

3. Bake 2 hours or until internal temperature reaches 145°F. Allow to cool.

4. Cut into twelve medallions and transfer two medallions to each of six separate airtight containers. Store in the refrigerator until ready to eat, up to one week.

PER SERVING Calories: 298 | Fat: 18 g | Protein: 29 g | Sodium: 462 mg | Fiber: 0 g | Carbohydrates: 0.5 g | Sugar: 0 g | Net Carbohydrates: 0.5 g

Pork Picadillo

Traditional picadillo, which originates from Latin America, uses raisins to add some sweetness, but this low-carb version gives you all the flavor without kicking you out of ketosis.

INGREDIENTS | SERVES 6

2 tablespoons butter-flavored coconut oil

1 medium yellow onion, peeled and diced

3 cloves garlic, minced

1½ pounds ground pork

1 teaspoon sea salt

½ teaspoon garlic salt

½ teaspoon freshly ground black pepper

1 medium yellow bell pepper, seeded and cut into strips

1 medium green bell pepper, seeded and cut into strips

1 medium red bell pepper, seeded and cut into strips

1 cup diced tomatoes, with liquid

6 cups chopped spinach

1. Heat coconut oil in a medium skillet over medium heat. Add onion and garlic and cook until softened, about 4 minutes.

2. Add pork and cook 3 minutes. Sprinkle sea salt, garlic salt, and black pepper onto pork and cook until no longer pink, about 7 minutes.

3. Add sliced peppers and cook 6 minutes or until vegetables are tender, but still crisp. Add tomatoes and spinach and cook until spinach is wilted, about 2 minutes. Remove from heat and allow to cool.

4. Divide into six equal portions and transfer each portion to a separate airtight container. Store in the refrigerator until ready to eat, up to one week.

PER SERVING Calories: 370 | Fat: 28 g | Protein: 20 g | Sodium: 672 mg | Fiber: 2.5 g | Carbohydrates: 7.5 g | Sugar: 3.5 g | Net Carbohydrates: 5 g

Pork Enchiladas

Use the Pork Carnitas or the Deconstructed Pork Tamales (see recipes in this chapter) for the perfect pork pairing for this recipe. You can make shredded pork in big batches, freeze, and then thaw in the refrigerator as you need it.

INGREDIENTS | SERVES 6

3 cups shredded cooked pork

1½ cups Creamy Taco Sauce (Chapter 9)

1½ cups full-fat sour cream

6 tablespoons chopped green chilies

2 cups shredded nacho cheese blend

1. Toss pork with Creamy Taco Sauce in a medium bowl and transfer ½ cup of mixture to each of six separate airtight containers.

2. Top each serving with ½ cup sour cream, 1 tablespoon green chilies, and ⅓ cup shredded cheese.

3. Cover and store in the refrigerator until ready to eat, up to one week.

PER SERVING Calories: 422 | Fat: 26 g | Protein: 27 g | Sodium: 949 mg | Fiber: 4 g | Carbohydrates: 6 g | Sugar: 1 g | Net Carbohydrates: 2 g

Deconstructed Pork Tamales

This pork is perfectly seasoned to go into a traditional Mexican tamale, but since corn is out for keto, you can pair it with some simple riced cauliflower when organizing your meal prep containers.

INGREDIENTS | SERVES 12

1½ pounds pork butt roast, fat trimmed and cut into chunks

2½ cups chicken broth

1 small white onion, peeled and roughly chopped

2 cloves garlic, crushed

1 bay leaf

1 teaspoon salt

1 teaspoon dried oregano

1 teaspoon cumin

½ teaspoon whole black peppercorns

1 dried red chili pepper

1. Place pork in a large pot. Add remaining ingredients and stir. Bring to a boil over high heat. Reduce heat to low, cover, and simmer 1 hour.

2. Remove meat from broth, allow to cool, then shred with a fork.

3. Divide into six equal portions then transfer each portion to a separate airtight container. Store in the refrigerator until ready to eat, up to one week.

PER SERVING Calories: 193 | Fat: 8.5 g | Protein: 24 g | Sodium: 504 mg | Fiber: 0.5 g | Carbohydrates: 3.5 g | Sugar: 1 g | Net Carbohydrates: 3 g

Zesty Ginger Pork

Coating the pork in flour before browning gives it a crispy outer texture, but if you don't have the carbs to spare, or just prefer a very low-carb keto diet, omit that step and continue with the rest of the recipe as written.

INGREDIENTS | SERVES 6

1½ pounds boneless pork loin, cubed

¾ cup Paleo flour

2 tablespoons butter-flavored coconut oil

¼ cup chicken broth

½ cup water

3 tablespoons coconut aminos

3 tablespoons sliced green onion

2 cloves garlic, minced

1 teaspoon granulated erythritol

1½ teaspoons ground ginger

½ teaspoon sea salt

¼ teaspoon freshly ground black pepper

What Is Paleo Flour?

Paleo flour typically combines almond flour, coconut flour, tapioca flour, and arrowroot starch to mimic the baking and cooking effects of all-purpose flour. Although technically not a low-carb food, using a small amount of Paleo flour in a recipe with several servings is perfectly acceptable for a keto diet. You can purchase Paleo flour already made for you or you can make your own by combining 1½ cups (sifted) almond flour, 1 cup arrowroot powder, 1 cup coconut flour, and ½ cup tapioca flour in a jar and storing it in an airtight container.

1. Combine pork and flour in a large resealable bag and shake until pork is coated.

2. Heat coconut oil in a medium skillet over medium-high heat. Add pork and brown on all sides. Remove with a slotted spoon.

3. Add chicken broth, water, and coconut aminos to skillet and stir. Add remaining ingredients and browned pork and bring to a boil over high heat. Reduce heat to low, cover, and simmer 15 minutes or until pork is tender.

4. Remove from heat and allow to cool.

5. Divide into six equal portions and transfer each portion to a separate airtight container. Store in the refrigerator until ready to eat, up to one week.

PER SERVING Calories: 293 | Fat: 20 g | Protein: 24 g | Sodium: 354 mg | Fiber: 5 g | Carbohydrates: 11 g | Sugar: 0 g | Net Carbohydrates: 6 g

Creamy Mushroom Pork

Make sure to use homemade Cream of Mushroom Soup (Chapter 11) in this recipe. The canned stuff contains artificial ingredients and added sugars that have no place in a healthy keto diet.

INGREDIENTS | SERVES 6

2 cloves garlic, minced

1 teaspoon sea salt

1 teaspoon freshly ground black pepper

1 teaspoon dried thyme

6 (4-ounce) pork chops

3 tablespoons butter-flavored coconut oil

1 large yellow onion, peeled and chopped

2 cups Cream of Mushroom Soup (Chapter 11)

1. Preheat oven to 350°F.

2. Combine garlic, salt, pepper, and thyme in a small bowl. Rub mixture over pork chops, coating as much as possible.

3. Heat coconut oil in a large skillet over medium-high heat. Brown pork chops, cooking 1 minute on each side.

4. Transfer pork chops to a 9" × 13" baking dish. Sprinkle onions on top and cover with Cream of Mushroom Soup.

5. Cover and bake 45 minutes. Remove cover and cook an additional 15 minutes. Remove from oven and cool.

6. Transfer each pork chop to a separate airtight container and store in the refrigerator until ready to eat, up to one week.

PER SERVING Calories: 283 | Fat: 15 g | Protein: 25 g | Sodium: 835 mg | Fiber: 1 g | Carbohydrates: 8 g | Sugar: 1.5 g | Net Carbohydrates: 7 g

Spiced Cubed Pork

When heating this pork up, drizzle a little oil in a pan, add the pork, cover, and cook over low heat. The trapped condensation from covering will ensure that the reheated pork retains its moisture.

INGREDIENTS | SERVES 6

1 tablespoon chili powder
½ teaspoon sea salt
1½ teaspoons ground cumin
2 teaspoons minced garlic
1 teaspoon dried cilantro
⅛ teaspoon freshly ground black pepper
1½ pounds pork loin, cubed
1 tablespoon olive oil

1. Preheat oven to 325°F.

2. Combine spices in a small bowl. Rub spice mixture over pork, covering as much as possible.

3. Drizzle olive oil on the bottom of a 9" × 13" pan. Place pork on top of oil. Bake 45 minutes, or until pork is no longer pink. Remove from oven and cool.

4. Divide into six equal portions and transfer each portion to a separate airtight container. Store in the refrigerator until ready to eat, up to one week.

PER SERVING Calories: 249 | Fat: 16 g | Protein: 22 g | Sodium: 289 mg | Fiber: 0.5 g | Carbohydrates: 1 g | Sugar: 0 g | Net Carbohydrates: 0.5 g

Pork Sloppy Joes

The sauciness of this recipe makes it an ideal pairing for cauliflower rice or cooked spaghetti squash. Throw a serving in your airtight container before piling some of these Pork Sloppy Joes on top and the veggies will absorb some of the flavor while it sits in the refrigerator.

INGREDIENTS | SERVES 6

1½ pounds ground pork
1 cup no-sugar-added ketchup
½ cup water
2 tablespoons white vinegar
1 tablespoon granulated erythritol
1 teaspoon coconut aminos
1 teaspoon dry mustard
1 teaspoon sea salt

1. Crumble pork in a medium skillet and cook over medium heat until pork is no longer pink, about 7 minutes. Drain excess fat.

2. Add remaining ingredients and stir until combined. Reduce heat to low and simmer 20 minutes.

3. Divide into six equal portions and transfer each portion to a separate airtight container. Allow to cool slightly. Store in the refrigerator until ready to eat, up to one week.

PER SERVING Calories: 311 | Fat: 23 g | Protein: 19 g | Sodium: 871 mg | Fiber: 0 g | Carbohydrates: 5 g | Sugar: 2 g | Net Carbohydrates: 5 g

Italian Pork Tenderloin

Pork tenderloin is considered the filet of the pork because it's so tender (hence its name). Because of this, it's often one of the most expensive cuts of pork as well. For a version that's slightly more budget-friendly, use pork loin instead.

INGREDIENTS | SERVES 6

2 tablespoons olive oil

¼ cup chopped prosciutto

1 teaspoon dried sage

1 teaspoon dried parsley

½ teaspoon dried oregano

½ teaspoon dried basil

3 tablespoons chopped sun-dried tomatoes

1 small yellow onion, peeled and diced

1½ pounds pork tenderloin, cut into 1" medallions

¾ cup chicken bone broth

¾ cup heavy cream

¼ teaspoon sea salt

½ teaspoon freshly ground black pepper

Dried in the Sun

Sun-dried tomatoes are fresh, ripe tomatoes that have been left outside, with a little salt sprinkled on top, to dry in the sun. This process strips them of their water content, which means there are more carbs per volume when compared to fresh tomatoes, exactly like fresh fruit versus dried fruit. Keep this in mind when using them in recipes and make sure not to overdo it.

1. Heat oil in a medium skillet over medium heat. Add prosciutto, dried herbs, sun-dried tomatoes, and onion, and cook until onion starts to soften, about 5 minutes.

2. Add pork to pan and cook 10 minutes, browning on all sides.

3. Stir in remaining ingredients and bring to a boil over medium-high heat. Reduce heat to low and simmer 20 minutes, stirring occasionally. Remove from heat and allow to cool.

4. Divide into six equal portions and transfer each portion to a separate airtight container. Store in the refrigerator until ready to eat, up to one week.

PER SERVING Calories: 280 | Fat: 18 g | Protein: 25 g | Sodium: 181 mg | Fiber: 0.5 g | Carbohydrates: 3 g | Sugar: 2 g | Net Carbohydrates: 2.5 g

Greek-Style Pork Tenderloin

This recipe calls for 4 hours of refrigeration to let the meat marinate, but you can prepare it the night before you plan to cook it and let it sit in the marinade overnight.

INGREDIENTS | SERVES 6

1½ cups fresh lime juice

¾ cup olive oil

8 cloves garlic, sliced

1½ teaspoons sea salt

5 tablespoons dried oregano

1½ pounds pork tenderloin

Why Marinate?

Letting your meat sit in marinade has two purposes: it tenderizes the meat and imparts flavor. The four main components of a good marinade are an oil, an acid (like lemon/lime juice, wine, or vinegar), seasoning, and salt. Of course, when a recipe calls for marinating, that usually means that you have to prepare in advance, so always read through recipes in their entirety before your planned cooking day.

1. Combine lime juice, olive oil, garlic, salt, and oregano in a large resealable bag and shake to mix. Add pork and massage to coat. Refrigerate 4 hours.

2. Preheat grill to medium heat.

3. Use a small amount of olive oil to oil grill grate. Remove pork from marinade and grill 25 minutes, turning once during cooking, or until pork reaches desired doneness. Remove from grill and allow to cool.

4. Cut into twelve medallions and transfer two medallions to each of six separate airtight containers. Store in the refrigerator until ready to eat, up to one week.

PER SERVING Calories: 386 | Fat: 29 g | Protein: 24 g | Sodium: 655 mg | Fiber: 1 g | Carbohydrates: 7 g | Sugar: 1.5 g | Net Carbohydrates: 6 g

Rosemary Pork Roast

To get a head start on your next meal prep, get two pork loins and after spreading the herb mixture on them, vacuum seal one of them and store it in the freezer. This will start the marinating process and make it easy to prepare a roast down the road.

INGREDIENTS | SERVES 6

2 tablespoons fresh rosemary
1½ teaspoons garlic salt
½ teaspoon dried thyme
¼ teaspoon dried marjoram
½ teaspoon freshly ground black pepper
1 tablespoon olive oil
1½ pounds boneless pork loin

1. Preheat oven to 350°F.

2. Combine herbs and spices in a small bowl.

3. Rub olive oil all over pork loin. Sprinkle herb mixture all over pork, covering as much as possible.

4. Cook 45 minutes or until pork reaches an internal temperature of 145°F. Remove from oven and allow to cool.

5. Cut into twelve medallions and transfer two medallions to each of six separate airtight containers. Store in the refrigerator until ready to eat, up to one week.

PER SERVING Calories: 243 | Fat: 16 g | Protein: 22 g | Sodium: 637 mg | Fiber: 0 g | Carbohydrates: 0 g | Sugar: 0 g | Net Carbohydrates: 0 g

Breaded Pork Cutlets

The breading on these pork cutlets is a mixture of Paleo flour and almond meal, which mimics the crispiness of bread crumbs, but without the carbohydrates.

INGREDIENTS | SERVES 6

1 teaspoon salt

½ teaspoon freshly ground black pepper

2 tablespoons Paleo flour

1½ pounds pork tenderloin, cut into 12 medallions

2 large eggs, beaten

2 cups almond meal

2 tablespoons grass-fed butter

Butter Is Back!

Butter used to be on the naughty list because of its high-saturated fat content, but like eggs, it's been let off the hook. High-quality butter, like the kind that comes from grass-fed cows, contains four hundred different fatty acids and the fat-soluble vitamins A, D, and K. It also contains conjugated linoleic acid, which helps the body store muscle instead of fat and has been shown to protect against certain types of cancer.

1. Combine salt, pepper, and Paleo flour in a medium bowl. Set aside.

2. Pound pork with a meat mallet to ½" thickness. Dredge pork in flour mixture. Dip coated pork in eggs and then cover in almond meal.

3. Heat butter in a medium skillet over medium heat. Add pork and cook until browned on both sides and pork is no longer pink, about 8 minutes. Remove from heat and allow to cool.

4. Transfer two pork medallions to each of six separate airtight containers and store in the refrigerator until ready to eat, up to one week.

PER SERVING Calories: 336 | Fat: 8.5 g | Protein: 30 g | Sodium: 471 mg | Fiber: 2.5 g | Carbohydrates: 9 g | Sugar: 0 g | Net Carbohydrates: 6.5 g

Garlic-Baked Pork Chops

If you prefer pork tenderloin over pork chops, you can replace the chops in this recipe. The basic garlic spread pairs well with chicken breasts and thighs too.

INGREDIENTS | SERVES 6

3 tablespoons grass-fed butter, melted
2 large eggs, lightly beaten
3 tablespoons full-fat coconut milk
6 (4-ounce) pork chops, butterflied
1 teaspoon granulated garlic
¼ teaspoon garlic salt

1. Preheat oven to 425°F. Drizzle melted butter into a 9" × 13" baking dish, covering the bottom.

2. Whisk together eggs and milk in a medium bowl. Dip pork chops into mixture then sprinkle with granulated garlic and garlic salt. Place pork chops in prepared baking dish.

3. Bake 10 minutes, flip, and bake another 10 minutes, or until pork is no longer pink. Remove from oven and cool.

4. Transfer each pork chop to a separate airtight container and store in the refrigerator until ready to eat, up to one week.

PER SERVING Calories: 234 | Fat: 13 g | Protein: 26 g | Sodium: 188 mg | Fiber: 0 g | Carbohydrates: 0.5 g | Sugar: 0 g | Net Carbohydrates: 0.5 g

Grecian Pulled Pork

This Grecian Pulled Pork comes together in minutes and freezes well, so if you want an easy way to fill your freezer, double or triple the recipe. The cooking time will stay the same, as long as you spread the pork out in the slow cooker.

INGREDIENTS | SERVES 6

1½ pounds pork tenderloin
1½ tablespoons Greek seasoning
1 (16-ounce) jar sliced pepperoncini peppers

Pickled Peppers

Pepperoncini peppers are popular in both Greek and Italian cooking. The Italian variety is not as sweet as the Greek variety, but they're both considered a medium-spiced pepper. The brine from jarred pepperoncini peppers contains vitamins, minerals, electrolytes, and probiotics, so don't discard it! You can use it in recipes or drink it to keep yourself hydrated.

1. Cover pork tenderloin in Greek seasoning. Transfer coated pork to a slow cooker, pour in jar of pepperoncini peppers and their juice, and cook on low for 8 hours.

2. Remove pork from slow cooker and shred with two forks. Return to slow cooker and cook another 30 minutes. Remove from heat and allow to cool.

3. Divide into six equal portions and transfer each portion to a separate airtight container. Store in the refrigerator until ready to eat, up to one week.

PER SERVING Calories: 151 | Fat: 2.5 g | Protein: 24 g | Sodium: 64 mg | Fiber: 1 g | Carbohydrates: 7 g | Sugar: 0 g | Net Carbohydrates: 6 g

Spicy Pork Meatballs

If you're not a fan of fish sauce or you don't have any on hand, you can double up the coconut aminos or use a tablespoon of Worcestershire sauce in its place.

INGREDIENTS | SERVES 6 (MAKES 24 MEATBALLS)

1½ teaspoons baking powder

1 tablespoon water

1½ pounds ground pork

1 tablespoon fish sauce

1 tablespoon coconut aminos

6 cloves garlic, minced

¾ teaspoon sea salt

¾ teaspoon freshly ground black pepper

1. In a small bowl dissolve baking powder in water.

2. Combine all ingredients together in a medium bowl and mix with your hands until incorporated. Refrigerate 1 hour.

3. Preheat oven to 325°F.

4. Form mixture into 1½" meatballs and arrange on a baking sheet. Bake 25 minutes or until pork is no longer pink. Remove from oven and cool.

5. Transfer four meatballs to each of six separate airtight containers. Store in the refrigerator until ready to eat, up to one week.

PER SERVING Calories: 151 | Fat: 2.5 g | Protein: 24 g | Sodium: 64 mg | Fiber: 1 g | Carbohydrates: 7 g | Sugar: 0 g | Net Carbohydrates: 6 g

Swedish Meatballs

The best way to heat up these Swedish meatballs is in a saucepan over low heat, covered, with some of their sauce; but if you're in a pinch or on the go, you can use the microwave instead.

INGREDIENTS | SERVES 6

⅓ cup almond meal

⅓ cup heavy cream

2 tablespoons grass-fed butter, divided

1 small yellow onion, peeled and minced

½ pound ground pork

½ pound ground beef

1 large egg, lightly beaten

1 teaspoon sea salt

¼ teaspoon freshly ground black pepper

¼ teaspoon ground allspice

¼ teaspoon ground nutmeg

3 tablespoons Paleo flour

1½ cups beef bone broth

⅓ cup full-fat sour cream

Bone Broth versus Stock

Bone broth and stock are similar in preparation but differ in how they're cooked. Stock is typically simmered for a couple hours, while bone broth is simmered 12–24 hours, depending on whether it's chicken or beef. The longer simmering time pulls all the nutrients from the bones—nutrients that aren't available in a lot of other foods. You can replace bone broth with stock in any recipe, but if you can find bone broth or make your own, the foods will be more nutritious.

1. Preheat oven to 350°F.

2. Combine almond meal with heavy cream in a small bowl and let sit for 20 minutes to absorb liquid. Drain any excess liquid.

3. Heat 1 tablespoon butter in a small skillet over medium heat and add onion. Cook until softened, about 4 minutes. Transfer to a large bowl and mix in almond meal mixture, pork, beef, egg, salt, pepper, and spices. Use your hands to mix until everything is evenly incorporated.

4. Form mixture into 1" meatballs.

5. Melt remaining butter in a medium skillet over medium heat. Cook meatballs in skillet until the outside is browned, about 5 minutes. Transfer to a rimmed baking tray lined with parchment paper and bake 30 minutes or until meatballs are cooked through.

6. Remove meatballs from baking sheet and transfer pan juices to a small saucepan over medium heat. Whisk in flour and beef broth and continue to cook until thickened, about 5 minutes. Remove from heat and stir in sour cream. Pour sauce over meatballs and toss to coat.

7. Divide meatballs evenly among six separate airtight containers and store in the refrigerator until ready to eat, up to one week.

PER SERVING Calories: 339 | Fat: 26 g | Protein: 16 g | Sodium: 677 mg | Fiber: 2.5 g | Carbohydrates: 10 g | Sugar: 1 g | Net Carbohydrates: 7.5 g

Pork Sausage–Stuffed Peppers

If you prefer a softer texture instead of a crispy one, you can blanch the peppers before stuffing them by putting them in boiling water for 3 minutes and then directly into an ice bath.

INGREDIENTS | SERVES 6

½ pound hot Italian sausage

1 pound 85/15 ground beef

1 (14.5-ounce) can fire-roasted tomatoes

¼ cup chopped Italian parsley

3 cloves garlic, minced

1 teaspoon sea salt

½ teaspoon freshly ground black pepper

⅛ teaspoon ground cayenne pepper

2 cups riced cauliflower

6 medium red bell peppers, tops cut off to form "cups" and seeded

1 cup grated Parmesan cheese

1. Preheat oven to 375°F.

2. Combine hot sausage and ground beef in a medium skillet over medium heat. Cook until no longer pink, about 7 minutes. Add tomatoes, parsley, garlic, salt, black pepper, cayenne pepper, and cauliflower and cook until cauliflower starts to soften, about 5 minutes.

3. Arrange peppers, cut side up, in a 9" × 13" baking dish. Divide sausage mixture into six equal portions and scoop each portion into each pepper. Sprinkle Parmesan cheese on top.

4. Bake 45 minutes or until mixture is hot and bubbly and peppers are tender. Remove from oven and allow to cool.

5. Transfer each pepper to a separate airtight container and store in the refrigerator until ready to eat, up to one week.

PER SERVING Calories: 392 | Fat: 25 g | Protein: 26 g | Sodium: 878 mg | Fiber: 4 g | Carbohydrates: 14 g | Sugar: 7 g | Net Carbohydrates: 10 g

Pork Burgers

The feta cheese in these pork burgers keeps them nice and moist and the hot sauce adds a little kick. If you prefer a burger without any kick, you can omit the hot sauce with no sacrifice to taste.

INGREDIENTS | SERVES 6

1½ pounds ground pork

1 small sweet onion, peeled and chopped

⅔ cup crumbled feta cheese

2 tablespoons Worcestershire sauce

1 teaspoon coconut aminos

2 tablespoons Frank's RedHot sauce

1 tablespoon minced garlic

1 teaspoon sea salt

¾ teaspoon freshly ground black pepper

2 tablespoons butter-flavored coconut oil

1. Combine all ingredients, except coconut oil, in a large bowl and mix with your hands until incorporated. Form mixture into six patties.

2. Heat coconut oil in a large skillet over medium heat. Add patties and cook 5 minutes on each side or until they reach desired level of doneness. Remove from heat and allow to cool slightly.

3. Transfer each patty to a separate airtight container and store in the refrigerator until ready to eat, up to one week.

PER SERVING Calories: 390 | Fat: 31 g | Protein: 21 g | Sodium: 659 mg | Fiber: 0.5 g | Carbohydrates: 3.5 g | Sugar: 2 g | Net Carbohydrates: 3 g

Sweet As Onions

Sweet onions contain less sulfur than other onion varieties, so they won't make you cry when you cut them. They're the perfect choice for eating raw, lightly cooking, or in relishes. The varieties of sweet onions include Vidalia, Texas, Maui, and Walla Walla.

CHAPTER 7

Vegetarian and Vegan

Cauliflower Zucchini Fritters

These fritters combine both cauliflower and zucchini, but you can make them with just cauliflower or only zucchini, if that's what you have on hand or that's what you prefer. Top them with an over-easy egg and an avocado for a meal that's perfectly balanced in macronutrients.

INGREDIENTS | SERVES 6 (MAKES 12 FRITTERS)

1 large head of cauliflower, riced and cooked

1 medium zucchini, shredded and squeezed dry

2 large eggs

⅔ cup almond flour

½ teaspoon garlic powder

½ teaspoon sea salt

¼ teaspoon freshly ground black pepper

3 tablespoons butter-flavored coconut oil

1. Combine all ingredients in a large bowl and mix well. Form into twelve patties.

2. Heat coconut oil in a medium skillet over medium-high heat. Cook each patty 4 minutes on each side, or until browned and crispy. Remove from heat and transfer to a paper towel–lined plate.

3. Allow to cool and transfer two fritters to each of six separate airtight containers. Store in the refrigerator until ready to eat, up to one week.

PER SERVING Calories: 165 | Fat: 9 g | Protein: 6 g | Sodium: 250 mg | Fiber: 2.5 g | Carbohydrates: 8 g | Sugar: 2.5 g | Net Carbohydrates: 5.5 g

Basil Vinaigrette

Several other dressings in Chapter 9 are also vegan, but this one is a standout vegan dressing that is great both on salads and as a marinade for roasted vegetables.

INGREDIENTS | SERVES 12 (MAKES ABOUT 1½ CUPS)

⅔ cup olive oil

⅔ cup apple cider vinegar

¼ cup granulated erythritol

3 tablespoons chopped fresh basil

3 cloves garlic, minced

1. Combine all ingredients, except garlic, in a food processor and process until combined. Strain through a fine-mesh cheesecloth to remove basil bits.

2. Stir in garlic and transfer to an airtight container. Store in the refrigerator until ready to use, up to one week.

PER SERVING Calories: 110 | Fat: 12 g | Protein: 0 g | Sodium: 1 mg | Fiber: 0 g | Carbohydrates: 2 g | Sugar: 0 g | Net Carbohydrates: 2 g

Red Pepper and Tomato Soup

*If you want to add a little spice and even more of a roasted flavor to this soup,
use a can of fire-roasted diced tomatoes in place of the regular version.*

INGREDIENTS | SERVES 6

2 teaspoons olive oil

1 medium onion, peeled and chopped

2 cloves garlic, minced

1 (14.5-ounce) can diced tomatoes

1 (24-ounce) jar roasted red peppers,
 drained and chopped

2 teaspoons paprika

1½ teaspoons dried thyme

¼ teaspoon granulated erythritol

6 cups vegetable broth

1 teaspoon sea salt

½ teaspoon freshly ground black pepper

⅛ teaspoon ground cayenne pepper

2 teaspoons Frank's RedHot sauce

½ teaspoon arrowroot powder

Roasting Your Red Peppers

If you prefer to roast your peppers fresh,
preheat the oven to 450°F, cut the peppers
in half, and remove the stems, seeds, and
membranes. Lay the peppers on a baking
sheet lined with parchment paper, cut side
down. Roast the peppers for 15–20
minutes or until the skins are dark and
sunken in. Let the peppers cool, remove
and discard the skins, then slice the
peppers. You can freeze roasted peppers
and keep them for several months.

1. Heat olive oil in a large skillet over medium heat. Add onion and garlic and cook until softened, about 5 minutes. Stir in tomato, roasted peppers, paprika, thyme, and erythritol. Cook, uncovered, 25 minutes or until most of the liquid has evaporated.

2. Stir in remaining ingredients, except arrowroot powder, and bring to a boil. Reduce heat to low and simmer 30 minutes.

3. Use an immersion blender to purée soup. Stir in arrowroot powder and cook over low heat another 10 minutes. Remove from heat and cool.

4. Divide into six equal portions and transfer each portion to a separate airtight container. Store in the refrigerator until ready to eat, up to one week.

PER SERVING Calories: 93 | Fat: 2 g | Protein: 3 g | Sodium: 927 mg | Fiber: 3.5 g | Carbohydrates: 15 g | Sugar: 10 g | Net Carbohydrates: 11.5 g

Zoodles with Avocado Cream Sauce

These zoodles require no cooking and are ready in 10 minutes flat. However, if you prefer your zoodles warm and slightly softened, you can sauté them in hot oil for a couple of minutes before tossing them with the sauce.

INGREDIENTS | SERVES 6

3 cups fresh basil

1 cup water

½ cup pine nuts

6 tablespoons lemon juice

½ teaspoon lemon zest

3 large avocados, peeled and pitted

3 large zucchini, spiralized

1½ cups cherry tomatoes, halved

1. Combine basil, water, pine nuts, lemon juice, lemon zest, and avocado in a food processor or blender. Blend until smooth.

2. Place zucchini noodles in a bowl and pour avocado cream sauce on top. Toss to coat. Add tomatoes and toss to combine.

3. Divide into six equal portions and transfer each portion to a separate airtight container. Store in the refrigerator until ready to eat, up to four days.

PER SERVING Calories: 266 | Fat: 2 g | Protein: 6.5 g | Sodium: 27 mg | Fiber: 10 g | Carbohydrates: 18 g | Sugar: 6 g | Net Carbohydrates: 8 g

Spiced Cauliflower Rice

Instead of using pre-riced cauliflower, you can rice your own by cutting 1½ large cauliflower heads into florets and pulsing them in a food processor.

INGREDIENTS | SERVES 6

2 tablespoons butter-flavored coconut oil

2 (12-ounce) bags riced cauliflower

2½ teaspoons California Gold Dust blend

½ teaspoon sea salt

¼ teaspoon freshly ground black pepper

¼ cup chopped fresh cilantro

A Spicy Blend

California Gold Dust is a blend of turmeric, cinnamon, ginger, black pepper, and chia seeds. In addition to providing a unique flavor, the spices help combat inflammation and balance blood sugar levels.

1. Heat coconut oil in a medium skillet over medium heat. Add cauliflower, California Gold Dust, salt, and pepper and cook until cauliflower is tender, about 7 minutes.

2. Remove from heat and stir in cilantro.

3. Allow to cool and divide into six equal-sized portions. Transfer each portion to an airtight container and store in the refrigerator until ready to eat, up to one week.

PER SERVING Calories: 68 | Fat: 4 g | Protein: 2 g | Sodium: 227 mg | Fiber: 2.5 g | Carbohydrates: 5.5 g | Sugar: 0.5 g | Net Carbohydrates: 3 g

Zucchini Lasagna

This vegan Zucchini Lasagna uses nuts to create the consistency of ricotta cheese. If you're vegetarian and eat dairy, you can replace the nuts with a blend of ricotta and cottage cheese.

INGREDIENTS | SERVES 6

3 cups raw cashews (soaked overnight)

2 tablespoons nutritional yeast

½ teaspoon garlic powder

1 teaspoon dried parsley

2 tablespoons lemon juice

1 tablespoon extra-virgin olive oil

1 teaspoon sea salt

½ teaspoon freshly ground black pepper

½ cup water

1 (28-ounce) jar no-sugar-added marinara sauce

3 large zucchini, sliced thinly with a mandoline

Soaking Nuts

Nuts can be hard to digest for many people, but they offer plenty of nutrients and a good dose of fat that fits in nicely on a keto diet. To make nuts more easily digestible, you can soak them, which breaks down phytic acid and neutralizes enzyme inhibitors. All you have to do is combine nuts with a little sea salt and enough water to cover them and leave them soaking overnight (or for a minimum of 7 hours).

1. Combine cashews, nutritional yeast, garlic powder, parsley, lemon juice, olive oil, salt, and pepper in a food processor and pulse until a coarse, moist meal is formed. Scrape down the sides of the food processor as you go.

2. Turn the food processor on low and slowly pour in water while the food processor is running. Continue processing 2 minutes, stopping to scrape the sides of the bowl down as necessary. Remove the bowl from food processor and set aside.

3. Preheat oven to 375°F.

4. Pour 1 cup marinara sauce into a 9" × 13" baking dish and spread out on bottom. Arrange zucchini slices over sauce in a single layer. Spread 1 cup cashew cheese on top of zucchini. Repeat layers until you run out of ingredients.

5. Bake, covered, for 45 minutes. Remove cover and bake another 15 minutes or until lasagna is hot and bubbly. Remove from oven and allow to cool.

6. Divide into six equal portions and transfer each portion to a separate airtight container. Store in the refrigerator until ready to eat, up to one week.

PER SERVING Calories: 507 | Fat: 42 g | Protein: 14 g | Sodium: 929 mg | Fiber: 8 g | Carbohydrates: 15 g | Sugar: 2 g | Net Carbohydrates: 7 g

Almond Cream Cheese–Stuffed Mushrooms

If you want to add some crisp back to these mushrooms when reheating, set your oven to broil and let them broil for a few minutes, but watch them carefully so they don't burn!

INGREDIENTS | SERVES 6

18 whole fresh mushrooms, cleaned

1 tablespoon olive oil

1½ tablespoons minced garlic

2 tablespoons minced onion

8 ounces almond milk cream cheese

½ teaspoon onion powder

½ teaspoon freshly ground black pepper

⅛ teaspoon cayenne pepper

¼ teaspoon sea salt

¼ cup chopped fresh basil

Making Your Own Almond Milk Cream Cheese

Several manufacturers make almond milk cream cheese that's typically available in the natural food section of your local grocery store. If you can't find any, you can make your own by combining 1⅓ cups soaked blanched almonds, ½ cup plain nondairy yogurt, 2 tablespoons lemon juice, 1 teaspoon sea salt, ¼ teaspoon onion powder, and 1½ teaspoons apple cider in a high-powered blender and blending on high until smooth.

1. Preheat oven to 350°F. Grease a baking sheet with olive oil cooking spray.

2. Break off mushroom stems and mince stems.

3. Heat olive oil in a medium skillet over medium heat. Add mushroom stems, garlic, and onion and cook until softened, about 4 minutes. Remove from heat and allow to cool.

4. Combine onion mixture with remaining ingredients and stir until fully incorporated. Fill each mushroom cap with equal parts of the mixture and arrange on prepared baking sheet.

5. Bake 20 minutes or until mushrooms are tender and stuffing starts to turn golden. Remove from oven and allow to cool.

6. Transfer three mushrooms to each of six separate airtight containers. Store in the refrigerator until ready to eat, up to one week.

PER SERVING Calories: 165 | Fat: 15 g | Protein: 4 g | Sodium: 236 mg | Fiber: 0.5 g | Carbohydrates: 4.5 g | Sugar: 2.5 g | Net Carbohydrates: 4 g

Peanut Butter Pancakes with Peanut Butter Drizzle

You can make these peanut-free by swapping the peanut butter for your favorite nut or seed butter in both the pancakes and the drizzle.

INGREDIENTS | SERVES 6 (MAKES 18 PANCAKES)

1¼ cups no-sugar-added creamy peanut butter, divided

1¾ cups unsweetened almond milk, divided

¼ cup plus 3 tablespoons granulated erythritol, divided

6 tablespoons ground flaxseed

6 tablespoons coconut flour

3 teaspoons baking powder

3 tablespoons butter-flavored coconut oil

1. Combine ¾ cup peanut butter, 1½ cups almond milk, and 3 tablespoons erythritol in a medium bowl and stir until smooth. In a separate bowl, combine flaxseed, coconut flour, and baking powder.

2. Fold flaxseed mixture into peanut butter mixture and stir until just incorporated.

3. Heat coconut oil in a skillet over medium heat. Spoon batter onto hot skillet. Cook 3 minutes on each side, or until golden brown and cooked through. Allow to cool then transfer three pancakes to each of six separate airtight containers.

4. Combine remaining erythritol, peanut butter, and almond milk in a small bowl and mix until smooth. Drizzle equal amounts on each portion of pancakes.

5. Store in the refrigerator until ready to eat, up to one week.

PER SERVING Calories: 450 | Fat: 38 g | Protein: 16 g | Sodium: 495 mg | Fiber: 10 g | Carbohydrates: 16 g | Sugar: 1 g | Net Carbohydrates: 6 g

Fudgy Brownies

You can make these brownies even "fudgier" by adding some stevia-sweetened chocolate chips to the batter or mixing some melted stevia-sweetened chocolate chips with heavy cream and spreading the mixture on top after cooling.

INGREDIENTS | SERVES 12

2 tablespoons ground flaxseed
5 tablespoons brewed coffee
½ cup butter-flavored coconut oil
½ cup water
¼ cup coconut milk yogurt
1 teaspoon vanilla extract
½ cup coconut flour
⅓ cup unsweetened cocoa powder
½ cup granulated erythritol
¼ teaspoon baking soda
¼ teaspoon sea salt

1. Preheat oven to 350°F. Line an 8" × 8" baking pan with parchment paper.

2. Whisk together flaxseed and coffee in a medium bowl and set aside to gel, about 10 minutes.

3. Combine flaxseed mixture with coconut oil, water, yogurt, and vanilla. Mix until just incorporated.

4. In a separate medium bowl, combine remaining ingredients. Fold dry ingredients into wet ingredients and mix until just blended.

5. Transfer mixture into prepared baking pan and spread out evenly. Bake 17 minutes or until set but slightly underdone. Remove from oven and allow to cool. Refrigerate overnight.

6. Cut into twelve equal-sized brownies and transfer each brownie to a separate airtight container or resealable bag. Store at room temperature until ready to eat, up to one week.

PER SERVING Calories: 103 | Fat: 10 g | Protein: 1.5 g | Sodium: 78 mg | Fiber: 4 g | Carbohydrates: 5 g | Sugar: 0.5 g | Net Carbohydrates: 1 g

Vegetarian Mexican Casserole

When you're ready to eat this Vegetarian Mexican Casserole, top it with some avocado, coconut sour cream, salsa, and fresh cilantro to make it a fresh, complete meal.

INGREDIENTS | SERVES 6

1 teaspoon ground cumin

2 teaspoons chili powder

½ teaspoon paprika

¼ teaspoon crushed red pepper flakes

¼ teaspoon dried oregano

¼ teaspoon garlic powder

¼ teaspoon onion powder

1 teaspoon sea salt

1 teaspoon freshly ground black pepper

2 tablespoons butter-flavored coconut oil

½ medium yellow onion, peeled and chopped

1 medium red bell pepper, seeded and diced

1 medium green bell pepper, seeded and diced

1 medium jalapeño, minced

1 large head cauliflower, riced

2 cups shredded four cheese Mexican blend

⅔ cup chopped Roma tomatoes

1. Preheat oven to 350°F.

2. Combine spices in a small bowl.

3. Heat coconut oil in a medium skillet over medium heat and add onion. Cook until starting to soften, about 3 minutes. Add bell peppers and jalapeño and cook another 4 minutes. Add cauliflower and combined spices and cook until cauliflower is tender, about 6 minutes.

4. Remove from heat and stir in 1 cup cheese. Transfer to a 9" × 13" baking dish.

5. Layer tomatoes on cauliflower mixture and sprinkle remaining cheese on top. Bake 30 minutes or until casserole is hot and bubbly and cheese is starting to turn golden. Remove from oven and cool.

6. Divide into six equal portions and transfer each portion to a separate airtight container. Store in the refrigerator until ready to eat, up to one week.

PER SERVING Calories: 266 | Fat: 20 g | Protein: 13 g | Sodium: 729 mg | Fiber: 3.5 g | Carbohydrates: 10 g | Sugar: 4 g | Net Carbohydrates: 6.5 g

Veggie Fajitas

The portobello mushrooms in this recipe give it a nice meaty texture, especially if you slice them thickly. When ready to eat, top with avocado and some coconut sour cream.

INGREDIENTS | SERVES 6

1 tablespoon butter-flavored coconut oil

2 cloves garlic, minced

2 medium green bell peppers, seeded and sliced

2 medium red bell peppers, seeded and sliced

1 medium yellow bell pepper, seeded and sliced

1 medium red onion, peeled and sliced

1 cup sliced portobello mushrooms

3 scallions, chopped

1 (4-ounce) can green chilies

1 teaspoon chili powder

1 teaspoon ground cumin

½ teaspoon garlic powder

½ teaspoon sea salt

½ teaspoon freshly ground black pepper

1. Heat coconut oil in a large skillet over medium heat. Add garlic and cook 1 minute. Add peppers and cook another 2 minutes. Stir in onions and cook another 2 minutes.

2. Add mushrooms, scallions, chilies, and all spices to the skillet. Cover and cook until vegetables are tender, another 5 minutes.

3. Remove from heat and cool. Divide into six equal portions and transfer each portion to a separate airtight container. Store in the refrigerator until ready to eat, up to one week.

PER SERVING Calories: 68 | Fat: 2.5 g | Protein: 2 g | Sodium: 215 mg | Fiber: 3 g | Carbohydrates: 10 g | Sugar: 5 g | Net Carbohydrates: 7 g

The Meaty Fungi

When you want a meaty taste without the meat, portobello mushrooms are the way to go. They have a rich, earthy, umami flavor that is very savory. They're also a great source of the phytochemicals L-ergothioneine and conjugated linoleic acid (or CLA), which help prevent cancer and aid in anti-aging. Mushrooms also have a detoxifying effect: they help eliminate toxins from the body and neutralize free radicals that contribute to chronic disease.

Cream Cheese Omelet

You don't often see cream cheese added to an omelet, but once you get a taste of the creamy texture, you'll never go back to anything else.

INGREDIENTS | SERVES 6

6 ounces cream cheese, softened
½ cup chopped scallions
1 teaspoon garlic salt
¼ cup grass-fed butter
12 large eggs, lightly beaten

1. Combine cream cheese, scallions, and salt in a bowl and mix well.

2. Heat half the butter in a medium skillet over medium heat. Pour in half the eggs and allow to cook, pushing the omelet toward one side of the pan as it cooks and allowing the raw egg to escape onto the bare side of the skillet.

3. When the egg is almost set, remove from heat and spread half the cream cheese mixture down the middle. Fold omelet over and remove from pan. Repeat with remaining butter, eggs, and cream cheese mixture.

4. Cut each omelet in three equal portions and transfer each portion to six separate airtight containers. Store in the refrigerator until ready to eat, up to one week.

PER SERVING Calories: 308 | Fat: 26 g | Protein: 14 g | Sodium: 634 mg | Fiber: 0 g | Carbohydrates: 2 g | Sugar: 1.5 g | Net Carbohydrates: 2 g

Broccoli Slaw

Broccoli Slaw is a great alternative to coleslaw and an excellent addition to any veggie burgers or portobello mushrooms burgers. It adds a creaminess and crunch that improves the texture of a veggie-rich meal.

INGREDIENTS | SERVES 6

⅓ cup coconut oil mayonnaise

1 tablespoon apple cider vinegar

1 teaspoon granulated erythritol

2 tablespoons lime juice

½ teaspoon sea salt

¼ teaspoon freshly ground black pepper

2 (12-ounce) bags broccoli slaw

1 small red onion, peeled and chopped

Use the Stalks

You can find broccoli slaw in the produce/deli section of your supermarket near the bags of coleslaw. If you can't find any precut broccoli slaw, you can make your own by julienning broccoli stalks. It's also a great way to use up the nutrient-rich stalks that you might otherwise throw in the trash.

1. Whisk mayonnaise, vinegar, erythritol, lime juice, salt, and pepper in a medium mixing bowl. Add broccoli slaw and red onion and toss to coat.

2. Divide into six equal portions and transfer each portion to a separate airtight container. Store in the refrigerator until ready to eat, up to one week.

PER SERVING Calories: 132 | Fat: 10 g | Protein: 3.5 g | Sodium: 302 mg | Fiber: 3 g | Carbohydrates: 9 g | Sugar: 2.5 g | Net Carbohydrates: 7 g

Mushroom Burgers

The key to turning mushrooms into burgers is to make a crumble that resembles ground beef. If the mushrooms just aren't sticking together, add a little vegetable broth at a time to moisten them.

INGREDIENTS | SERVES 6

1 tablespoon ground flaxseed

3 tablespoons water

2 tablespoons butter-flavored coconut oil, divided

1 pound fresh portobello mushrooms, finely chopped

1 large yellow onion, peeled and minced

3 cloves garlic, minced

2 tablespoons coconut aminos

1 teaspoon salt

½ teaspoon freshly ground black pepper

Flax Eggs

In baking, eggs help hold baked products together, providing structure and helping to leaven, but since eggs aren't suitable for a vegan diet, "flax eggs" were born. Flax eggs are made of water and ground flaxseed, which forms a gel that mimics the effect of eggs but without getting any animals involved. To make a flax egg, combine 1 tablespoon flaxseed meal with 2½ to 3 tablespoons water. Use one of these flax eggs in place of each egg called for in a recipe.

1. Combine flaxseed and water in a small bowl and let sit for 15 minutes until mixture gels.

2. Heat 1 tablespoon coconut oil in a medium skillet over medium heat. Add mushrooms, onion, and garlic and cook 4 minutes. Add coconut aminos and cook 1 more minute. Remove from pan and allow to cool.

3. Transfer mixture to a food processor and pulse until large crumbles form. Add flaxseed mixture, salt, and pepper and pulse again.

4. Divide mixture into six equal portions and form into patties. Heat remaining coconut oil in skillet and cook patties 5 minutes, flipping once, or until patties are browned and crispy on both sides. Remove from heat and allow to cool slightly.

5. Transfer each burger to a separate airtight container and store in the refrigerator until ready to eat, up to one week.

PER SERVING Calories: 74 | Fat: 5 g | Protein: 2 g | Sodium: 395 mg | Fiber: 2 g | Carbohydrates: 6 g | Sugar: 3 g | Net Carbohydrates: 4 g

Cheese and Egg–Stuffed Peppers

This basic recipe gives lots of room for creative freedom. Add any low-carb veggies you want or switch up the herbs for some easy variation in your meal prep rotation.

INGREDIENTS | SERVES 6

6 large eggs

¾ cup whole milk ricotta cheese

¾ cup shredded Cheddar cheese

¾ cup grated vegetarian Parmesan cheese, divided

1 teaspoon garlic powder

½ teaspoon dried parsley

¾ cup baby spinach, chopped

3 medium red bell peppers, seeded and sliced in half lengthwise

1. Heat oven to 375°F. Line a baking sheet with parchment paper.

2. Combine eggs, ricotta cheese, Cheddar cheese, ½ cup Parmesan cheese, garlic powder, parsley, and spinach in a food processor and process until mixed well.

3. Pour equal amounts of egg mixture into each pepper half. Place peppers on baking sheet and bake 40 minutes.

4. Sprinkle remaining Parmesan cheese on top and broil 4 minutes or until cheese is bubbly and starts to brown. Remove from oven and cool.

5. Transfer each pepper to a separate airtight container and store in the refrigerator until ready to eat, up to one week.

PER SERVING Calories: 268 | Fat: 18 g | Protein: 19 g | Sodium: 401 mg | Fiber: 1.5 g | Carbohydrates: 6 g | Sugar: 3 g | Net Carbohydrates: 4.5 g

Very Veggie Spaghetti Squash Lasagna

This Very Veggie Spaghetti Squash Lasagna is the perfect base for any low-carb veggies that you have on hand. Put it in your rotation any time you need to get rid of extra vegetables or clear your refrigerator out for the next round of meal prep.

INGREDIENTS | SERVES 6

2 tablespoons butter-flavored coconut oil

2 cloves garlic, minced

1 small yellow onion, peeled and chopped

2 cups chopped white mushrooms

2 cups chopped spinach

1½ cups whole milk ricotta cheese

1 large egg

½ cup grated vegetarian Parmesan cheese

1 teaspoon Italian seasoning

1 teaspoon dried basil

½ teaspoon dried parsley

½ teaspoon garlic powder

½ teaspoon sea salt

¼ teaspoon freshly ground black pepper

6 cups cooked spaghetti squash

3 cups no-sugar-added marinara sauce

2 cups shredded mozzarella cheese

1. Preheat oven to 375°F.

2. Heat coconut oil in a medium skillet over medium heat. Add garlic and onions and cook until softened, about 4 minutes. Add mushrooms and cook another 4 minutes. Add spinach and cook until wilted, about 2 minutes. Remove from heat and set aside.

3. In a medium bowl, combine ricotta, egg, Parmesan, herbs, salt, and pepper and stir to combine.

4. Spread 3 cups spaghetti squash on the bottom of a 9" × 13" baking dish. Spread half vegetable mixture on top. Pour 1½ cups marinara over vegetables and sprinkle 1 cup mozzarella cheese on top. Repeat layers with remaining ingredients.

5. Bake 45 minutes or until hot and bubbly and cheese starts to turn golden brown. Remove from oven and allow to cool.

6. Divide into six equal portions and transfer each portion to a separate airtight container. Store in the refrigerator until ready to eat, up to one week.

PER SERVING Calories: 443 | Fat: 26 g | Protein: 23 g | Sodium: 1,065 mg | Fiber: 9 g | Carbohydrates: 20 g | Sugar: 6 g | Net Carbohydrates: 11 g

Four Cheese Pesto "Pasta"

*If you're pescatarian or a meat eater, you can stir in two cans of tuna
with the broccoli and make it a protein-rich tuna casserole.*

INGREDIENTS | SERVES 6

12 ounces mascarpone cheese

½ cup grated vegetarian Parmesan
cheese

¼ cup grated Asiago cheese

¾ teaspoon sea salt

½ teaspoon freshly ground black pepper

⅛ teaspoon ground nutmeg

½ cup pesto

8 cups raw zucchini noodles

¾ cup bite-sized broccoli florets, lightly
steamed

1½ cups grated mozzarella cheese

1. Preheat oven to 400°F.

2. Combine marscapone, Parmesan, Asiago, salt, pepper,
   nutmeg, and pesto in a large saucepan over low heat.
   Stir until melted and combined. Add zucchini and stir
   over heat 2 minutes. Remove from heat and transfer to
   a 9" × 13" pan.

3. Stir in broccoli florets and spread out evenly in pan.
   Sprinkle mozzarella cheese on top.

4. Bake 10 minutes or until hot and bubbly. Remove from
   oven and cool.

5. Divide into six equal portions and transfer each
   portion to a separate airtight container. Store in the
   refrigerator until ready to eat, up to one week.

PER SERVING Calories: 429 | Fat: 36 g | Protein: 17 g | Sodium:
773 mg | Fiber: 3 g | Carbohydrates: 11 g | Sugar: 6.5 g | Net
Carbohydrates: 8 g

Deconstructed Egg Roll

Traditional fried egg rolls aren't keto-approved, but this deconstructed version gives you all the taste without the extra carbs. If you have room in your macronutrient breakdown, you can add some julienned carrots to the mix too.

INGREDIENTS | SERVES 6

2 tablespoons butter-flavored coconut oil

1 large red onion, peeled and thinly sliced

1 cup broccoli slaw

8 medium stalks celery, chopped

12 cups shredded cabbage

1½ cups sliced white mushrooms

⅓ cup coconut aminos

¾ teaspoon sea salt

¼ teaspoon freshly ground black pepper

1 tablespoon water

1 tablespoon toasted sesame oil

2 tablespoons chopped scallions

2 tablespoons sesame seeds

1. Heat coconut oil in a large skillet over medium-high heat. Add onion and cook until softened, about 5 minutes.

2. Add broccoli slaw, celery, cabbage, mushrooms, coconut aminos, salt, pepper, and water. Cover and reduce heat to low. Cook 10 minutes or until vegetables reach desired level of doneness.

3. Remove from heat and stir in sesame oil, scallions, and sesame seeds. Allow to cool.

4. Divide into six equal portions and transfer each portion to a separate airtight container. Store in the refrigerator until ready to eat, up to one week.

PER SERVING Calories: 162 | Fat: 8.5 g | Protein: 5 g | Sodium: 398 mg | Fiber: 8 g | Carbohydrates: 19 g | Sugar: 9 g | Net Carbohydrates: 11 g

Creamy Shirataki with Spinach

To make this recipe vegan, you can use almond milk cream cheese in place of the dairy version and omit the Parmesan cheese. If you want a cheesier flavor, add a little nutritional yeast in its place.

INGREDIENTS | SERVES 6

1 tablespoon butter-flavored coconut oil

2 cloves garlic, minced

1 small yellow onion, peeled and diced

2 cups frozen chopped spinach, thawed and drained

6 ounces cream cheese

¼ cup grated vegetarian Parmesan cheese

1 teaspoon sea salt

½ teaspoon freshly ground black pepper

2 (7-ounce) packages shirataki noodles, rinsed thoroughly

1. Heat coconut oil in a medium skillet over medium heat. Add garlic and onion and cook until softened, about 4 minutes. Add spinach and cook until heated through, about 2 minutes.

2. Add cream cheese, Parmesan cheese, salt, and pepper and stir until melted and smooth.

3. Stir in shirataki noodles and toss to coat. Remove from heat.

4. Divide into six equal portions and transfer each portion to a separate airtight container. Store in the refrigerator until ready to eat, up to one week.

PER SERVING Calories: 236 | Fat: 13 g | Protein: 10 g | Sodium: 592 mg | Fiber: 1.5 g | Carbohydrates: 8 g | Sugar: 1.5 g | Net Carbohydrates: 6.5 g

Greek Buddha Bowl

Buddha bowls are typically made with various veggies, beans, and a grain, but this version omits the beans and replaces the grain with cauliflower rice. You can top it with nuts, seeds, or whatever keto-friendly ingredients you want.

INGREDIENTS | SERVES 6

6 ounces coconut yogurt

1 teaspoon paprika

1 teaspoon garlic powder

3 teaspoons lime juice

2 teaspoons butter-flavored coconut oil

3 cups riced cauliflower

1½ cups diced tomatoes

1½ cups diced zucchini

6 scallions, chopped

6 tablespoons cilantro, chopped

2 large avocados, peeled, pitted, and diced

1. In a small bowl, combine coconut yogurt, paprika, garlic powder, and lime juice and mix well. Set aside.

2. Heat coconut oil in a medium skillet over medium heat and add cauliflower. Cook 3 minutes or until cauliflower is softened, but not mushy. Stir in tomatoes and zucchini and cook for 2 more minutes. Remove from heat and stir in scallions and cilantro.

3. Divide cauliflower evenly between six separate airtight containers. Top each serving with an equal portion of coconut yogurt mixture. Place ⅙ of diced avocado on top.

4. Cover and store in the refrigerator until ready to eat, up to one week.

PER SERVING Calories: 171 | Fat: 13 g | Protein: 5 g | Sodium: 41 mg | Fiber: 7 g | Carbohydrates: 13 g | Sugar: 5 g | Net Carbohydrates: 6 g

CHAPTER 8

Salads

Seedy Broccoli Mason Jar Salad

As the raw broccoli sits in the mayonnaise mixture in the refrigerator, it will start to soften and soak in the vinegar flavors, so you don't have to cook it.

INGREDIENTS | SERVES 6

3 tablespoons white wine vinegar

2 tablespoons granulated erythritol

1 cup coconut oil mayonnaise

1 large head raw broccoli, cut into bite-sized florets

6 slices no-sugar-added bacon, cooked and crumbled

6 tablespoons minced red onion

6 tablespoons sunflower seeds

1. Combine vinegar, erythritol, and mayonnaise in a small bowl and whisk until incorporated. Transfer equal portions of mixture to the bottom of each of six quart-sized Mason jars.

2. Layer each Mason jar with equal amounts of broccoli, ⅙ crumbled bacon, 1 tablespoon onion, and 1 tablespoon sunflower seeds.

3. Store in the refrigerator until ready to eat, up to one week. When ready to eat, shake vigorously to combine ingredients and coat with dressing.

PER SERVING Calories: 449 | Fat: 44 g | Protein: 7 g | Sodium: 408 mg | Fiber: 2 g | Carbohydrates: 6 g | Sugar: 1.5 g | Net Carbohydrates: 4 g

Roasted Beet and Goat Cheese Mason Jar Salad

To save time on preparation and cleanup, purchase beets already peeled and roasted. You can find them in the refrigerated section of most produce departments.

INGREDIENTS | SERVES 6

12 tablespoons Basic Herb and Garlic Dressing (Chapter 9)

6 tablespoons chopped roasted beets

6 tablespoons chopped walnuts

6 tablespoons crumbled goat cheese

6 cups mixed baby salad greens

1. Pour 2 tablespoons dressing into the bottom of each of six separate quart-sized Mason jars.

2. Layer each jar with 1 tablespoon chopped beets, 1 tablespoon chopped walnuts, 1 tablespoon goat cheese, and 1 cup salad greens.

3. Store in the refrigerator until ready to eat, up to one week. When ready to eat, shake vigorously to combine ingredients and coat with dressing.

PER SERVING Calories: 253 | Fat: 21 g | Protein: 10 g | Sodium: 427 mg | Fiber: 1 g | Carbohydrates: 7 g | Sugar: 4 g | Net Carbohydrates: 6 g

Cheeseburger Mason Jar Salad

Thousand Island Dressing is often used as a "special sauce" on burgers, but if you want a more basic cheeseburger taste, you can use no-sugar-added ketchup and mustard in place of the dressing.

INGREDIENTS | SERVES 6

1½ pounds 85/15 ground beef

1 teaspoon sea salt

¼ teaspoon freshly ground black pepper

½ teaspoon garlic powder

½ teaspoon onion powder

12 tablespoons Thousand Island Dressing (Chapter 9)

6 tablespoons minced yellow onion

6 tablespoons diced tomatoes

6 tablespoons minced dill pickles

6 tablespoons shredded Cheddar cheese

6 cups chopped Romaine lettuce

1. Crumble beef in a medium skillet over medium-high heat and add seasonings. Cook until no longer pink, about 8 minutes. Allow to cool.

2. Pour 2 tablespoons of dressing into the bottom of each of six separate quart-sized Mason jars.

3. Layer equal amounts of beef, 1 tablespoon minced onion, 1 tablespoon tomatoes, 1 tablespoon pickles, 1 tablespoon Cheddar cheese, and 1 cup chopped Romaine lettuce.

4. Store in the refrigerator until ready to eat, up to one week. When ready to eat, shake vigorously to combine ingredients and coat with dressing.

PER SERVING Calories: 366 | Fat: 27 g | Protein: 22 g | Sodium: 528 mg | Fiber: 1.5 g | Carbohydrates: 10 g | Sugar: 8 g | Net Carbohydrates: 8.5 g

Mexican Cauliflower Mason Jar Salad

If you want to keep your avocado from turning brown, you can chop it and add it right before you eat the salad instead of adding it in during meal prep. However, if you keep the jar tightly sealed, it will delay the browning process.

INGREDIENTS | SERVES 6

1½ pounds 85/15 ground beef

1½ tablespoons taco seasoning

12 tablespoons Creamy Taco Sauce (Chapter 9)

3 small plum tomatoes, chopped

6 tablespoons scallions, chopped

6 tablespoons chopped avocado

6 tablespoons shredded Cheddar cheese

3 cups raw riced cauliflower

Homemade Taco Seasoning

Many of the taco seasonings found in the store have unappealing added ingredients, like cornstarch, MSG, and sugar. You can avoid all of that by making a batch of your own, plus it tastes better too! Just mix 1 tablespoon chili powder, 1½ teaspoons ground cumin, ½ teaspoon paprika, 1 teaspoon sea salt, 1 teaspoon freshly ground black pepper, ¼ teaspoon dried oregano, ¼ teaspoon red pepper flakes, ¼ teaspoon garlic powder, and ¼ teaspoon onion powder.

1. Crumble beef into a medium skillet over medium heat and cook until starting to brown, about 5 minutes. Add taco seasoning and cook until no longer pink, about 5 more minutes. Remove from heat and allow to cool.

2. Pour 2 tablespoons of Creamy Taco Sauce into the bottom of each of six separate quart-sized Mason jars.

3. Divide beef evenly between six jars and place on top of dressing.

4. Layer ⅙ of chopped plum tomatoes, 1 tablespoon scallions, 1 tablespoon chopped avocado, 1 tablespoon cheese, and ½ cup riced cauliflower in each jar. Cover and refrigerate.

5. Store in the refrigerator until ready to eat, up to one week. When ready to eat, shake vigorously to combine ingredients and coat with sauce.

PER SERVING Calories: 380 | Fat: 26 g | Protein: 23 g | Sodium: 395 mg | Fiber: 2.5 g | Carbohydrates: 10 g | Sugar: 2.5 g | Net Carbohydrates: 7.5 g

Greek Cauliflower Mason Jar Salad

Kalamata olives have pits, so keep that in mind when prepping this salad. Remove the pits and then mince the olives. If you prefer the taste of black olives, use those instead.

INGREDIENTS | SERVES 6

12 tablespoons Creamy Greek Dressing (Chapter 9)

1½ cups cooked chopped chicken

1½ cups chopped cucumbers

3 small plum tomatoes, diced

6 scallions, chopped

1½ cups chopped green bell pepper

6 tablespoons minced pitted Kalamata olives

3 cups raw riced cauliflower

1½ cups chopped kale

1. Pour 2 tablespoons dressing into the bottom of each of six separate quart-sized Mason jars.

2. Layer ¼ cup cooked chicken, ¼ cup chopped cucumber, ⅙ of chopped tomatoes, ⅙ of chopped scallions, ¼ cup bell pepper, 1 tablespoon olives, ½ cup cauliflower, and ¼ cup kale in each jar. Cover.

3. Store in the refrigerator until ready to eat, up to one week. When ready to eat, shake vigorously to combine ingredients and coat with dressing.

PER SERVING Calories: 180 | Fat: 9 g | Protein: 12 g | Sodium: 345 mg | Fiber: 3 g | Carbohydrates: 13 g | Sugar: 7 g | Net Carbohydrates: 10 g

Cauliflower Cobb Mason Jar Salad

If you want to make this a true cobb salad, swap out the cauliflower rice and use 1 cup of your favorite lettuce in each Mason jar.

INGREDIENTS | SERVES 6

12 tablespoons Jalapeño Ranch Dressing (Chapter 9)

1½ pounds cooked chopped chicken

6 slices no-sugar-added bacon, cooked and crumbled

6 large hardboiled eggs, chopped

3 small plum tomatoes, chopped

6 tablespoons chopped avocado

6 tablespoons crumbled blue cheese

1½ cups raw riced cauliflower

1. Pour 2 tablespoons dressing into the bottom of each of six separate quart-sized Mason jars.

2. Layer 4 ounces chicken, ⅙ crumbled bacon, ⅙ chopped eggs, ⅙ chopped tomatoes, 1 tablespoon avocado, 1 tablespoon blue cheese, and ¼ cup cauliflower in each jar. Cover.

3. Store in the refrigerator until ready to eat, up to one week. When ready to eat, shake vigorously to combine ingredients and coat with dressing.

PER SERVING Calories: 564 | Fat: 41 g | Protein: 45 g | Sodium: 679 mg | Fiber: 1.5 g | Carbohydrates: 6 g | Sugar: 3 g | Net Carbohydrates: 4.5 g

Deconstructed Burrito Mason Jar Salad

You can use the Pork Carnitas or Pork Enchiladas (see recipes in Chapter 6) in place of the shredded chicken in this recipe to give it a more authentic burrito taste.

INGREDIENTS | SERVES 6

12 tablespoons Spicy Chipotle Sauce (Chapter 9)

1½ pounds cooked shredded chicken

6 tablespoons minced red onion

¾ cup chopped roasted red peppers

6 tablespoons chopped avocado

6 tablespoons shredded Cheddar cheese

¾ cup chopped fresh cilantro

6 cups chopped iceberg lettuce

1. Pour 2 tablespoons Spicy Chipotle Sauce into the bottom of each of six separate quart-sized Mason jars.

2. Layer 4 ounces chicken, 1 tablespoon onion, ⅛ cup red peppers, 1 tablespoon avocado, 1 tablespoon Cheddar cheese, ⅛ cup cilantro, and 1 cup lettuce. Cover.

3. Store in the refrigerator until ready to eat, up to one week. When ready to eat, shake vigorously to combine ingredients and coat with sauce.

PER SERVING Calories: 286 | Fat: 12 g | Protein: 35 g | Sodium: 160 mg | Fiber: 2 g | Carbohydrates: 6 g | Sugar: 3 g | Net Carbohydrates: 4 g

Caprese Mason Jar Salad

Make sure to use the fresh balls of mozzarella cheese for this recipe and not the shredded cheese or the blocks of the cheese. Using the fresh stuff will give you a more authentic caprese flavor.

INGREDIENTS | SERVES 6

12 tablespoons Basil Vinaigrette (Chapter 7)

1½ cups grape tomatoes, halved

1½ cups chopped fresh mozzarella

1½ cups chopped fresh basil

6 cups chopped Romaine lettuce

1. Pour 2 tablespoons vinaigrette into the bottom of each of six separate quart-sized Mason jars.

2. Layer ¼ cup grape tomatoes, ¼ cup mozzarella, ¼ cup basil, and 1 cup lettuce in each jar. Cover.

3. Store in the refrigerator until ready to eat, up to one week. When ready to eat, shake vigorously to combine ingredients and coat with vinaigrette.

PER SERVING Calories: 246 | Fat: 22 g | Protein: 7.5 g | Sodium: 182 mg | Fiber: 1.5 g | Carbohydrates: 5 g | Sugar: 3 g | Net Carbohydrates: 3.5 g

Ranch Burgers (Chapter 5)

Roasted Beet and Goat Cheese Mason Jar Salad
(Chapter 8)

Jerk Chicken (Chapter 4)

Chicken Florentine Soup (Chapter 11)

Greek Buddha Bowl (Chapter 7)

Pepper Steak (Chapter 12)

Chicken Cordon Bleu
with Creamy Lemon Butter Sauce (Chapter 17)

Pumpkin Cheesecake Bars (Chapter 16)

Jalapeño Popper Fat Bombs (Chapter 15)

Bolognese-Stuffed Peppers (Chapter 5)

Gouda and Bacon–Stuffed Pork Tenderloin
(Chapter 17)

Spanakorizo (Chapter 10)

Spinach and Artichoke Dip (Chapter 13)

Coconut Berry Fat Bombs (Chapter 15)

Pork Picadillo (Chapter 6)

Pesto Chicken Pinwheels (Chapter 17)

Sausage, Spinach, and Pepper Soup (Chapter 11)

Nacho Pepper Boats (Chapter 14)

Southwest Egg and Cheese Muffins (Chapter 3)

Blackened Salmon (Chapter 17)

Tomato and Zucchini Bake (Chapter 10)

Key Lime Bars (Chapter 16)

Zucchini Pizza Bites (Chapter 14)

Spicy Pork Meatballs (Chapter 6)

Thai Peanut Mason Jar Salad

You can use raw plain broccoli slaw in this Thai Peanut Mason Jar Salad or add another dimension by using the Broccoli Slaw recipe (Chapter 7), which offers a little creaminess to the salad.

INGREDIENTS | SERVES 6

12 tablespoons Asian-Inspired Salad Dressing (Chapter 9)

1½ pounds cooked cubed chicken

1½ cups diced cucumber

1½ cups chopped red bell peppers

1½ cups broccoli slaw

6 tablespoons chopped cilantro

6 tablespoons chopped peanuts

6 cups chopped Romaine lettuce

1. Pour 2 tablespoons dressing into the bottom of each of six separate quart-sized Mason jars.

2. Layer 4 ounces cooked chicken, ¼ cup cucumber, ¼ cup red pepper, ¼ cup broccoli slaw, 1 tablespoon cilantro, 1 tablespoon peanuts, and 1 cup lettuce in each jar. Cover.

3. Store in the refrigerator until ready to eat, up to one week. When ready to eat, shake vigorously to combine ingredients and coat with dressing.

PER SERVING Calories: 372 | Fat: 22 g | Protein: 36 g | Sodium: 281 mg | Fiber: 3 g | Carbohydrates: 9 g | Sugar: 5 g | Net Carbohydrates: 6 g

Greek Zoodle Mason Jar Salad

Make sure to put the zoodles in last when putting this salad together. Zucchini contains a lot of moisture, so if you let it sit in dressing in the refrigerator it will get soggy.

INGREDIENTS | SERVES 6

12 tablespoons Creamy Greek Dressing (Chapter 9)

1½ cups chopped yellow bell pepper

1½ cups grape tomatoes, halved

¾ cup diced celery

6 tablespoons minced pitted Kalamata olives

6 tablespoons crumbled feta

6 tablespoons chopped avocado

6 cups spiralized zucchini

1. Pour 2 tablespoons dressing into the bottom of each of six separate quart-sized Mason jars.

2. Layer ¼ cup yellow pepper, ¼ cup tomatoes, ⅛ cup celery, 1 tablespoon olives, 1 tablespoon feta, 1 tablespoon avocado, and 1 cup zucchini in each jar. Cover.

3. Store in the refrigerator until ready to eat, up to one week. When ready to eat, shake vigorously to combine ingredients and coat with dressing.

PER SERVING Calories: 157 | Fat: 10 g | Protein: 4 g | Sodium: 404 mg | Fiber: 3.5 g | Carbohydrates: 14 g | Sugar: 9 g | Net Carbohydrates: 10.5 g

Bacon Turkey Club Mason Jar Salad

Always make sure to check your deli meat labels! Sugar and other sweeteners are often hidden in deli meats to make them last longer. If you're getting them from the deli counter, ask them if you can read the ingredient list before ordering.

INGREDIENTS | SERVES 6

12 tablespoons Jalapeño Ranch Dressing (Chapter 9)

1½ cups cherry tomatoes, halved

12 slices no-sugar-added bacon, cooked and crumbled

1½ pounds sliced turkey, chopped

¾ cup shredded Cheddar cheese

6 cups chopped Romaine lettuce

1. Pour 2 tablespoons dressing into the bottom of each of six separate quart-sized Mason jars.

2. Layer ¼ cup tomatoes, ⅙ crumbled bacon, 4 ounces chopped turkey, ⅛ cup cheese, and 1 cup lettuce in each jar. Cover.

3. Store in the refrigerator until ready to eat, up to one week. When ready to eat, shake vigorously to combine ingredients and coat with dressing.

PER SERVING Calories: 525 | Fat: 41 g | Protein: 42 g | Sodium: 919 mg | Fiber: 1.5 g | Carbohydrates: 6 g | Sugar: 3.5 g | Net Carbohydrates: 4.5 g

Greek Cobb Salad

If you want a true Greek gyro type of flavor, use some ground lamb for the protein in this salad in place of the chicken.

INGREDIENTS | SERVES 6

12 tablespoons Creamy Cilantro Dressing (Chapter 9)

1½ pounds cooked chopped chicken

6 large hardboiled eggs, chopped

6 slices no-sugar-added bacon, cooked and crumbled

¾ cup chopped tomatoes

6 tablespoons crumbled feta

6 tablespoons chopped avocado

6 cups baby spinach

1. Pour 2 tablespoons dressing into the bottom of each of six separate quart-sized Mason jars.

2. Layer 4 ounces chicken, ⅙ chopped hardboiled eggs, ⅙ crumbled bacon, ⅛ cup tomato, 1 tablespoon feta, 1 tablespoon avocado, and 1 cup spinach in each jar. Cover.

3. Store in the refrigerator until ready to eat, up to one week. When ready to eat, shake vigorously to combine ingredients and coat with dressing.

PER SERVING Calories: 522 | Fat: 33 g | Protein: 44 g | Sodium: 756 mg | Fiber: 1.5 g | Carbohydrates: 7 g | Sugar: 4 g | Net Carbohydrates: 5.5 g

Antipasto Mason Jar Salad

If you can't find garlic-stuffed green olives, you can substitute them with any green olives of your choice.

INGREDIENTS | SERVES 6

12 tablespoons Basic Herb and Garlic Dressing (Chapter 9)

1½ cups roasted red peppers

1½ cups grape tomatoes, halved

1½ cups diced cucumbers

¾ cup garlic-stuffed green olives

¾ cup chopped pepperoncini

¾ cup chopped artichoke hearts

6 tablespoons minced pepperoni

6 tablespoons minced salami

¾ cup chopped fresh mozzarella

6 cups chopped iceberg lettuce

1. Pour 2 tablespoons dressing into the bottom of each of six separate quart-sized Mason jars.

2. Layer ¼ cup red peppers, ¼ cup tomatoes, ¼ cup cucumbers, ⅛ cup olives, ⅛ cup pepperoncini, ⅛ cup artichoke hearts, 1 tablespoon pepperoni, 1 tablespoon salami, ⅛ cup mozzarella, and 1 cup lettuce in each jar. Cover.

3. Store in the refrigerator until ready to eat, up to one week. When ready to eat, shake vigorously to combine ingredients and coat with dressing.

PER SERVING Calories: 257 | Fat: 17 g | Protein: 10 g | Sodium: 824 mg | Fiber: 4 g | Carbohydrates: 16 g | Sugar: 5 g | Net Carbohydrates: 12 g

Southwestern Mason Jar Salad

Nacho blend cheese contains Cheddar, Colby, and Monterey jack cheeses, which all have mild flavors that tend to be crowd pleasers, combined with a Mexican spice blend.

INGREDIENTS | SERVES 6

12 tablespoons Creamy Cilantro Dressing (Chapter 9)

1½ pounds cooked cubed chicken

1½ cups chopped green bell pepper

1½ cups cherry tomatoes, halved

6 tablespoons minced black olives

¾ cup chopped avocado

¾ cup shredded nacho blend cheese

6 cups baby spinach

1. Pour 2 tablespoons dressing into the bottom of each of six separate quart-sized Mason jars.

2. Layer each jar with 4 ounces chicken, ¼ cup bell pepper, ¼ cup cherry tomato, 1 tablespoon olives, ⅛ cup avocado, ⅛ cup cheese, and 1 cup spinach. Cover.

3. Store in the refrigerator until ready to eat, up to one week. When ready to eat, shake vigorously to combine ingredients and coat with dressing.

PER SERVING Calories: 411 | Fat: 23 g | Protein: 38 g | Sodium: 584 mg | Fiber: 3 g | Carbohydrates: 10 g | Sugar: 5 g | Net Carbohydrates: 7 g

Bacon and Cheddar Mason Jar Salad

The iceberg lettuce in this salad gives it a satisfying crunch, but it's not the most nutritious of the greens. If you want to up the micronutrient content, use a blend of iceberg and mixed greens or swap the iceberg out and use baby spinach or baby kale instead.

INGREDIENTS | SERVES 6

12 tablespoons Jalapeño Ranch Dressing (Chapter 9)

12 slices no-sugar-added bacon, cooked and crumbled

1½ cups cherry tomatoes, halved

6 tablespoons minced red onion

1½ cups chopped avocado

1½ cups shredded Cheddar cheese

6 cups shredded iceberg lettuce

1. Pour 2 tablespoons dressing into the bottom of each of six separate quart-sized Mason jars.

2. Layer each jar with ⅙ crumbled bacon, ¼ cup tomatoes, 1 tablespoon red onion, ¼ cup avocado, ¼ cup shredded cheese, and 1 cup lettuce.

3. Store in the refrigerator until ready to eat, up to one week. When ready to eat, shake vigorously to combine ingredients and coat with dressing.

PER SERVING Calories: 475 | Fat: 49 g | Protein: 17 g | Sodium: 766 mg | Fiber: 4 g | Carbohydrates: 10 g | Sugar: 5 g | Net Carbohydrates: 6 g

Creamy Zoodle Mason Jar Salad

Combining the Dill Sauce with this salad makes the zoodles perfectly creamy and adds an antioxidant punch too.

INGREDIENTS | SERVES 6

12 tablespoons Dill Sauce (Chapter 9)

3 (5-ounce) cans tuna

¾ cup chopped roasted red peppers

¾ cup slivered almonds

¾ cup crumbled feta cheese

6 cups spiralized zucchini

Getting Down with Dill

Dill contains special compounds called monoterpene effects, which help antioxidants attach to free radicals to neutralize them so they can't cause damage to the body.

1. Pour 2 tablespoons Dill Sauce into the bottom of each of six separate quart-sized Mason jars.

2. Layer each jar with ½ can tuna, ⅛ cup peppers, ⅛ cup almonds, ⅛ cup feta cheese, and 1 cup of zucchini. Cover.

3. Store in the refrigerator until ready to eat, up to one week. When ready to eat, shake vigorously to combine ingredients and coat with Dill Sauce.

PER SERVING Calories: 390 | Fat: 25 g | Protein: 28 g | Sodium: 666 mg | Fiber: 4 g | Carbohydrates: 13 g | Sugar: 7 g | Net Carbohydrates: 9 g

Mediterranean Broccoli Mason Jar Salad

You can keep the broccoli in this salad raw, but if you prefer cooked broccoli, lightly steam it, about 5 minutes, so that it retains most of its crunch and wait until it cools down to seal the Mason jar. If you trap the heat inside, it will make everything soggy.

INGREDIENTS | SERVES 6

12 tablespoons Creamy Greek Dressing (Chapter 9)

¾ cup minced red onion

¾ cup chopped artichoke hearts

6 cups bite-sized broccoli florets

6 tablespoons roasted sunflower seeds

6 tablespoons minced sun-dried tomatoes

6 tablespoons crumbled feta

1. Pour 2 tablespoons dressing into the bottom of each of six separate quart-sized Mason jars.

2. Layer ⅛ cup onion, ⅛ cup artichoke hearts, 1 cup broccoli, 1 tablespoon sunflower seeds, 1 tablespoon sun-dried tomatoes, and 1 tablespoon feta. Cover.

3. Store in the refrigerator until ready to eat, up to one week. When ready to eat, shake vigorously to combine ingredients and coat with dressing.

PER SERVING Calories: 198 | Fat: 12 g | Protein: 7 g | Sodium: 380 mg | Fiber: 5 g | Carbohydrates: 14 g | Sugar: 5 g | Net Carbohydrates: 9 g

Chef Mason Jar Salad

Sometimes it can be difficult to find no-sugar-added deli meats behind the deli counter. Stores like Trader Joe's and Wegmans carry the Applegate brand, which has lots of keto-friendly options and is located with the pre-sliced packaged deli meats.

INGREDIENTS | SERVES 6

12 tablespoons Jalapeño Ranch Dressing (Chapter 9)

6 slices no-sugar-added bacon, cooked and crumbled

12 slices no-sugar-added ham, chopped

12 slices no-sugar-added turkey, chopped

12 slices Swiss cheese, chopped

6 large hardboiled eggs, chopped

¾ cup chopped avocado

6 cups spring salad mix

1. Pour 2 tablespoons dressing into the bottom of each of six separate quart-sized Mason jars.

2. Layer ⅙ crumbled bacon, ⅙ chopped ham, ⅙ chopped turkey, ⅙ chopped Swiss cheese, ⅙ chopped hardboiled egg, ⅛ chopped avocado, and 1 cup spring salad mix in each jar. Cover.

3. Store in the refrigerator until ready to eat, up to one week. When ready to eat, shake vigorously to combine ingredients and coat with dressing.

PER SERVING Calories: 624 | Fat: 49 g | Protein: 51 g | Sodium: 1026 mg | Fiber: 2 g | Carbohydrates: 7 g | Sugar: 3 g | Net Carbohydrates: 5 g

Roasted Vegetable Mason Jar Salad

Although this recipe is written as a salad, the roasted vegetable combo also makes a great side dish for any of the basic protein main dishes.

INGREDIENTS | SERVES 6

3 cups bite-sized cauliflower florets

1 medium zucchini, diced

1 small red bell pepper, seeded and sliced thinly

1 cup cherry tomatoes, halved

3 tablespoons olive oil

1 teaspoon garlic salt

½ teaspoon freshly ground black pepper

12 tablespoons Basic Herb and Garlic Dressing (Chapter 9)

1½ pounds cooked cubed chicken

6 tablespoons grated Parmesan cheese

1. Preheat oven to 400°F.

2. Combine cauliflower, zucchini, red pepper, and tomatoes on a rimmed baking sheet. Drizzle with olive oil and sprinkle with garlic salt and pepper. Roast for 20 minutes. Remove and cool.

3. Pour 2 tablespoons dressing into the bottom of each of six separate quart-sized Mason jars.

4. Layer each jar with equal amounts of roasted vegetables, 4 ounces of chicken, and 1 tablespoon Parmesan cheese.

5. Store in the refrigerator until ready to eat, up to one week. When ready to eat, shake vigorously to combine ingredients and coat with dressing.

PER SERVING Calories: 367 | Fat: 21 g | Protein: 36 g | Sodium: 709 mg | Fiber: 2 g | Carbohydrates: 8 g | Sugar: 6 g | Net Carbohydrates: 6 g

Chicken and Roasted Red Pepper Mason Jar Salad

You can use jarred roasted red peppers or peppers that you roast yourself for this salad. If you use jarred, pour a little of the brine into the dressing for added pepper flavor.

INGREDIENTS | SERVES 6

12 tablespoons Creamy Cilantro Dressing (Chapter 9)

1½ pounds cooked shredded chicken

1½ cups roasted red peppers, chopped

¾ cup crumbled feta

6 cups baby spinach

1. Pour 2 tablespoons dressing into the bottom of each of six separate quart-sized Mason jars.

2. Layer each jar with 4 ounces chicken, ¼ cup red peppers, ⅛ cup feta cheese, and 1 cup spinach. Cover.

3. Store in the refrigerator until ready to eat, up to one week. When ready to eat, shake vigorously to combine ingredients and coat with dressing.

PER SERVING Calories: 390 | Fat: 22 g | Protein: 37 g | Sodium: 465 mg | Fiber: 1.5 g | Carbohydrates: 5 g | Sugar: 3 g | Net Carbohydrates: 3.5 g

CHAPTER 9

Sauces and Dressings

Thousand Island Dressing

Thousand Island Dressing typically contains sugar and sweet relish, which has sugar in it, but this version combines a keto-friendly sweetener with fresh dill pickles.

INGREDIENTS | SERVES 12 (MAKES ABOUT 1½ CUPS)

1 cup coconut oil mayonnaise

2 tablespoons no-sugar-added ketchup

1 tablespoon raw apple cider vinegar

2 tablespoons minced dill pickle, divided

2 tablespoons minced white onion, divided

¼ teaspoon minced garlic

1 tablespoon powdered erythritol

⅛ teaspoon sea salt

⅛ teaspoon freshly ground black pepper

1. Add all ingredients, except 1 tablespoon pickles and 1 tablespoon onions, to a high-powered blender. Blend until smooth, about 1 minute.

2. Transfer to an airtight container and stir in remaining pickles and onions.

3. Refrigerate until ready to eat, up to one week.

PER SERVING Calories: 127 | Fat: 14 g | Protein: 0.5 g | Sodium: 162 mg | Fiber: 0 g | Carbohydrates: 1 g | Sugar: 1 g | Net Carbohydrates: 1 g

Jalapeño Ranch Dressing

This recipe calls for pickled jalapeños, but you can absolutely use fresh if you prefer them. If you want the dressing really spicy, add some of the seeds as well. If you want a milder jalapeño flavor, use only the flesh of the pepper.

INGREDIENTS | SERVES 12 (MAKES ABOUT 1½ CUPS)

½ cup coconut oil mayonnaise

½ cup full-fat sour cream

¼ cup heavy cream

2 tablespoons white vinegar

2 cloves garlic, minced

2 tablespoons chopped fresh dill

1 tablespoon chopped fresh parsley

1 teaspoon chopped fresh chives

1 teaspoon onion powder

1 teaspoon sea salt

½ tablespoon minced fresh cilantro

2 tablespoons minced pickled jalapeños

1 small tomato, diced

½ small avocado, peeled, pitted, and roughly chopped

1. Combine mayonnaise, sour cream, heavy cream, vinegar, garlic, dill, parsley, chives, onion powder, and salt in a high-powered blender. Blend until smooth. Add remaining ingredients and blend until incorporated.

2. Transfer to an airtight container and refrigerate at least 2 hours before serving.

3. Store in the refrigerator for up to one week.

PER SERVING Calories: 102 | Fat: 10 g | Protein: 0.5 g | Sodium: 252 mg | Fiber: 0 g | Carbohydrates: 1 g | Sugar: 0.5 g | Net Carbohydrates: 1 g

Creamy Greek Dressing

You'll get a creamier result with this dressing if you use fresh blocks of feta cheese and crumble it yourself, rather than buying the feta cheese that's already crumbled for you. Make sure to use full-fat cheese!

INGREDIENTS | SERVES 12 (MAKES ABOUT 1½ CUPS)

½ cup coconut oil mayonnaise

½ cup full-fat sour cream

¼ cup heavy cream

2 tablespoons white vinegar

2 cloves garlic, minced

2 tablespoons chopped fresh dill

1 tablespoon chopped fresh parsley

1 teaspoon chopped fresh chives

1 teaspoon onion powder

1 teaspoon sea salt

¼ cup crumbled feta cheese

2 tablespoons minced cucumber, seeded

2 tablespoons minced green bell pepper, seeded

2 tablespoons minced red onion

1 tablespoon minced Kalamata olives, pitted

¾ teaspoon dried oregano

¾ teaspoon dried basil

¼ teaspoon freshly ground black pepper

1. Combine mayonnaise, sour cream, heavy cream, vinegar, garlic, dill, parsley, chives, onion powder, and salt in a high-powered blender. Blend until smooth. Transfer mixture to an airtight container.

2. Combine remaining ingredients in blender and blend until smooth. Stir feta mixture into ranch dressing mixture until smooth.

3. Refrigerate at least 2 hours before serving. Store in the refrigerator up to one week.

PER SERVING Calories: 111 | Fat: 11 g | Protein: 1 g | Sodium: 281 mg | Fiber: 0 g | Carbohydrates: 1.5 g | Sugar: 0.5 g | Net Carbohydrates: 1.5 g

Creamy Taco Sauce

If you want to kick this Creamy Taco Sauce up a notch, use the Jalapeño Ranch Dressing (see recipe in this chapter) in place of regular ranch dressing.

INGREDIENTS | SERVES 12 (MAKES ABOUT 1½ CUPS)

½ cup full-fat sour cream
¼ cup ranch dressing
½ cup salsa, liquid drained
¼ teaspoon chili powder
¼ teaspoon taco seasoning

1. Combine all ingredients in a bowl and stir until combined.

2. Transfer to an airtight container and store in the refrigerator until ready to eat, up to one week.

PER SERVING Calories: 40 | Fat: 3.5 g | Protein: 0.5 g | Sodium: 139 mg | Fiber: 0 g | Carbohydrates: 1 g | Sugar: 1 g | Net Carbohydrates: 1 g

Lemon Poppy Seed Dressing

Poppy seeds give this dressing some color and texture, but they're not just for looks. Poppy seeds can help improve digestion, assist in red blood cell formation, and improve cognitive performance.

INGREDIENTS | SERVES 12 (MAKES ABOUT 1½ CUPS)

½ cup fresh lemon juice
⅓ cup granulated erythritol
2 teaspoons diced white onion
1 teaspoon Dijon mustard
½ teaspoon sea salt
⅔ cup avocado oil
1 tablespoon poppy seeds

1. Combine lemon juice, erythritol, onion, mustard, and salt in a food processor and process until smooth.

2. While food processor is running, slowly pour avocado oil into the mixture until smooth.

3. Add poppy seeds and pulse slightly to incorporate into the dressing.

4. Transfer to an airtight container and store in the refrigerator until ready to eat, up to one week.

PER SERVING Calories: 113 | Fat: 12 g | Protein: 0 g | Sodium: 103 mg | Fiber: 0 g | Carbohydrates: 1 g | Sugar: 0 g | Net Carbohydrates: 1 g

Fresh versus Bottled

It's tempting to use bottled lemon juice in place of fresh since it's easier to just pour it from the bottle instead of squeezing the lemons, but try to resist the urge. Not only is the flavor of bottled lemon juice different from the real thing, it also contains preservatives since the juice isn't fresh. On the other hand, fresh lemon juice contains only lemon and has the taste to prove it.

Asian-Inspired Salad Dressing

If you don't want the olive flavor in your dressing, you can use avocado oil in place of the extra virgin olive oil. It has a milder flavor, but the fatty acid profile is still excellent.

INGREDIENTS | SERVES 12 (MAKES ABOUT 1½ CUPS)

¼ cup minced celery

2 tablespoons grated fresh ginger

⅓ cup minced white onion

¼ cup coconut aminos

1 tablespoon fresh lime juice

1½ tablespoons granulated erythritol

1 tablespoon no-sugar-added ketchup

¼ teaspoon freshly ground black pepper

½ cup olive oil

1 tablespoon sesame oil

Choosing an Olive Oil

Olive oil comes in extra virgin, virgin, and light. Extra virgin olive oil is produced by cold pressing and doesn't use any chemical processing. There's also no heat used in the refining process, so the fatty acids and nutrients remain intact. Virgin olive oil is extra virgin olive oil that has been cold pressed a second time. Light olive oil is made from refined oil and usually a mixture of other, cheaper vegetable oils. It's typically chemically processed, as well. Although extra virgin olive oil has a stronger olive flavor, it's the preferred type.

1. Combine celery, ginger, and onion in a food processor and pulse until combined. Scrape down sides of food processor.

2. Add coconut aminos, lime juice, erythritol, ketchup, and black pepper and process until combined, about 30 seconds.

3. Combine olive oil and sesame oil in a small bowl. While food processor is running, slowly pour oil into the mixture and continue processing until smooth.

4. Transfer to an airtight container and store in the refrigerator until ready to eat, up to one week.

PER SERVING Calories: 94 | Fat: 9 g | Protein: 0 g | Sodium: 115 mg | Fiber: 0 g | Carbohydrates: 3 g | Sugar: 0.5 g | Net Carbohydrates: 3 g

Creamy Cilantro Dressing

Make sure to use fresh cilantro in this dressing, not dried. The fresh cilantro gives it a better flavor and texture.

INGREDIENTS | SERVES 12 (MAKES ABOUT 1½ CUPS)

¾ cup coconut oil mayonnaise

6 tablespoons avocado oil

2½ tablespoons roasted pumpkin seeds

2 tablespoons water

2 tablespoons red wine vinegar

2 tablespoons crumbled Manchego cheese

1 (4.5-ounce) can roasted chilies

1 clove garlic, minced

¼ teaspoon sea salt

⅛ teaspoon freshly ground black pepper

½ cup chopped fresh cilantro

1. Combine all ingredients, except cilantro, in a food processor and process until smooth.

2. Add cilantro and process until fully incorporated.

3. Transfer dressing to an airtight container and store in the refrigerator until ready to eat, up to one week.

PER SERVING Calories: 173 | Fat: 18 g | Protein: 1 g | Sodium: 158 mg | Fiber: 0.5 g | Carbohydrates: 1.5 g | Sugar: 0.5 g | Net Carbohydrates: 1 g

Creamy Tahini Dressing

If you're sensitive to yeast, you can simply omit it from this recipe. It gives the finished product a cheesy taste, but it's not necessary and the dressing will come together just fine without it.

INGREDIENTS | SERVES 12 (MAKES ABOUT 1½ CUPS)

⅔ cup extra-light olive oil

⅓ cup fresh lemon juice

⅓ cup tahini

1 tablespoon nutritional yeast

¼ cup tamari

1 tablespoon granulated erythritol

½ teaspoon dried oregano

1 clove garlic, minced

1 tablespoon whole plain Greek yogurt

½ teaspoon sea salt

¼ teaspoon freshly ground black pepper

1. Combine all ingredients in a food processor or high-powered blender and process until smooth.

2. Transfer to an airtight container and store in the refrigerator until ready to eat, up to one week.

PER SERVING Calories: 154 | Fat: 15 g | Protein: 2 g | Sodium: 444 mg | Fiber: 0.5 g | Carbohydrates: 1.5 g | Sugar: 0.5 g | Net Carbohydrates: 1 g

Basic Herb and Garlic Dressing

If you can't find white balsamic vinegar, you can substitute regular balsamic vinegar instead, but it will give the finished dressing a sweeter flavor and a syrupier texture.

INGREDIENTS | SERVES 12 (MAKES ABOUT 1½ CUPS)

1 cup extra-light olive oil
4 tablespoons white balsamic vinegar
1 teaspoon granulated erythritol
8 cloves garlic, minced
1 tablespoon lemon juice
1 teaspoon sea salt
½ teaspoon freshly ground black pepper
1 teaspoon dried parsley
¼ teaspoon dried basil
¼ teaspoon celery seed
¼ teaspoon dried oregano

1. Combine all ingredients in a bowl and whisk until combined.

2. Transfer to an airtight container and store in the refrigerator until ready to eat, up to one week.

PER SERVING Calories: 167 | Fat: 18 g | Protein: 0 g | Sodium: 196 mg | Fiber: 0 g | Carbohydrates: 1.5 g | Sugar: 0.5 g | Net Carbohydrates: 1.5 g

Spicy Sesame Dressing

Don't be alarmed by the rice wine vinegar. Even though it's made by fermenting the sugars in rice, rice wine vinegar doesn't contain any carbohydrates.

INGREDIENTS | SERVES 12 (MAKES ABOUT 1½ CUPS)

¼ cup rice wine vinegar
1 cup extra-virgin olive oil
¼ cup coconut aminos
1½ tablespoons sesame oil
2 cloves garlic, crushed
1 teaspoon red pepper flakes
2 tablespoons granulated erythritol

1. Combine all ingredients in a food processor and process until smooth and erythritol is dissolved and red pepper flakes are broken up, about 2 minutes.

2. Strain through a fine-mesh cheesecloth into an airtight container.

3. Store in the refrigerator until ready to eat, up to one week.

PER SERVING Calories: 176 | Fat: 19 g | Protein: 0 g | Sodium: 96 mg | Fiber: 0 g | Carbohydrates: 0.5 g | Sugar: 0 g | Net Carbohydrates: 0.5 g

Basic Vegetable Dip

As written, this recipe comes out thick like a dip, but if you want to turn it into a creamy, basic dressing, you can thin it out with a little cream or nondairy milk.

INGREDIENTS | SERVES 12 (MAKES ABOUT 1½ CUPS)

¾ cup coconut oil mayonnaise

¾ cup full-fat sour cream

1 teaspoon sea salt

½ teaspoon freshly ground black pepper

1. Combine all ingredients in a bowl and whisk until smooth.

2. Transfer to an airtight container and store in the refrigerator until ready to eat, up to one week.

PER SERVING Calories: 122 | Fat: 13 g | Protein: 0.5 g | Sodium: 277 mg | Fiber: 0 g | Carbohydrates: 0.5 g | Sugar: 0.5 g | Net Carbohydrates: 0.5 g

Dill Sauce

Fresh dill works best for this recipe, but if you're in a pinch and have only dried dill, you can use 2 teaspoons in its place.

INGREDIENTS | SERVES 12 (MAKES ABOUT 1½ CUPS)

¾ cup full-fat sour cream

¾ cup coconut oil mayonnaise

¼ cup Dijon mustard

3 tablespoons lemon juice

2 tablespoons chopped fresh dill

1 teaspoon granulated erythritol

1. Combine all ingredients in a bowl and whisk until smooth.

2. Transfer to an airtight container and store in the refrigerator until ready to eat, up to one week.

PER SERVING Calories: 125 | Fat: 13 g | Protein: 0.5 g | Sodium: 140 mg | Fiber: 0.5 g | Carbohydrates: 1.5 g | Sugar: 0.5 g | Net Carbohydrates: 1 g

Dissolving Erythritol

Sometimes granulated erythritol doesn't dissolve well. If the grainy texture bothers you, you can use powdered erythritol in its place or use a high-speed blender and blend the ingredients together until the erythritol dissolves.

Creamy Gorgonzola Sauce

This Creamy Gorgonzola Sauce is an ideal accompaniment for steak. Just scoop some on top after it's done cooking and then store it in the refrigerator until you're ready to eat.

INGREDIENTS | SERVES 12 (MAKES ABOUT 1 CUP)

⅓ cup grass-fed butter

⅔ cup crumbled Gorgonzola cheese

3 scallions, minced

3 cloves garlic, minced

¼ teaspoon freshly ground black pepper

1. Combine all ingredients in a small saucepan over low heat. Whisk until combined and warmed through, about 5 minutes.

2. Remove from heat and transfer to an airtight container. Store in the refrigerator until ready to eat, up to four days.

PER SERVING Calories: 77 | Fat: 7 g | Protein: 2 g | Sodium: 48 mg | Fiber: 0 g | Carbohydrates: 0.5 g | Sugar: 0 g | Net Carbohydrates: 0.5 g

Spicy Chipotle Sauce

Always choose plain, full-fat yogurt when making keto recipes. Flavored yogurts often contain as much sugar as a can of soda and low-fat versions are lacking in vitamins, flavor, and fat, of course.

INGREDIENTS | SERVES 12 (MAKES ABOUT 1½ CUPS)

¾ cup full-fat plain Greek yogurt

¾ cup coconut oil mayonnaise

1 tablespoon puréed chipotle peppers in adobo sauce

1 teaspoon cumin

⅛ teaspoon paprika

¼ teaspoon freshly ground black pepper

½ teaspoon granulated erythritol

1. Combine all ingredients in a food processor and process until smooth.

2. Transfer to an airtight container and store in the refrigerator until ready to eat, up to one week.

PER SERVING Calories: 109 | Fat: 11 g | Protein: 0.5 g | Sodium: 97 mg | Fiber: 0 g | Carbohydrates: 1 g | Sugar: 1 g | Net Carbohydrates: 1 g

Tomato Cream Sauce

You can make this Tomato Cream Sauce dairy-free by using coconut cream in place of heavy cream and ghee in place of butter.

INGREDIENTS | SERVES 6

¼ cup olive oil

2 medium yellow onions, peeled and diced

6 cloves garlic, minced

2 (14.5-ounce) can Italian-style diced tomatoes

1 (6-ounce) can tomato paste

2 tablespoons dried basil leaves

2 teaspoons granulated erythritol

½ teaspoon dried oregano

½ teaspoon sea salt

¼ teaspoon freshly ground black pepper

1 cup heavy cream

2 tablespoons grass-fed butter

1. Heat olive oil in a medium saucepan over medium heat. Add onion and garlic and sauté until fragrant, about 5 minutes.

2. Add remaining ingredients, except cream and butter, stir to combine, and bring to a boil over medium-high heat. Allow sauce to boil until slightly thickened, about 5 minutes.

3. Reduce heat to low and stir in cream and butter until combined. Simmer 5 minutes.

4. Remove from heat and use an immersion blender to pulse until sauce reaches desired consistency.

5. Allow to cool and transfer to an airtight container. Store in the refrigerator for up to four days.

PER SERVING Calories: 158 | Fat: 14 g | Protein: 2 g | Sodium: 294 mg | Fiber: 2 g | Carbohydrates: 6 g | Sugar: 2 g | Net Carbohydrates: 4 g

Fontina Parmesan Sauce

Fontina cheese is approximately 45 percent fat. It provides about 79 percent of the recommended amount of vitamin K$_2$, which is vital for healthy bones and arteries.

INGREDIENTS | SERVES 6

1 cup unsalted grass-fed butter

1 heaping tablespoon minced garlic

1 tablespoon coconut flour

4 cups heavy cream

¼ cup whole milk

1 cup shredded Parmesan cheese

¼ cup shredded Fontina cheese

½ teaspoon salt

1 teaspoon freshly ground black pepper

¼ teaspoon ground nutmeg

What Is Fontina Cheese?

Fontina is an Italian cow's milk cheese that has a buttery, nutty flavor. It's rich and creamy with both a sweet and pungent taste. Most versions of Fontina are made without any additives, but you should always check your labels to make sure. If you can't find Fontina, you can use provolone or Gruyere in its place. Although the flavor won't be an exact match, they'll give you a tasty end product as well.

1. Melt butter in a large stockpot over medium heat. Add garlic and coconut flour and cook until garlic is fragrant, about 1 minute.

2. Whisk in heavy cream and milk, whisking constantly until the mixture starts to thicken, about 10 minutes. Make sure the mixture doesn't come to a boil.

3. Gradually whisk in cheeses and stir until smooth. Stir in salt, pepper, and nutmeg.

4. Reduce heat to low and simmer until sauce is thickened, about 15 minutes.

5. Remove from heat and allow to cool slightly. Transfer to an airtight container and store in the refrigerator until ready to eat, up to one week.

PER SERVING Calories: 465 | Fat: 48 g | Protein: 6 g | Sodium: 277 mg | Fiber: 0.5 g | Carbohydrates: 3.5 g | Sugar: 2.5 g | Net Carbohydrates: 3 g

Cilantro Serrano Cream Sauce

Serrano peppers register between 10,000 and 25,000 Scoville Heat Units, which makes them almost four times as spicy as jalapeños, but ten times less spicy than habanero peppers. If you want to tone down the spiciness of this recipe, use jalapeños instead.

INGREDIENTS | SERVES 12 (MAKES ABOUT 1½ CUPS)

½ cup chopped fresh cilantro

3 serrano chili peppers, seeded and minced

3 cloves garlic, minced

¾ cup coconut oil mayonnaise

¾ cup full-fat sour cream

1 tablespoon fresh lime juice

½ teaspoon sea salt

¼ teaspoon freshly ground black pepper

1. Combine all ingredients in a food processor and process until smooth.

2. Transfer to an airtight container and refrigerate until ready to eat, up to one week.

PER SERVING Calories: 123 | Fat: 13 g | Protein: 0.5 g | Sodium: 181 mg | Fiber: 0 g | Carbohydrates: 1 g | Sugar: 0.5 g | Net Carbohydrates: 1 g

Garlic Parmesan Seasoned Butter

You can store this Garlic Parmesan Seasoned Butter in the refrigerator for several months, so feel free to make a bunch, because once you taste it, you're going to want to put it on everything!

INGREDIENTS | SERVES 12 (MAKES ABOUT 1½ CUPS)

1 cup grass-fed unsalted butter, softened

¼ cup grated Parmesan cheese

1 tablespoon minced garlic

1 teaspoon garlic salt

2 teaspoons garlic powder

1 teaspoon dried basil

1. Combine all ingredients in a medium bowl and stir until incorporated.

2. Store in the refrigerator until ready to eat, up to two months.

PER SERVING Calories: 123 | Fat: 13 g | Protein: 0.5 g | Sodium: 181 mg | Fiber: 0 g | Carbohydrates: 1 g | Sugar: 0.5 g | Net Carbohydrates: 1 g

Thai Satay Sauce

The crunchy peanut butter adds a little texture to the finished recipe, but you can use creamy peanut butter in its place if that's all you have.

INGREDIENTS | SERVES 12 (MAKES ABOUT 1½ CUPS)

1 (10-ounce) can full-fat coconut cream

½ cup no-sugar-added crunchy peanut butter

½ small yellow onion, peeled and finely minced

2 cloves garlic, minced

1 tablespoon coconut aminos

1 teaspoon granulated erythritol

1 teaspoon red pepper flakes

1. Combine all ingredients in a medium saucepan over medium-high heat. Bring to a boil while stirring frequently.

2. Remove from heat and allow to cool. Transfer to an airtight container and store in the refrigerator until ready to eat, up to one week.

PER SERVING Calories: 119 | Fat: 10 g | Protein: 3 g | Sodium: 99 mg | Fiber: 1 g | Carbohydrates: 3 g | Sugar: 0 g | Net Carbohydrates: 2 g

Jalapeño Hot Sauce

The granulated erythritol cuts the heat in this hot sauce a little bit, so don't omit it. It makes the finished product more enjoyable.

INGREDIENTS | SERVES 12

1 teaspoon extra-light olive oil

15 fresh jalapeños, seeded and diced

3 cloves garlic, minced

¼ cup minced yellow onions

½ teaspoon sea salt

1½ cups water

1 tablespoon granulated erythritol

¼ cup distilled white vinegar

1. Combine olive oil, jalapeños, garlic, onion, and salt in a medium saucepan over high heat. Sauté until peppers are slightly softened, about 5 minutes.

2. Add water and erythritol, reduce heat to medium-high, and continue to cook 20 minutes, stirring frequently.

3. Remove from heat and allow sauce to cool. Transfer the mixture to a food processor or high-powered blender and process until smooth.

4. With the blender or food processor running, slowly add vinegar until incorporated.

5. Store in an airtight glass jar in the refrigerator until ready to eat, up to six months.

PER SERVING Calories: 11 | Fat: 0.5 g | Protein: 0 g | Sodium: 98 mg | Fiber: 0.5 g | Carbohydrates: 1.5 g | Sugar: 0.5 g | Net Carbohydrates: 1 g

CHAPTER 10

Sides

Cauliflower Risotto

If you want to save some time, use a couple bags of frozen riced cauliflower in place of the fresh cauliflower rice. You can stock up when they're on sale and store them in your freezer for easy meal prep.

INGREDIENTS | SERVES 6

¼ cup grass-fed butter

2 shallots, minced

3 cloves garlic, minced

6 cups cauliflower rice

1½ cups sliced baby bella mushrooms

¾ cup half-and-half

½ cup grated Parmesan cheese

1 teaspoon sea salt

½ teaspoon freshly ground black pepper

¼ teaspoon ground nutmeg

Risotto: an Italian Favorite

Traditional risotto is an Italian dish that's made with rice that's been toasted and creamed instead of boiled. Although risotto is out for a keto diet, you can mimic the taste and texture with riced cauliflower, combined with cream and cheese. Risotto can be served as a side dish or you can add a protein, like chicken or seafood, to make it a complete meal.

1. Heat butter in a medium skillet over medium heat. Add shallots and garlic and cook until softened, about 5 minutes. Add cauliflower rice and mushrooms and cook until tender, about 6 minutes.

2. Stir in remaining ingredients and cook 6 more minutes, or until cauliflower reaches desired doneness and ingredients are melted together.

3. Remove from heat and allow to cool. Divide into six equal portions and transfer each portion to a separate airtight container. Store in the refrigerator until ready to eat, up to one week.

PER SERVING Calories: 179 | Fat: 13 g | Protein: 6 g | Sodium: 586 mg | Fiber: 3 g | Carbohydrates: 9 g | Sugar: 4 g | Net Carbohydrates: 6 g

Cauliflower Casserole

This Cauliflower Casserole is delicious as is, but you can also use it as a base to create your own masterpiece. Add your favorite low-carb veggies or some cooked chicken for a complete meal.

INGREDIENTS | SERVES 6

½ cup full-fat sour cream

½ cup coconut oil mayonnaise

2 cloves garlic, minced

1 teaspoon sea salt

½ teaspoon freshly ground black pepper

1 large head cauliflower, cut into small florets and lightly steamed

1 cup Cheddar cheese, divided

1 cup mozzarella cheese, divided

6 slices no-sugar-added bacon, cooked and crumbled

¼ cup fresh chives, divided

1. Preheat oven to 400°F.

2. Combine sour cream, mayonnaise, garlic, salt, and pepper in a bowl and stir to mix. Add cauliflower, ½ cup Cheddar cheese, ½ cup mozzarella cheese, bacon, and ⅛ cup chives and stir to incorporate.

3. Transfer to a 9" × 13" baking dish and sprinkle remaining cheese and chives on top.

4. Bake 25 minutes or until bubbling and cheese starts to turn golden brown. Remove from oven and allow to cool.

5. Divide into six equal portions and transfer each portion to a separate airtight container. Store in the refrigerator until ready to eat, up to one week.

PER SERVING Calories: 451 | Fat: 40 g | Protein: 15 g | Sodium: 973 mg | Fiber: 2 g | Carbohydrates: 7 g | Sugar: 3 g | Net Carbohydrates: 5 g

Green Bean Casserole

This Green Bean Casserole replaces fried onions with crispy pork rinds to make the traditional side keto-friendly and easy to incorporate into your meal prep.

INGREDIENTS | SERVES 6

1 pound fresh green beans, trimmed and cut in half

2 tablespoons grass-fed butter

1 large shallot, diced

3 cloves garlic, minced

½ cup chicken bone broth

½ cup heavy cream

¼ cup grated Parmesan cheese

½ cup crushed pork rinds

The Bean That's Not a Bean

Despite their name, green beans are not categorized as a bean; they're considered a vegetable. One cup of green beans contains only 7 grams of carbohydrates, 3.5 of which come from fiber, and they're a good source of vitamin A, vitamin C, vitamin K, and protein. They also contain a high amount of chlorophyll, which can help prevent cancer.

1. Preheat oven to 400°F.

2. Fill a large pot with water and a pinch of salt. Bring to a boil. Add green beans and boil 5 minutes or until green beans are tender, but crisp. Remove from water and set aside.

3. Heat butter in a medium skillet over medium heat. Add shallot and garlic and cook until softened, about 5 minutes.

4. Add chicken broth and cream. Bring to a boil over high heat and then reduce heat to low and simmer until sauce starts to thicken, about 5 minutes. Stir in Parmesan cheese. Once cheese has melted, add cooked green beans.

5. Transfer mixture to a 9" × 13" baking dish. Sprinkle pork rinds on top.

6. Bake 15 minutes or until bubbly and pork rinds turn golden brown. Remove from oven and allow to cool.

7. Divide into six equal portions and transfer each portion to an airtight container. Store in the refrigerator until ready to eat, up to one week.

PER SERVING Calories: 169 | Fat: 12 g | Protein: 3.5 g | Sodium: 94 mg | Fiber: 2 g | Carbohydrates: 7 g | Sugar: 3 g | Net Carbohydrates: 5 g

Greek Spinach

This recipe calls for spinach, but you can use whatever greens you have on hand. Swiss chard makes a great base for these flavors and tends to hold its structure more than spinach.

INGREDIENTS | SERVES 6

2 tablespoons grass-fed butter

3 large shallots, minced

4 cloves garlic, minced

2 (10-ounce) packages frozen spinach, thawed and squeezed dry

1 teaspoon dried oregano

1 teaspoon lemon zest

2 tablespoons lemon juice

½ cup crumbled feta

1. Heat butter in a medium skillet over medium heat. Add shallots and garlic and cook until softened, about 3 minutes.

2. Add spinach, oregano, lemon zest, and lemon juice and cook until heated through, about 3 more minutes.

3. Sprinkle feta on top and toss to combine. Remove from heat and allow to cool.

4. Divide into six equal portions and transfer each portion to an airtight container. Store in the refrigerator until ready to eat, up to one week.

PER SERVING Calories: 98 | Fat: 7 g | Protein: 5 g | Sodium: 185 mg | Fiber: 3 g | Carbohydrates: 5 g | Sugar: 1 g | Net Carbohydrates: 2 g

Lemon Pepper Green Beans

You can add some variety to your meal prep by swapping out the green beans in this recipe for another of your low-carb favorites, like asparagus.

INGREDIENTS | SERVES 6

1 pound fresh green beans, trimmed

2 tablespoons grass-fed butter

1 tablespoon lemon juice

1 teaspoon lemon pepper

¼ teaspoon sea salt

¼ teaspoon freshly ground black pepper

1. Place green beans in a steaming basket over boiling water. Cook on high heat until tender, but still crisp, about 8 minutes. Drain and set aside.

2. Melt butter in a medium skillet over medium heat. Add green beans and lemon juice and toss to combine. Sprinkle with lemon pepper, salt, and black pepper and toss to coat.

3. Remove from heat, allow to cool slightly, and divide into six equal portions. Transfer each portion to an airtight container and store in the refrigerator until ready to eat, up to one week.

PER SERVING Calories: 57 | Fat: 4 g | Protein: 1.5 g | Sodium: 102 mg | Fiber: 2 g | Carbohydrates: 5 g | Sugar: 2 g | Net Carbohydrates: 3 g

Spanakorizo

Traditional Spanakorizo combines white rice with spinach, but this recipe substitutes cauliflower instead for a lower-carb version that pairs well with any protein main course.

INGREDIENTS | SERVES 6

2 tablespoons grass-fed butter

1 large yellow onion, peeled and diced

3 cloves garlic, minced

1 (10-ounce) package frozen chopped spinach, thawed and squeezed dry

1 (12-ounce) bag frozen riced cauliflower, thawed

1 teaspoon sea salt

½ teaspoon freshly ground black pepper

½ teaspoon dried dill

½ cup crumbled feta

The Greek Side Dish

A typical Spanakorizo recipe includes long-grain white rice, fresh spinach, dill, cumin, and feta cheese. In Greece, the dish is enjoyed either warm or cold, which makes it an excellent choice for meal prep—you don't even have to heat it up! It's also often served with a fried egg, so if you want to add some protein to balance out your macronutrients, throw an egg on top!

1. Heat butter in a medium skillet over medium heat. Add onion and garlic and cook until softened, about 3 minutes.

2. Add spinach and cook until heated through, another 2 minutes. Stir in remaining ingredients except feta and cook until cauliflower is tender, about 7 minutes.

3. Remove from heat and sprinkle feta on top. Allow to cool, then divide into six equal portions. Transfer each portion to a separate airtight container and store in the refrigerator until ready to eat, up to one week.

PER SERVING Calories: 104 | Fat: 6 g | Protein: 5 g | Sodium: 557 mg | Fiber: 3 g | Carbohydrates: 8 g | Sugar: 3 g | Net Carbohydrates: 5 g

Roasted Garlic Cauliflower

This Roasted Garlic Cauliflower is the perfect side for any protein dish, but it's also delicious cold. Eat it right out of the fridge or add it to any of the Mason jar salads.

INGREDIENTS | SERVES 6

2 tablespoons minced garlic

3 tablespoons olive oil

1 large head cauliflower, cut into bite-sized florets

1 teaspoon sea salt

½ teaspoon freshly ground black pepper

¾ teaspoon onion powder

1 tablespoon chopped fresh parsley

¼ cup grated Parmesan cheese

1. Preheat oven to 450°F. Grease a 9" × 13" baking dish with olive oil cooking spray.

2. Whisk together garlic and olive oil in a mixing bowl. Add cauliflower and toss to coat. Sprinkle salt, pepper, onion powder, and parsley on cauliflower and toss again.

3. Transfer cauliflower to prepared baking dish and cover. Bake 15 minutes, stir, and then continue baking 10 more minutes. Sprinkle Parmesan cheese on top and turn oven to broil. Broil 3 minutes or until cheese is bubbly and golden brown.

4. Remove from oven and allow to cool. Divide into six equal portions and transfer each portion to a separate airtight container. Store in the refrigerator until ready to eat, up to one week.

PER SERVING Calories: 107 | Fat: 8 g | Protein: 3 g | Sodium: 493 mg | Fiber: 2 g | Carbohydrates: 6 g | Sugar: 2 g | Net Carbohydrates: 4 g

Italian-Style Mushrooms and Spinach

Make sure to use mature spinach and not baby spinach in this recipe. The mature spinach holds up better to heat and lends a better texture to the finished meal.

INGREDIENTS | SERVES 6

2 tablespoons avocado oil

2 small shallots, diced

3 cloves garlic, minced

1 pound sliced baby bella mushrooms

¼ cup keto-friendly white wine

1 (16-ounce) bag fresh spinach, roughly chopped

1 tablespoon balsamic vinegar

1 teaspoon sea salt

½ teaspoon freshly ground black pepper

1. Heat avocado oil in a medium skillet over medium-high heat. Add shallots and garlic and cook until softened, about 3 minutes. Add mushrooms and cook until they start to soften, about 4 minutes.

2. Pour wine into skillet, scraping garlic and shallots off the pan. Reduce heat to low and cook until wine reduces, about 7 minutes.

3. Add spinach and vinegar and stir into wine. Allow to cook until remaining liquid is absorbed, about 3 minutes.

4. Remove from heat and sprinkle salt and pepper on top.

5. Divide into six equal portions and transfer each portion to an airtight container. Store in the refrigerator until ready to eat, up to one week.

PER SERVING Calories: 86 | Fat: 5 g | Protein: 4 g | Sodium: 454 mg | Fiber: 3 g | Carbohydrates: 6 g | Sugar: 2 g | Net Carbohydrates: 3 g

Broccoli Cheese Bake

To make this even more portable, you can scoop the broccoli into the wells of a muffin tin and pour the sauce on it before baking.

INGREDIENTS | SERVES 6

6 cups broccoli florets, lightly steamed
⅓ cup grass-fed butter
2 tablespoons Paleo flour
1 small yellow onion, peeled and diced
1¼ cups half-and-half
½ teaspoon sea salt
¼ teaspoon freshly ground black pepper
½ teaspoon garlic powder
3 cups shredded sharp Cheddar cheese
1 cup shredded Gruyere cheese
2 large eggs, beaten

Experimenting with Cheeses

Experimenting with different cheeses is (arguably) one of the best parts of the keto diet. Gruyere cheese is a nutty, Swiss-like cheese that is great for melting. In addition to using it in bakes, you can use it to make cauliflower "mac" and cheese or any cheesy dip. If you can't find Gruyere, you can substitute Swiss cheese or Emmentaler.

1. Preheat oven to 325°F.

2. Arrange broccoli in a 9" × 13" baking dish.

3. Melt butter in a medium saucepan over medium heat. Whisk in flour and stir until bubbly. Add onion and half-and-half and stir until combined. Bring to a boil, whisking 1 minute, then remove from heat. Stir in salt, pepper, and garlic powder.

4. Allow to cool slightly, then add cheese and egg, whisking until cheese is melted and fully incorporated.

5. Pour sauce over broccoli and stir to combine. Spread mixture out and bake 30 minutes or until heated through and bubbly.

6. Remove from oven and allow to cool. Divide into six equal portions and transfer each portion to a separate airtight container. Store in the refrigerator until ready to eat, up to one week.

PER SERVING Calories: 578 | Fat: 47 g | Protein: 28 g | Sodium: 836 mg | Fiber: 4 g | Carbohydrates: 12 g | Sugar: 4 g | Net Carbohydrates: 8 g

Okra with Tomatoes and Bacon

Okra is a low-carbohydrate vegetable that belongs to the same family as cocoa, hibiscus, and cotton. It's commonly used in stews and gumbos, and can be stir-fried with other similar veggies like zucchini or bell peppers.

INGREDIENTS | SERVES 6

3 slices no-sugar-added bacon

1 (12-ounce) bag frozen sliced okra, thawed

1 small yellow onion, peeled and diced

1 small red bell pepper, seeded and diced

2 medium stalks celery, diced

1 (14.5-ounce) can stewed tomatoes

½ teaspoon sea salt

¼ teaspoon freshly ground black pepper

A Healthy Gut with Okra

Okra is an excellent source of fiber, which keeps your digestive system healthy and regular. When cooked, okra develops a gelatinous texture that's especially helpful for keeping your gut happy and healthy. One cup of okra contains only 7 grams of carbohydrates, 3 of which come from fiber, and 44 percent of the total amount of vitamin K you need for the entire day.

1. Cook bacon in a medium skillet over medium-high heat until crispy, about 8 minutes. Remove from pan, reserving grease, and transfer to a paper towel–lined plate.

2. Add okra and onion to pan and cook 3 minutes. Add bell pepper and celery and continue cooking until softened, about 4 more minutes.

3. Add tomatoes, salt, and pepper and cook until tomatoes are heated through, about 2 minutes. Remove from heat.

4. Crumble bacon and stir into okra mixture.

5. Divide into six equal portions and transfer each portion to an airtight container. Store in the refrigerator until ready to eat, up to one week.

PER SERVING Calories: 99 | Fat: 6 g | Protein: 4 g | Sodium: 386 mg | Fiber: 4 g | Carbohydrates: 9 g | Sugar: 4 g | Net Carbohydrates: 5 g

Shredded Brussels Sprouts

If you're not the biggest fan of Brussels sprouts, soak them in salt water for an hour before shredding them. This neutralizes some of the bitter taste that turns people off.

INGREDIENTS | SERVES 6

6 slices no-sugar-added bacon
¼ cup grass-fed butter
2 cloves garlic, minced
1½ pounds Brussels sprouts, shredded
2 scallions, minced
½ teaspoon sea salt
¼ teaspoon freshly ground black pepper

1. Cook bacon in a medium skillet over medium-high heat until crispy, about 8 minutes. Remove, reserving bacon grease, and transfer to a paper towel–lined plate.

2. Add butter to bacon grease and reduce heat to medium. Add garlic and sauté until fragrant, about 1 minute. Add shredded Brussels sprouts and scallions and cook until tender, about 8 minutes.

3. While Brussels sprouts are cooking, chop bacon into small pieces. Add to Brussels sprouts along with salt and pepper and stir to combine.

4. Remove from heat and divide into six equal portions. Place each portion in a separate airtight container and store in the refrigerator until ready to eat, up to one week.

PER SERVING Calories: 235 | Fat: 19 g | Protein: 8 g | Sodium: 408 mg | Fiber: 4.5 g | Carbohydrates: 10 g | Sugar: 3 g | Net Carbohydrates: 5.5 g

Garlic and Parmesan Broccoli Rabe

If you can't find broccoli rabe in your supermarket, you can substitute any other bitter green. Turnip greens are a good choice, but don't substitute broccoli. Although the names are similar, they're not related.

INGREDIENTS | SERVES 6

1½ pounds broccoli rabe, trimmed

⅓ cup grass-fed butter

3 cloves garlic, minced

2 tablespoons grated Parmesan cheese

¼ teaspoon crushed red pepper

Wait, It's Not Broccoli?

Although broccoli rabe looks like it's the trimmings from broccoli, it's actually not related. In fact, it's closely related to the turnip. The entire plant—the stems, leaves, and broccoli-like buds—are all edible. When using broccoli rabe in recipes, try to incorporate as much of it as you can. It's best to cook it like you would any other bitter leafy green, like mustard greens, turnip greens, or dandelion greens.

1. Fill a pot with water and a pinch of salt and bring to a boil over high heat. Add broccoli rabe to the water and cover. Cook until tender but still slightly crisp, about 6 minutes. Drain and set aside.

2. Heat butter in a medium skillet over medium heat. Add garlic and cook until fragrant, about 1 minute.

3. Add broccoli rabe and cook another 12 minutes or until it reaches desired doneness.

4. Sprinkle Parmesan cheese and crushed red pepper on top and toss to coat.

5. Remove from heat and divide into six equal portions. Transfer each portion to a separate airtight container and store in the refrigerator until ready to eat, up to one week.

PER SERVING Calories: 139 | Fat: 11 g | Protein: 4 g | Sodium: 76 mg | Fiber: 3 g | Carbohydrates: 8 g | Sugar: 2 g | Net Carbohydrates: 5 g

Green Beans with Blue Cheese and Bacon

Blue cheese is very rich, containing 39 grams of fat in one cup. It's a great way to add some intense flavor to low-carb vegetables.

INGREDIENTS | SERVES 6

1½ pounds green beans, trimmed and cut into 2" pieces

6 slices no-sugar-added bacon

⅓ cup crumbled blue cheese

½ teaspoon sea salt

¼ teaspoon freshly ground black pepper

1. Place green beans in a steamer basket over boiling water. Boil over medium-high heat for 5 minutes or until green beans are tender but still crisp. Remove from heat and drain.

2. Cook bacon in a medium skillet over medium-high heat until crispy, about 8 minutes. Remove bacon from skillet, reserving bacon grease, and transfer to a paper towel–lined plate.

3. Add green beans to bacon grease and cook 3 more minutes, or until green beans are tender. Remove from heat and add blue cheese, salt, and pepper. Toss to coat and allow to cool slightly. Crumble the reserved bacon and sprinkle on top.

4. Divide into six equal portions and transfer each portion to an airtight container. Store in the refrigerator until ready to eat, up to one week.

PER SERVING Calories: 177 | Fat: 13 g | Protein: 7 g | Sodium: 471 mg | Fiber: 3 g | Carbohydrates: 8 g | Sugar: 3 g | Net Carbohydrates: 5 g

Caramelized Bell Pepper Medley

You can use any combination of bell peppers that you want for this recipe. You can use all green or all red, but keep in mind that using a variety of colors will also give you a variety of different nutrients.

INGREDIENTS | SERVES 6

3 tablespoons grass-fed butter

1 medium red bell pepper, seeded and sliced lengthwise

1 medium yellow bell pepper, seeded and sliced lengthwise

1 medium orange bell pepper, seeded and sliced lengthwise

2 medium red onions, cut into thin strips

¼ teaspoon sea salt

¼ teaspoon freshly ground black pepper

½ teaspoon Italian seasoning

1. Heat butter in a medium skillet over medium heat. Add peppers and onion and sauté until they begin to soften, about 8 minutes.

2. Sprinkle seasonings over peppers and onions and toss to coat. Remove from heat.

3. Divide into six equal portions, allow to cool slightly, and transfer each portion to a separate airtight container. Store in the refrigerator until ready to eat, up to one week.

PER SERVING Calories: 79 | Fat: 6 g | Protein: 1 g | Sodium: 101 mg | Fiber: 2 g | Carbohydrates: 6 g | Sugar: 3 g | Net Carbohydrates: 4 g

Creamed Cucumber

You can choose whether or not you want to peel the cucumber in this recipe. If you leave the peel on, it will up the fiber content of the dish, but the end product has a smoother, creamier texture without it.

INGREDIENTS | SERVES 6

1½ cups coconut oil mayonnaise

¼ cup heavy cream

1 teaspoon granulated erythritol

¾ teaspoon white vinegar

½ teaspoon dried dill

½ teaspoon sea salt

¼ teaspoon freshly ground black pepper

2 large cucumbers, sliced into coins

1. Add mayonnaise, cream, erythritol, vinegar, dill, salt, and pepper to a medium bowl and whisk until combined. Add cucumber slices and toss to coat.

2. Divide into six equal portions and transfer each portion to a separate airtight container. Store in the refrigerator until ready to eat, up to one week.

PER SERVING Calories: 442 | Fat: 47 g | Protein: 1 g | Sodium: 512 mg | Fiber: 0.5 g | Carbohydrates: 4 g | Sugar: 2 g | Net Carbohydrates: 3.5 g

Lemon Butter and Dill Zucchini

You can make this recipe vegan, without sacrificing any richness or flavor, by using butter-flavored coconut oil in place of the grass-fed butter.

INGREDIENTS | SERVES 6

¼ cup grass-fed butter

4 medium zucchini, sliced into coins

2 teaspoons dried dill

1 tablespoon lemon juice

½ teaspoon sea salt

¼ teaspoon freshly ground black pepper

Go Grass-Fed

Conjugated linoleic acid, or CLA, is a fatty acid that's been linked to a reduced risk of cancer, stronger bones, and increased muscle mass. Grass-fed butter contains five times more CLA than butter from grain-fed cows. Grass-fed butter is also much higher in omega-3 fatty acids and vitamin K, a fat-soluble vitamin.

1. Heat butter in a medium skillet over medium heat. Add zucchini and cook until tender, but still slightly crispy, about 4 minutes.

2. Add dill, lemon juice, salt, and pepper and toss to coat. Cook another 2 minutes then remove from heat.

3. Divide into six equal portions and transfer each portion to an airtight container. Store in the refrigerator until ready to eat, up to one week.

PER SERVING Calories: 91 | Fat: 8 g | Protein: 2 g | Sodium: 206 mg | Fiber: 1.5 g | Carbohydrates: 4 g | Sugar: 3 g | Net Carbohydrates: 2.5 g

Parmesan Cabbage Casserole

You can make this recipe creamier by using heavy cream in place of the half-and-half. You can also use coconut cream, but it does add a sweet, coconutty flavor.

INGREDIENTS | SERVES 6

1 cup half-and-half
2 tablespoons Paleo flour
2 tablespoons grass-fed butter
¼ teaspoon sea salt
⅛ teaspoon freshly ground black pepper
⅛ teaspoon crushed red pepper flakes
1 large head cabbage, shredded
¾ cup shredded Asiago cheese
¼ cup grated Parmesan cheese

1. Preheat oven to 350°F.

2. Combine half-and-half, flour, butter, salt, black pepper, and red pepper in a small saucepan over medium heat and whisk constantly until thickened, about 6 minutes. Remove from heat and set aside.

3. Put cabbage in a steaming basket over boiling water and steam until tender, but still firm, about 8 minutes.

4. Transfer cabbage to an 8" × 8" baking dish. Pour sauce over cabbage and sprinkle cheeses on top. Toss to combine.

5. Bake 30 minutes or until bubbly and turning golden brown. Remove from heat and allow to cool.

6. Divide into six equal portions and transfer each portion to a separate airtight container. Store in the refrigerator until ready to eat, up to one week.

PER SERVING Calories: 213 | Fat: 15 g | Protein: 8 g | Sodium: 322 mg | Fiber: 5 g | Carbohydrates: 13 g | Sugar: 6 g | Net Carbohydrates: 8 g

Creamed Onions

*Creamed Onions make an excellent side dish, but they're also perfect
for some added flavor on top of any basic grilled meat.*

INGREDIENTS | SERVES 6

4 tablespoons grass-fed butter

2 large yellow onions, peeled and sliced

2 cloves garlic, minced

1 cup half-and-half

½ teaspoon sea salt

¼ teaspoon freshly ground black pepper

⅔ cup shredded Parmesan cheese

¼ cup shredded mozzarella cheese

Choosing an Onion

Yellow onions are considered the "all-purpose" onion because they have a nice balance of flavors and they become sweeter the longer they cook. When you're not sure of what type of onion to use in a recipe, going with a yellow onion is typically the safest choice. White onions are more pungent than yellow onions and red onions have a distinct flavor that isn't as universal.

1. Preheat oven to 425°F.

2. Heat butter in a medium skillet over medium heat. Add onions and garlic and cook until softened, about 5 minutes. Transfer to a 9" × 9" baking dish.

3. Combine half-and-half, salt, and pepper in a small bowl and whisk until foamy. Pour over onions.

4. Sprinkle cheeses on top and bake 15 minutes or until hot and bubbly. Remove from oven and allow to cool.

5. Divide into six equal portions and transfer each portion to a separate airtight container. Store in the refrigerator until ready to eat, up to one week.

PER SERVING Calories: 205 | Fat: 16 g | Protein: 7 g | Sodium: 417 mg | Fiber: 1 g | Carbohydrates: 7 g | Sugar: 4 g | Net Carbohydrates: 6 g

Tomato and Zucchini Bake

It's a good idea to squeeze out any excess moisture from the zucchini before adding them to the skillet. It's not imperative, but it will help prevent the bake from getting soggy as it's stored in the refrigerator.

INGREDIENTS | SERVES 6

2 tablespoons butter-flavored coconut oil

1 large yellow onion, peeled and diced

3 cloves garlic, minced

3 large zucchini, sliced into coins

1 (14.5-ounce) can Italian seasoned diced tomatoes, drained

1 teaspoon Italian seasoning

½ teaspoon sea salt

¼ teaspoon freshly ground black pepper

½ cup shredded mozzarella cheese

1. Preheat oven to 350°F.

2. Heat coconut oil in a medium skillet over medium heat. Add onion and garlic and cook until softened, about 4 minutes. Add zucchini and cook until tender, but still crisp.

3. Stir in tomatoes and spices. Transfer mixture to a 9" × 13" pan and sprinkle mozzarella cheese on top.

4. Bake 20 minutes. Turn oven to broil and cook another 2 minutes.

5. Remove from oven and cool. Divide into six equal portions and transfer each portion to a separate airtight container. Store in the refrigerator until ready to eat, up to one week.

PER SERVING Calories: 120 | Fat: 7 g | Protein: 5 g | Sodium: 352 mg | Fiber: 3.5 g | Carbohydrates: 10 g | Sugar: 3 g | Net Carbohydrates: 6.5 g

Zucchini and Onion Fritters

These Zucchini and Onion Fritters perfectly complement any protein dish, but they truly shine when topped with a couple over-easy or soft-boiled eggs.

INGREDIENTS | SERVES 6

3 large zucchini

1 large yellow onion, peeled

1 teaspoon garlic salt

¼ teaspoon onion powder

¼ cup grated Parmesan cheese

1 large egg

3 tablespoons butter-flavored coconut oil

Hydrating Foods

Zucchini contains approximately 95 percent water, so it's one of those foods that can help hydrate you. That also means that recipes made with zucchini can occasionally get a little soggy. To combat this, sprinkle sea salt on top of cut or shredded zucchini and let it sit for at least 30 minutes in a strainer before using in a recipe. The salt pulls out the excess moisture and gives you a drier zucchini base to work with.

1. Shred zucchini and onion using a shredding attachment on a food processor (or by hand with a cheese grater).

2. In a large bowl, combine shredded zucchini and onion with garlic salt, onion powder, Parmesan cheese, and egg. Mix until incorporated.

3. Form mixture into twelve equal-sized patties.

4. Heat coconut oil in a medium skillet over medium-high heat. Add prepared patties and cook 5 minutes on each side, or until both sides are golden brown.

5. Place fritters on a paper towel–lined plate to absorb excess oil.

6. Transfer two fritters to each of six separate airtight containers and store in the refrigerator until ready to eat, up to one week.

PER SERVING Calories: 126 | Fat: 9 g | Protein: 5 g | Sodium: 488 mg | Fiber: 2 g | Carbohydrates: 8 g | Sugar: 3 g | Net Carbohydrates: 6 g

CHAPTER 11

Soups and Chili

Italian Sausage and Zucchini Soup

If you don't want this soup to be spicy, use regular pork sausage instead of hot Italian sausage, just make sure to check the ingredient list because many prepared sausages contain added sugar.

INGREDIENTS | SERVES 6

1½ pounds hot Italian sausage, casings removed

2 cups chopped celery

6 medium zucchini, cut into ¼"-thick medallions

2 (28-ounce) cans petite-diced tomatoes

1 medium green bell pepper, seeded and diced

1 medium red bell pepper, seeded and diced

1 cup chopped yellow onion

2 teaspoons salt

1 teaspoon dried oregano

1 teaspoon dried basil

1 teaspoon dried parsley

½ teaspoon granulated garlic

1. Crumble sausage into a large skillet and bring to medium-high heat. Cook until browned, about 6 minutes. Add celery and cook until softened, about 7 more minutes.

2. Transfer sausage and celery to a slow cooker and add remaining ingredients. Stir to combine.

3. Cook on low 5 hours.

4. Remove from heat and allow to cool. Transfer six equal portions to airtight containers and store in the refrigerator until ready to eat, up to one week.

PER SERVING Calories: 372 | Fat: 21 g | Protein: 23 g | Sodium: 1,255 mg | Fiber: 7 g | Carbohydrates: 14 g | Sugar: 4 g | Net Carbohydrates: 7 g

Low-Carb Celery

Like cucumbers, celery is another keto favorite because it contains virtually no carbohydrates—one stalk contains only 1.2 grams—and it's hydrating and crispy. You can whip up some easy snacks during your meal prep by topping celery with peanut butter, cream cheese, or prepared tuna or chicken salad.

Ground Pork and Bacon Chili

Thick-cut bacon has a pancetta-like texture that lends well to this thick and meaty chili. You won't even miss the beans!

INGREDIENTS | SERVES 6

1½ pounds ground pork

½ teaspoon salt

¼ teaspoon freshly ground black pepper

¼ teaspoon granulated garlic

¼ teaspoon granulated onion

⅛ teaspoon ground cayenne pepper (optional)

10 thick-cut slices no-sugar-added bacon, roughly chopped

1 (14.5 ounce) can fire-roasted diced tomatoes

1 (6-ounce) can tomato paste

½ cup beef broth

½ cup tomato sauce

1 medium yellow onion, peeled and diced

2 small green bell peppers, seeded and diced

1 small red bell pepper, seeded and diced

1 package chili seasoning

1. Crumble pork into a medium skillet and bring up to medium-high heat. Add salt, black pepper, granulated garlic, granulated onion, and cayenne pepper (if using) and stir. Cook until browned, about 6 minutes, stirring occasionally. Drain excess grease and transfer cooked pork to a slow cooker.

2. Add bacon to hot skillet and cook over medium-high heat until browned and crispy, about 10 minutes. Discard excess grease and transfer cooked bacon to slow cooker.

3. Add remaining ingredients to slow cooker and stir to combine.

4. Cook on low 6 hours.

5. Remove from heat and allow to cool. Transfer six equal portions to separate airtight containers and store in the refrigerator until ready to eat, up to one week.

PER SERVING Calories: 546 | Fat: 42 g | Protein: 27 g | Sodium: 1,037 mg | Fiber: 4 g | Carbohydrates: 13 g | Sugar: 8 g | Net Carbohydrates: 9 g

Homemade Chili Seasoning

The chili seasoning mix packets that you find in the store may be convenient, but they also frequently contain added sugars and undesirable added ingredients like cornstarch. You can make your own chili seasoning at home by combining 1 tablespoon chili powder, 1 teaspoon ground cumin, ¼ teaspoon cayenne pepper, ¼ teaspoon garlic powder, ½ teaspoon onion powder, 1 teaspoon sea salt, and ¼ teaspoon freshly ground black pepper. These amounts will give you the same volume that you'd get in one chili seasoning packet. You can triple or quadruple the recipe if you want to prepare some in advance to use during your meal prep at a later time.

Meaty Jambalaya

This low-carb jambalaya has all the flavor of the traditional dish but replaces the rice with extra veggies to fill you up without kicking you out of ketosis. If you can't find andouille sausage without sugar in it, replace it with a chicken sausage flavor of your choice.

INGREDIENTS | SERVES 6

2 tablespoons butter-flavored coconut oil

1 large yellow onion, peeled and diced

½ pound no-sugar-added andouille sausage, cut into rounds

3 teaspoons minced garlic

1 (14.5-ounce) can petite-diced tomatoes

2 medium green bell peppers, seeded and diced

1 medium zucchini, diced

1 (12-ounce) bag frozen cut okra, thawed

2 tablespoons Cajun seasoning

2 teaspoons Frank's RedHot sauce

1 cup chicken bone broth

1 pound chicken breast, cooked and cubed

1. Heat coconut oil in a Dutch oven over medium heat. Add onion and sausage and cook until onion starts to caramelize, about 7 minutes. Add garlic and cook until fragrant, about 1 minute.

2. Add remaining ingredients, except chicken, and bring to a boil over medium-high heat. Reduce heat to low and simmer, uncovered, 20 minutes or until most of the liquid has evaporated and jambalaya has thickened.

3. Stir in chicken and remove from heat.

4. Allow to cool and divide into six equal portions. Transfer each portion to a separate airtight container and store in the refrigerator until ready to eat, up to one week.

PER SERVING Calories: 278 | Fat: 14 g | Protein: 26 g | Sodium: 371 mg | Fiber: 4.5 g | Carbohydrates: 13 g | Sugar: 5 g | Net Carbohydrates: 8.5 g

A True Jambalaya

The staple ingredients in jambalaya, which is popular and well loved in Louisiana, are rice, meat, and vegetables. Rice is out on the keto diet, so while you can't create a true jambalaya, you can get pretty close to the flavors by combining some Cajun seasoning, andouille sausage, and low-carb veggies. If you can't find andouille sausage without added sugar, you can substitute with chorizo or kielbasa (but don't tell any die-hard jambalaya fans).

Spicy Sausage Soup

This soup freezes very well, so if you can fit it in your stockpot, you may want to double up. You can meal prep some for now and stock your freezer up with the rest for later. It will keep up to six months frozen.

INGREDIENTS | SERVES 6

1 tablespoon grass-fed butter

1 pound hot Italian sausage

2 cloves garlic, minced

1 small yellow onion, peeled and diced

6 cups beef bone broth

1 (15-ounce) can fire-roasted diced tomatoes

½ teaspoon sea salt

¼ teaspoon freshly ground black pepper

2 medium zucchini, cubed

1 (10-ounce) package frozen chopped spinach, thawed and drained

1. Heat butter in a large stockpot over medium heat. Add sausage, garlic, and onions and cook until sausage is no longer pink, about 7 minutes.

2. Stir in beef broth, tomatoes, salt, and pepper and reduce heat to medium-low. Simmer 15 minutes. Add zucchini and simmer another 15 minutes.

3. Stir in spinach, cover, and remove from heat. Allow to sit 5 minutes.

4. Divide soup into six equal portions and transfer each portion to an airtight container. Store in the refrigerator until ready to eat, up to one week.

PER SERVING Calories: 248 | Fat: 16 g | Protein: 17 g | Sodium: 1,287 mg | Fiber: 3 g | Carbohydrates: 9 g | Sugar: 4 g | Net Carbohydrates: 6 g

Cream of Mushroom Soup

This Cream of Mushroom Soup can (and should) be used in any recipes that call for canned cream of mushroom soup. The canned varieties are not only higher in carbohydrates, they contain artificial (and gross) ingredients.

INGREDIENTS | SERVES 6

5 cups sliced baby bella mushrooms

1½ cups chicken bone broth

½ cup chopped yellow onion

¼ teaspoon dried thyme

3 tablespoons grass-fed butter

3 tablespoons coconut flour

½ teaspoon arrowroot powder

¼ teaspoon sea salt

¼ teaspoon freshly ground black pepper

1 cup heavy cream

1. Combine mushrooms, broth, onion, and thyme in a large stockpot and stir. Cook until mushrooms are tender, about 15 minutes.

2. Use an immersion blender to purée mixture until it reaches a smooth consistency. Set aside.

3. Heat butter in a medium saucepan over medium heat and whisk in flour and arrowroot powder. Add remaining ingredients and mushroom mixture and allow to come to a boil, stirring constantly.

4. Remove from heat and allow to cool. Divide into six equal portions and transfer each portion to a separate airtight container. Store in the refrigerator until ready to eat, up to one week.

PER SERVING Calories: 226 | Fat: 21 g | Protein: 4 g | Sodium: 137 mg | Fiber: 3.5 g | Carbohydrates: 8 g | Sugar: 3.5 g | Net Carbohydrates: 4.5 g

Cheeseburger Soup

After reheating this Cheeseburger Soup, top it with a dollop of sour cream and some pickled jalapeños.

INGREDIENTS | SERVES 6

4 tablespoons grass-fed butter, divided
1 pound 85/15 ground beef
¾ cup chopped yellow onion
1 cup chopped celery
1 teaspoon dried basil
1 teaspoon dried parsley
½ teaspoon sea salt
¼ teaspoon freshly ground black pepper
3 cups beef bone broth
⅛ cup coconut flour
½ teaspoon arrowroot powder
1½ cups heavy cream
1 cup shredded Cheddar cheese
¼ cup full-fat sour cream

1. Heat 1 tablespoon butter in a large stockpot over medium heat. Add beef, onion, celery, basil, parsley, salt, and pepper and cook until beef is no longer pink, about 7 minutes.

2. Add broth and allow to simmer 15 minutes.

3. While soup is simmering, heat remaining butter in a medium saucepan over medium heat. Whisk in flour, arrowroot powder, and cream and whisk until smooth and starting to thicken.

4. Slowly add cream mixture to soup, stirring constantly. Bring to a boil and reduce heat to low. Stir in cheese. Once cheese is melted, remove from heat and stir in sour cream.

5. Allow to cool and then divide into six equal portions. Transfer each portion to an airtight container and store in the refrigerator until ready to eat, up to one week.

PER SERVING Calories: 579 | Fat: 53 g | Protein: 22 g | Sodium: 873 mg | Fiber: 2.5 g | Carbohydrates: 6.5 g | Sugar: 3 g | Net Carbohydrates: 4 g

Thai Coconut Soup

Shiitake mushrooms have a rich flavor, but if you prefer a milder flavor, you can use white mushrooms instead.

INGREDIENTS | SERVES 6

1 tablespoon coconut oil

2 tablespoons fresh grated ginger

2 stalks lemongrass, minced

2 teaspoons red curry paste

4 cups chicken bone broth

3 tablespoons fish sauce

2 teaspoons granulated erythritol

3 (13.6-ounce) cans full-fat coconut milk

8 ounces sliced shiitake mushrooms

2 tablespoons fresh lime juice

1 teaspoon lime zest

½ teaspoon salt

Ten Times the Flavor

Shiitake mushrooms are known for their smoky, rich flavor. Compared to white mushrooms, shiitake mushrooms have ten times the flavor. When selecting shiitake mushrooms, make sure they're firm and not moist and wrinkled. To clean them, wipe them with a clean, damp cloth instead of letting water run over them. Washing mushrooms under running water can make them soggy.

1. Heat coconut oil in a large stockpot over medium heat. Add ginger, lemongrass, and curry paste and cook 1 minute.

2. Stir in chicken broth, fish sauce, and erythritol and simmer 15 minutes. Stir in coconut milk and mushrooms and allow to simmer until mushrooms are soft, about 5 minutes. Stir in lime juice, lime zest, and salt.

3. Remove from heat and allow to cool. Divide into six equal portions and transfer each portion to a separate airtight container. Store in the refrigerator until ready to eat, up to one week.

PER SERVING Calories: 445 | Fat: 44 g | Protein: 9 g | Sodium: 487 mg | Fiber: 1 g | Carbohydrates: 11 g | Sugar: 1.5 g | Net Carbohydrates: 10 g

Cabbage and Beef Soup

One medium raw head of cabbage yields about 8 to 8½ cups chopped cabbage. Since this recipe uses only 6 cups, try to plan your meal prep to use the other 2 to 3. You can make this soup alongside the Deconstructed Cabbage Roll Casserole (Chapter 5).

INGREDIENTS | SERVES 6

2 tablespoons butter-flavored coconut oil

1 pound 85/15 ground beef

2 teaspoons minced garlic

½ large yellow onion, peeled and chopped

6 cups chopped cabbage

2 cups beef bone broth

1 (15-ounce) can tomato sauce

1 (8-ounce) can tomato paste

1 teaspoon ground cumin

1 teaspoon sea salt

1 teaspoon freshly ground black pepper

1. Heat oil in a large stockpot over medium-high heat. Add beef, garlic, and onion and cook until beef is no longer pink, about 7 minutes. Transfer to a slow cooker.

2. Add remaining ingredients, stir, and cover.

3. Cook on low 7 hours, stirring occasionally.

4. Allow to cool and divide into six equal portions. Transfer each portion to an airtight container and store in the refrigerator until ready to eat, up to one week.

PER SERVING Calories: 297 | Fat: 18 g | Protein: 17 g | Sodium: 1,175 mg | Fiber: 5 g | Carbohydrates: 15 g | Sugar: 8 g | Net Carbohydrates: 10 g

Buffalo Chicken Soup

It's best to reheat this Buffalo Chicken Soup over low heat on the stovetop. When it's nice and hot, add some crumbled blue cheese on top or drizzle some ranch dressing into it.

INGREDIENTS | SERVES 6

¼ cup grass-fed butter

3 medium stalks celery, diced

1 small white onion, peeled and diced

¼ cup Paleo flour

¾ cup heavy cream

3 cups chicken bone broth

½ teaspoon garlic powder

2 cups shredded cooked chicken

½ cup Frank's RedHot sauce

1 cup shredded sharp Cheddar cheese

½ cup pepper jack cheese

½ teaspoon sea salt

¼ teaspoon freshly ground black pepper

1. Melt butter in a large stockpot over medium-high heat. Add celery and onion and cook until softened, about 6 minutes.

2. Add flour and cook until flour absorbs most of the moisture, about 3 minutes. Stir in cream and chicken broth. Add remaining ingredients and stir until cheese is melted and mixture is smooth.

3. Reduce heat to medium-low. Simmer 10 minutes, stirring occasionally. Allow to cool.

4. Divide into six equal portions and transfer each portion to an airtight container. Store in the refrigerator until ready to eat, up to one week.

PER SERVING Calories: 434 | Fat: 34 g | Protein: 25 g | Sodium: 520 mg | Fiber: 4 g | Carbohydrates: 8 g | Sugar: 2 g | Net Carbohydrates: 4 g

Egg Drop Soup

Make sure to pour the eggs into this soup slowly so they can create ribbon-like strands that are reminiscent of a traditional egg drop soup.

INGREDIENTS | SERVES 6

6 cups chicken bone broth, divided
1 tablespoon coconut aminos
2 cloves garlic, crushed
1 (1") piece fresh ginger, peeled
3 tablespoons chopped scallions
2 teaspoons arrowroot starch
3 large eggs
2 large egg yolks

1. Combine broth, coconut aminos, garlic, ginger, and scallions in a large stockpot over medium-high heat. Bring to a boil and reduce heat to medium. Allow to simmer 10 minutes. Remove garlic, ginger, and scallions from both and discard.

2. Whisk arrowroot starch into broth, stirring constantly until thickened, about 5 minutes.

3. Combine eggs and egg yolks in a medium bowl and beat lightly.

4. Slowly pour eggs into broth in a steady stream and let sit until cooked, about 1 minute.

5. Remove from heat and allow to cool slightly. Separate into six equal portions and transfer each portion to a separate airtight container. Store in the refrigerator until ready to eat, up to one week.

PER SERVING Calories: 94 | Fat: 5 g | Protein: 9 g | Sodium: 257 mg | Fiber: 0 g | Carbohydrates: 3.5 g | Sugar: 0.5 g | Net Carbohydrates: 3.5 g

Spicy Thai Chicken Soup

Using lemongrass paste is an easy way to get the flavor of lemongrass without having to go through the added step of straining the fibrous stalks out of the soup; however, you can use fresh lemongrass in its place, if you prefer. Use 1 tablespoon fresh lemongrass to replace every tablespoon of paste.

INGREDIENTS | SERVES 6

1 tablespoon coconut oil

2 teaspoons lemongrass paste

4 cloves garlic, minced

1 (2") piece fresh ginger, minced

2 pounds boneless, skinless chicken breasts, cubed

8 ounces sliced shiitake mushrooms

1½ tablespoons red curry paste

3 tablespoons fish sauce

2 tablespoons lime juice

6 cups chicken bone broth

1 (13.6-ounce) can full-fat coconut milk

1 medium red onion, peeled and roughly chopped

½ cup chopped cilantro

Working with Lemongrass

If you're using fresh lemongrass, remove the top and base, which is tough and fibrous, from the stalks and use only the bottom 4 inches. Peel off any dry or tough layers and then chop or mince and add to your recipe. If you can't find fresh lemongrass, check the freezer section. Since lemongrass freezes well, you can often luck out and find a frozen package (which will keep longer too).

1. Heat coconut oil in a large stockpot over medium heat. Add lemongrass paste, garlic, and ginger and cook until softened, about 3 minutes. Add chicken and cook until starting to brown, about 5 minutes. Add mushrooms and continue cooking until mushrooms are softened and chicken is no longer pink, about 5 more minutes.

2. Stir in curry paste, fish sauce, and lime juice and mix until combined. Add chicken broth and coconut milk and reduce heat to medium-low. Simmer 20 minutes.

3. Add red onion and simmer until onion softens, about 5 minutes.

4. Remove from heat and stir in cilantro.

5. Allow to cool and divide into six equal portions. Transfer each portion to an airtight container and store in the refrigerator until ready to eat, up to one week.

PER SERVING Calories: 393 | Fat: 21 g | Protein: 42 g | Sodium: 369 mg | Fiber: 1.5 g | Carbohydrates: 10 g | Sugar: 2 g | Net Carbohydrates: 8.5 g

Taco Turkey Soup

This soup is a great way to use any leftover turkey you may have from Thanksgiving. If you don't have any turkey and aren't planning to make any soon, you can replace it with shredded chicken.

INGREDIENTS | SERVES 6

2 tablespoons butter-flavored coconut oil

1 large yellow onion, peeled and roughly chopped

3 cloves garlic, minced

2 cups shredded turkey

4 cups chicken bone broth

1 (28-ounce) can stewed tomatoes

1 (4-ounce) can chopped green chili peppers

1 tablespoon lime juice

¾ teaspoon ground cumin

½ teaspoon cayenne pepper

½ teaspoon sea salt

½ teaspoon freshly ground black pepper

½ cup fresh chopped cilantro

1. Heat oil in a large stockpot over medium heat. Add onion and garlic and cook until softened, about 4 minutes. Add remaining ingredients, except cilantro, and bring to a boil.

2. Reduce heat to low and simmer 20 minutes. Remove from heat and stir in cilantro.

3. Allow to cool and divide into six equal portions. Transfer each portion to an airtight container and store in the refrigerator until ready to eat, up to one week.

PER SERVING Calories: 176 | Fat: 8 g | Protein: 12 g | Sodium: 386 mg | Fiber: 3 g | Carbohydrates: 9 g | Sugar: 5 g | Net Carbohydrates: 6 g

Homemade Chicken Bone Broth

You can use chicken stock in any recipe that calls for bone broth, but bone broth has more amino acids and collagen, which is a powerhouse nutrient for your gut. To make chicken bone broth, combine 2 pounds of chicken bones, 2 chicken feet (optional), 1 chopped medium onion, 2 chopped medium carrots, 2 stalks chopped celery, 2 tablespoons apple cider vinegar, 2 cloves garlic and 1 teaspoon whole peppercorns in a slow cooker with just enough water to cover everything. Set to low and allow to cook at least 12 hours. Strain the bone and reserve it for use in soups and whatever recipes you want.

White Chicken Chili

This White Chicken Chili may thicken as it sits. If you want to thin it out a little, you can add more half-and-half and/or chicken broth right before you eat it, depending on the texture you want.

INGREDIENTS | SERVES 6

1 tablespoon butter-flavored coconut oil

1 medium white onion, peeled and roughly chopped

3 cloves garlic, minced

1 pound boneless, skinless chicken thighs, cut into cubes

2½ cups chicken bone broth

2 (4-ounce) cans chopped green chilies

1 teaspoon sea salt

½ teaspoon freshly ground black pepper

1 teaspoon ground cumin

1 teaspoon dried oregano

⅛ teaspoon cayenne pepper

¾ cup full-fat sour cream

½ cup half-and-half

1. Heat coconut oil in a large stockpot over medium heat, add onion and garlic and cook until they start to soften, about 4 minutes. Add chicken and cook until no longer pink, about 10 minutes.

2. Add remaining ingredients, except sour cream and half-and-half, and bring to a boil. Reduce heat to low and simmer 1 hour.

3. Remove from heat and stir in remaining ingredients. Allow to cool.

4. Divide into six equal portions and transfer each portion to a separate airtight container. Store in the refrigerator until ready to eat, up to one week.

PER SERVING Calories: 225 | Fat: 13 g | Protein: 18 g | Sodium: 512 mg | Fiber: 1 g | Carbohydrates: 9 g | Sugar: 4 g | Net Carbohydrates: 8 g

Chorizo and Beef Chili

This tomato-based Chorizo and Beef Chili gets even better after sitting in the refrigerator for a few days as the flavors are allowed to develop. You may want to make it a night or two before you plan to eat it.

INGREDIENTS | SERVES 6

2 tablespoons butter-flavored coconut oil

3 medium stalks celery, chopped

1 medium yellow onion, peeled and roughly chopped

3 cloves garlic, minced

1 pound 85/15 ground beef

½ pound ground chorizo

1 (28-ounce) can tomato sauce

1 (14.5-ounce) can fire-roasted diced tomatoes

1 (14.5-ounce) can petite diced tomatoes

1 (6-ounce) can tomato paste

1 (4-ounce) can chopped green chilies

1½ tablespoons chili seasoning mix

1. Heat coconut oil in a large stockpot over medium-high heat. Add celery, onion, and garlic and cook until softened, about 6 minutes.

2. Add ground beef and chorizo and cook until no longer pink, about 7 minutes. Add remaining ingredients and stir to mix. Bring to a boil and then reduce heat to low and simmer 2 hours.

3. Remove from heat and allow to cool. Divide into six equal portions and transfer each portion to an airtight container. Store in the refrigerator until ready to eat, up to one week.

PER SERVING Calories: 482 | Fat: 33 g | Protein: 26 g | Sodium: 1,231 mg | Fiber: 6 g | Carbohydrates: 12 g | Sugar: 4 g | Net Carbohydrates: 6 g

Chorizo in a Pinch

If you can't find chorizo without added sugar or unwanted ingredients, you can make your own version by combining hot Italian sausage with 1 teaspoon smoked paprika and 1 tablespoon apple cider vinegar per pound of meat. This version isn't true chorizo, which is made with a vinegar-based chili paste and dried Mexican chilies, but the flavor is close enough to hold you over until you can find the real thing.

Hamburger Stew

Baby kale has a milder flavor and more delicate texture than mature, chopped kale, but you can use either one in this stew. You can also use spinach if you prefer it over kale.

INGREDIENTS | SERVES 6

2 tablespoons avocado oil

4 medium stalks celery, chopped

1 small yellow onion, peeled and chopped

3 cloves garlic, minced

1½ pounds 85/15 ground beef

4 cups beef bone broth

½ cup pumpkin purée

1 teaspoon sea salt

1 teaspoon freshly ground black pepper

1 teaspoon dried oregano

1 teaspoon dried basil

1 teaspoon dried parsley

½ teaspoon dried sage

3 cups baby kale

1. Heat oil in a large stockpot over medium heat. Add celery, onion, and garlic and cook until softened, about 5 minutes. Crumble beef into onion mixture and cook until no longer pink, about 7 minutes.

2. Add remaining ingredients, except kale, increase heat to medium-high and bring to a boil. Reduce heat to low and simmer, covered, 30 minutes.

3. Stir in kale and cook an additional 10 minutes. Remove from heat and allow to cool.

4. Divide into six equal portions and transfer each portion to a separate airtight container. Store in the refrigerator until ready to eat, up to one week.

PER SERVING Calories: 335 | Fat: 25 g | Protein: 22 g | Sodium: 1,090 mg | Fiber: 1.5 g | Carbohydrates: 4 g | Sugar: 1.5 g | Net Carbohydrates: 2.5 g

Baby Kale versus Mature Kale

Like the name implies, baby kale are the immature leaves of the kale plant. Baby kale has a peppery flavor that's similar to arugula. One of the major differences between baby kale and mature kale is that baby kale is a lot easier to eat raw because mature kale is tougher and more fibrous. Both baby kale and mature kale are very low-carb vegetables, weighing in at only 7 grams per cup (3 of which come from fiber).

Creamy Taco Soup

You can also make this Creamy Taco Soup with ground beef instead of chicken. Cook ground beef in a skillet with spices, drain, add to a slow cooker, and then follow the rest of the recipe as written.

INGREDIENTS | SERVES 6

1½ pounds boneless, skinless chicken breasts

1 small yellow onion, peeled and diced

4 cloves garlic, minced

1 tablespoon cumin

1 teaspoon chili powder

½ teaspoon paprika

1 teaspoon onion powder

½ teaspoon sea salt

1 tablespoon lemon juice

2 tablespoons lime juice

2½ cups chicken bone broth

8 ounces cream cheese

½ cup chopped cilantro

1. Add chicken, onion, garlic, cumin, chili powder, paprika, onion powder, salt, lemon juice, lime juice, and chicken broth to slow cooker.

2. Cover and cook on low 5 hours. Remove chicken and shred.

3. Stir cream cheese into broth mixture and mix until incorporated.

4. Return chicken to slow cooker. Stir in cilantro.

5. Allow to cool and divide into six equal portions. Transfer each portion to a separate airtight container and store in the refrigerator until ready to eat, up to one week.

PER SERVING Calories: 294 | Fat: 16 g | Protein: 30 g | Sodium: 427 mg | Fiber: 0.5 g | Carbohydrates: 6 g | Sugar: 2 g | Net Carbohydrates: 5.5 g

Jalapeño Popper Soup

When working with peppers, always make sure to use gloves. If you get capsaicin on your hands and then rub your eyes, you'll be in for an unwelcome surprise.

INGREDIENTS | SERVES 6

2 tablespoons grass-fed butter

3 cloves garlic, minced

1 small yellow onion, peeled and diced

1½ pounds boneless, skinless chicken breasts, cut into cubes

2 teaspoons red chili paste

1 teaspoon ground cumin

1 teaspoon sea salt

1 teaspoon freshly ground black pepper

½ teaspoon dried oregano

¼ teaspoon paprika

4 medium jalapeño peppers, seeded and sliced

2 cups chicken bone broth

1 cup heavy cream

6 ounces cream cheese

1 cup shredded sharp Cheddar cheese

1 cup shredded pepper jack cheese

1. Heat butter in a large stockpot. Add garlic and onion and cook until softened, about 5 minutes. Add chicken and cook until no longer pink, about 8 minutes.

2. Add red chili paste, cumin, salt, black pepper, oregano, paprika, and jalapeño peppers and cook 2 more minutes. Pour in chicken broth and bring to a boil. Reduce heat to low and simmer 30 minutes.

3. Add heavy cream and cream cheese and stir until melted. Add remaining cheeses and stir until melted.

4. Remove from heat and allow to cool. Divide into six equal portions and transfer each portion to a separate airtight container. Store in the refrigerator until ready to eat, up to one week.

PER SERVING Calories: 595 | Fat: 44 g | Protein: 40 g | Sodium: 845 mg | Fiber: 0.5 g | Carbohydrates: 6 g | Sugar: 3 g | Net Carbohydrates: 5.5 g

You Don't Know Jack

Pepper jack cheese is Monterey jack that's been flavored with habanero peppers, sweet peppers, rosemary, garlic, and jalapeños. If you prefer your dishes less spicy, you can replace any amount of pepper jack cheese with Monterey jack. It has the same buttery texture as pepper jack but without any of the kick.

Chicken Chowder

If you don't have a pressure cooker, you can make this chowder in a slow cooker. Follow the directions as written, but instead of adding ingredients to the pressure cooker, add them to a slow cooker and cook on low for 8 hours. When done cooking, stir in the cream, spinach, and bacon.

INGREDIENTS | SERVES 6

1½ pounds boneless skinless thighs

8 ounces cream cheese

3 teaspoons minced garlic

½ cup chopped yellow onion

½ cup chopped celery

½ cup sliced baby bella mushrooms

¼ cup grass-fed butter

3 cups chicken bone broth

1 teaspoon dried thyme

½ teaspoon sea salt

¼ teaspoon freshly ground black pepper

1 cup heavy cream

2 cups fresh spinach, chopped

¾ pound no-sugar-added bacon, cooked crispy and crumbled

1. Add chicken, cream cheese, garlic, onion, celery, mushrooms, butter, chicken broth, thyme, salt, and pepper to the pot of a pressure cooker.

2. Set to 30 minutes using the Soup setting. Allow pressure to release naturally.

3. Once pressure has released, stir in heavy cream. Stir in spinach and then bacon.

4. Allow to cool. Divide into six equal portions and transfer each portion to a separate airtight container. Store in the refrigerator until ready to eat, up to one week.

PER SERVING Calories: 735 | Fat: 62 g | Protein: 35 g | Sodium: 876 mg | Fiber: 1 g | Carbohydrates: 7 g | Sugar: 6 g | Net Carbohydrates: 6 g

Chicken Florentine Soup

This recipe calls for coconut cream, but if you're not a fan of the slightly sweet flavor it adds, you can replace it with heavy cream or half-and-half.

INGREDIENTS | SERVES 6

1 tablespoon butter-flavored coconut oil

3 cloves garlic, minced

½ large yellow onion, peeled and diced

1 teaspoon Italian seasoning

¼ teaspoon dried basil

¼ teaspoon dried parsley

¼ teaspoon dried oregano

4 cups chicken bone broth

1½ pounds cooked shredded chicken

1 (10-ounce) package frozen chopped spinach, thawed and drained

1 teaspoon sea salt

½ teaspoon freshly ground black pepper

1 cup coconut cream

4 ounces cream cheese

1. Melt coconut oil in a large stockpot over medium heat. Add garlic and onion and cook until softened, about 6 minutes.

2. Add remaining ingredients, except coconut cream and cream cheese, and allow to simmer 10 minutes.

3. Add coconut cream and cream cheese and stir until melted. Allow to cool.

4. Divide into six equal portions and transfer each portion to a separate airtight container. Store in the refrigerator until ready to eat, up to one week.

PER SERVING Calories: 432 | Fat: 27 g | Protein: 39 g | Sodium: 643 mg | Fiber: 2 g | Carbohydrates: 8 g | Sugar: 6 g | Net Carbohydrates: 6 g

Homemade Italian Seasoning

Most spice manufacturers make an Italian seasoning blend that's all ready to go for you, but if you prefer to make your own, combine 2 tablespoons dried basil, 2 tablespoons dried oregano, 2 tablespoons dried rosemary, 2 tablespoons dried marjoram, 2 tablespoons dried cilantro, 2 tablespoons dried thyme, 2 tablespoons dried savory, and 2 tablespoons red pepper flakes. You can also adjust these spices to reduce the flavors you don't love and increase the ones you do. Use what you want and store the rest for later.

Sausage, Spinach, and Pepper Soup

Use mature chopped spinach in this recipe instead of baby spinach. Baby spinach wilts quickly and develops a slimy texture, whereas mature spinach will soften, but still give you a nice texture.

INGREDIENTS | SERVES 6

2 tablespoons butter-flavored coconut oil

1½ pounds pork sausage

1 medium red bell pepper, seeded and diced

3 medium stalks celery, diced

2 teaspoons Italian seasoning

2 teaspoons chili powder

1 teaspoon ground cumin

¼ teaspoon red pepper flakes

1 teaspoon sea salt

½ teaspoon freshly ground black pepper

6 cups chicken bone broth

2 cups chopped spinach

1. Heat oil in a large stockpot over medium-high heat. Add sausage and cook until no longer pink, about 7 minutes.

2. Add red pepper, celery, and spices and continue cooking until softened, about 5 minutes.

3. Pour in chicken broth and reduce heat to medium-low. Simmer 1 hour.

4. Stir in spinach and cook 5 more minutes.

5. Remove from heat and allow to cool. Divide into six equal portions and transfer each portion to a separate airtight container. Store in the refrigerator until ready to eat, up to one week.

PER SERVING Calories: 432 | Fat: 27 g | Protein: 39 g | Sodium: 643 mg | Fiber: 2 g | Carbohydrates: 8 g | Sugar: 6 g | Net Carbohydrates: 6 g

Slow Cooker Meals

Slow Cooker Whole Chicken

It's often helpful to cook a whole chicken in the slow cooker the night before your meal prep cooking day. You can shred the chicken when it's done cooking and use it in the recipes that called for cooked shredded chicken.

INGREDIENTS | SERVES 6

1 large yellow onion, peeled and cut into quarters

3 cloves garlic, crushed

1 (3-pound) whole roasting chicken

1 teaspoon sea salt

½ teaspoon freshly ground black pepper

½ teaspoon garlic powder

1 teaspoon paprika

1 cup chicken bone broth

1. Place cut onion and garlic into open cavity of chicken. Transfer chicken to slow cooker.

2. Sprinkle salt, black pepper, garlic powder, and paprika all over chicken. Pour broth on the bottom of the slow cooker.

3. Cover and cook on low 10 hours or until chicken is cooked through.

4. Remove meat from bones and divide into six equal portions. Transfer each portion to a separate airtight container and store in the refrigerator until ready to eat, up to one week.

PER SERVING Calories: 287 | Fat: 7 g | Protein: 49 g | Sodium: 573 mg | Fiber: 0.5 g | Carbohydrates: 3 g | Sugar: 1 g | Net Carbohydrates: 2.5 g

Balsamic Pork Tenderloin

When selecting a balsamic vinaigrette, check the ingredient list and make sure that there's no added sugar and it's keto-friendly. If you can't find one, you can use 2 cups of homemade dressing in its place.

INGREDIENTS | SERVES 6

1 (3-pound) pork tenderloin

1 (10-ounce) bottle balsamic vinaigrette dressing

Homemade Balsamic Vinaigrette

Dressing is one of the most difficult items to find without added high-carbohydrate sweeteners. If you're having trouble, you can make your own balsamic vinaigrette by combining 1 cup olive oil, ½ cup balsamic vinegar, 2 teaspoons powdered erythritol, 2 teaspoons Dijon mustard, 2 minced shallots, 2 minced cloves garlic, ½ teaspoon sea salt, and ¼ teaspoon freshly ground black pepper and whisking until incorporated.

1. Place pork in slow cooker. Pour balsamic dressing over pork.

2. Cook on low 11 hours or until pork is cooked through.

3. Divide into six equal servings and place each portion into a separate airtight container. Store in the refrigerator until ready to eat, up to one week.

PER SERVING Calories: 356 | Fat: 14 g | Protein: 47 g | Sodium: 582 mg | Fiber: 0 g | Carbohydrates: 3 g | Sugar: 3 g | Net Carbohydrates: 3 g

Buffalo Wings

This recipe does require you to use the oven in addition to the slow cooker, but the extra step is necessary to get the crispiness for which buffalo wings are known.

INGREDIENTS | SERVES 6

1 (12-ounce) bottle Frank's RedHot sauce

½ cup grass-fed butter

2 tablespoons coconut aminos

2 teaspoons dried oregano

2 teaspoons onion powder

2 teaspoons garlic powder

4 pounds chicken wing pieces

½ teaspoon arrowroot powder

1. Combine all ingredients, except chicken and arrowroot powder, in a medium saucepan over medium-heat. Bring to a boil, reduce heat to low, and allow to simmer 5 minutes.

2. Place chicken wings in slow cooker, pour sauce on top, and stir to coat. Cover and cook on high 1 hour. Reduce heat to low and cook 1 more hour.

3. Preheat oven to 400°F.

4. Grease two rimmed baking sheets and transfer wings with a slotted spoon from slow cooker. Bake 30 minutes, turning once during cooking, or until wings are crispy and slightly browned.

5. While wings are cooking in the oven, transfer sauce from the slow cooker to a medium saucepan. Stir in arrowroot powder and simmer on low until sauce thickens, about 5 minutes.

6. Transfer sauce to a large mixing bowl. Remove wings from oven and add them to the mixing bowl. Toss to coat.

7. Allow to cool. Divide wings into six equal portions and place each portion in an airtight container. Store in the refrigerator until ready to eat, up to one week.

PER SERVING Calories: 819 | Fat: 54 g | Protein: 53 g | Sodium: 294 mg | Fiber: 0.5 g | Carbohydrates: 2.5 g | Sugar: 0.5 g | Net Carbohydrates: 2 g

Pork and Sauerkraut

Make sure to reserve and use the juices from the sauerkraut. The brine that the kraut ferments in is rich in probiotics that feed the good bacteria in your gut and keep your whole body healthy.

INGREDIENTS | SERVES 6

1½ pound pork tenderloin

4 cups sauerkraut, with juices

1½ cups chicken bone broth

½ teaspoon sea salt

¼ teaspoon freshly ground black pepper

10 tablespoons grass-fed butter, cubed

1. Place pork in a slow cooker and cover with sauerkraut, juices, and chicken bone broth.

2. Sprinkle with salt and pepper and arrange butter cubes all over pork.

3. Cook on low 10 hours, or until pork is tender and comes apart easily with a fork.

4. Allow to cool and divide into six equal portions. Transfer each portion to an airtight container and store in the refrigerator until ready to eat, up to one week.

PER SERVING Calories: 319 | Fat: 22 g | Protein: 25 g | Sodium: 899 mg | Fiber: 3 g | Carbohydrates: 4 g | Sugar: 1 g | Net Carbohydrates: 1 g

Mongolian Beef

Flank steak has great flavor, but it can be a little tough at times. It's perfect for slow cooking, since the extended cooking time softens the meat making it easier to chew and digest.

INGREDIENTS | SERVES 6

¾ cup beef bone broth

¾ cup coconut aminos

½ cup powdered erythritol

3 scallions, chopped

2 tablespoons olive oil

3 cloves garlic, minced

½ teaspoon minced fresh ginger

1½ pounds beef flank steak

1. Combine all ingredients except the steak in a slow cooker and stir to mix. Add steak.

2. Cover and cook on low 5 hours or until beef is cooked through and tender.

3. Allow to cool, then divide into six equal portions. Transfer each portion to a separate airtight container and store in the refrigerator until ready to eat, up to one week.

PER SERVING Calories: 219 | Fat: 12 g | Protein: 24 g | Sodium: 193 mg | Fiber: 0 g | Carbohydrates: 1 g | Sugar: 0 g | Net Carbohydrates: 1 g

Chicken Fajitas

When meal prepping, pair these Chicken Fajitas with some basic cauliflower rice and store them in the same container until ready to eat.

INGREDIENTS | SERVES 6

1½ pounds boneless, skinless chicken breast

1 small white onion, peeled and thinly sliced

1 small red bell pepper, seeded and cut into thin strips

1 small yellow bell pepper, seeded and cut into thin strips

1 small orange bell pepper, seeded and cut into thin strips

½ cup no-sugar-added salsa

1 package no-sugar-added fajita seasoning mix

⅛ teaspoon cayenne pepper

Homemade Fajita Seasoning

Fajita seasoning and taco seasoning are very similar, but there's one subtle difference. Fajita seasoning has more cumin added to it, while taco seasoning favors chili powder. If you can't find fajita seasoning with clean, keto-approved ingredients, you can use taco seasoning instead or you can make your own by combining 1¼ teaspoons ground cumin, 1 teaspoon chili powder, 1 teaspoon paprika, 1 teaspoon garlic powder, ½ teaspoon dried oregano, 1 teaspoon sea salt, and ¼ teaspoon freshly ground black pepper.

1. Place chicken breasts in the bottom of a slow cooker. Add onions and peppers on top of chicken.

2. In a small bowl, combine salsa, fajita seasoning mix, and cayenne pepper and pour on top of chicken.

3. Cook on low 7 hours or until chicken is cooked through and tender. Remove chicken from slow cooker, shred with a fork, and return to slow cooker. Stir to combine.

4. Divide into six equal portions and then transfer each portion to an airtight container. Store in the refrigerator until ready to eat, up to one week.

PER SERVING Calories: 154 | Fat: 3 g | Protein: 26 g | Sodium: 221 mg | Fiber: 1 g | Carbohydrates: 4 g | Sugar: 2 g | Net Carbohydrates: 3 g

Pepper Steak

Avocado oil is one of the best oils to cook with because it has a high smoke point and can withstand temperatures up to 400°F. Like the avocados it comes from, it's also rich in monounsaturated fats.

INGREDIENTS | SERVES 6

1 teaspoon garlic powder

1½ teaspoons sea salt, divided

½ teaspoon freshly ground black pepper

1½ pounds beef sirloin, cut into strips

2 tablespoons avocado oil

¼ cup beef bone broth

½ cup chopped yellow onion

1 large green bell pepper, seeded and cut into strips

1 large red bell pepper, seeded and cut into strips

2 cloves garlic, minced

1 (14.5-ounce) can stewed tomatoes

3 tablespoons coconut aminos

1 teaspoon granulated erythritol

½ teaspoon red pepper flakes (optional)

1. Sprinkle garlic powder, ½ teaspoon salt, and black pepper over beef strips. Heat avocado oil in a medium skillet over medium-high heat and add seasoned beef. Cook until beef is browned on all sides.

2. While beef is browning, add remaining ingredients to slow cooker and stir to combine. Add beef to slow cooker and stir again. Cover and cook on low 7 hours or until beef is cooked through and tender.

3. Allow to cool and divide into six equal portions. Transfer each portion to an airtight container and store in the refrigerator until ready to eat, up to one week.

PER SERVING Calories: 226 | Fat: 10 g | Protein: 25 g | Sodium: 765 mg | Fiber: 2.5 g | Carbohydrates: 6 g | Sugar: 2 g | Net Carbohydrates: 3.5 g

Barbecue Pork

The best way to reheat this Barbecue Pork is to add some extra sauce with the pork to a small saucepan, cover it, and warm it up over low temperature until it reaches your desired temperature.

INGREDIENTS | SERVES 6

1 teaspoon granulated garlic

1 teaspoon granulated onion

1 teaspoon sea salt

½ teaspoon freshly ground black pepper

1 (2-pound) pork tenderloin

3 cups no-sugar-added barbecue sauce, divided

Homemade Barbecue Sauce

If you can't find barbecue sauce without added sugar, you can make your own combining 1½ cups Golden Monk Fruit Sugar Substitute, 1½ cups no-sugar-added ketchup, ½ cup red wine vinegar, ½ cup water, 1 tablespoon Worcestershire sauce, 2½ tablespoons dry mustard, 2 teaspoons paprika, 2 teaspoons sea salt, 1½ teaspoons freshly ground black pepper, and 1 teaspoon Frank's RedHot sauce in a blender and blending until smooth.

1. Sprinkle garlic, onion, salt, and pepper on pork and place in a slow cooker. Pour 2 cups barbecue sauce on top of pork and cook on low 8 hours or until pork falls apart easily.

2. Remove pork from slow cooker, shred with a fork, and return to slow cooker. Add remaining barbecue sauce and stir.

3. Cook 1 additional hour.

4. Allow to cool, then divide into six equal portions. Transfer each portion to an airtight container and store in the refrigerator until ready to eat, up to one week.

PER SERVING Calories: 400 | Fat: 5 g | Protein: 32 g | Sodium: 1,264 mg | Fiber: 1.5 g | Carbohydrates: 9 g | Sugar: 1 g | Net Carbohydrates: 6.5 g

Beef Carnitas

Beef Carnitas are the perfect foundation for a homemade, keto-friendly burrito bowl. Top some cauliflower rice with Beef Carnitas, then pile shredded cheese, sour cream, avocado, salsa, and some fresh cilantro on top.

INGREDIENTS | SERVES 6

2 pounds chuck roast
1 tablespoon chili powder
½ teaspoon dried oregano
½ teaspoon ground cumin
½ (4-ounce) can green chili peppers
3 cloves garlic, minced
1 teaspoon salt
2 cups beef bone broth
3 medium jalapeño peppers, seeded and minced

1. Season chuck roast with chili powder, oregano, and cumin. Transfer to slow cooker.

2. Add remaining ingredients, cover, and cook on low 6 hours, or until beef is cooked through and tender. Remove meat from slow cooker and shred with a fork. Return to slow cooker and stir. Allow to cool.

3. Divide into six equal portions and transfer each portion to an airtight container. Store in the refrigerator until ready to eat, up to one week.

PER SERVING Calories: 258 | Fat: 9 g | Protein: 39 g | Sodium: 834 mg | Fiber: 1 g | Carbohydrates: 2 g | Sugar: 0.5 g | Net Carbohydrates: 1 g

Buffalo Chicken

If you prefer the richer flavor, and higher fat content, of dark meat, you can use chicken thighs instead of chicken breasts.

INGREDIENTS | SERVES 6

1½ pounds boneless, skinless chicken breasts
1 (12-ounce) bottle Frank's RedHot sauce
1 tablespoon ranch dressing seasoning mix
2 tablespoons grass-fed butter, melted

1. Place chicken in a slow cooker. Combine remaining ingredients in a medium bowl and then pour over chicken.

2. Cook on low 6 hours. Remove chicken, shred with a fork, and return to slow cooker. Cook for 1 additional hour.

3. Allow to cool and then divide into six equal portions. Transfer each portion to an airtight container and store in the refrigerator until ready to eat, up to one week.

PER SERVING Calories: 184 | Fat: 7 g | Protein: 26 g | Sodium: 150 mg | Fiber: 0 g | Carbohydrates: 1 g | Sugar: 1 g | Net Carbohydrates: 1 g

Zesty Barbecue Chicken

*Make sure both the barbecue sauce and the Italian dressing that
you use for this chicken don't have any added sugar.*

INGREDIENTS | SERVES 6

1½ pounds boneless, skinless chicken
  breasts
½ cup diced yellow onion
2 cups no-sugar-added barbecue sauce
½ cup no-sugar-added Italian dressing
2 tablespoons coconut aminos

1. Place chicken and onions in a slow cooker.

2. Combine remaining ingredients in a medium bowl and then pour over chicken and onions.

3. Cover and cook 7 hours on low or until chicken is cooked through and tender.

4. Remove chicken from slow cooker, shred with a fork, and return to slow cooker. Stir and allow to cook 1 more hour.

5. Allow to cool. Divide into six equal portions and transfer each portion to a separate airtight container. Store in the refrigerator until ready to eat, up to one week.

PER SERVING Calories: 342 | Fat: 7 g | Protein: 26 g | Sodium: 1,076 mg | Fiber: 1 g | Carbohydrates: 4 g | Sugar: 1 g | Net Carbohydrates: 3 g

Italian Beef

The Italian dressing mix in this recipe gives this beef a zesty tang that pairs well with the rich flavor of the beef bone broth.

INGREDIENTS | SERVES 6

2 cups beef bone broth

1 teaspoon sea salt

1 teaspoon freshly ground black pepper

1 teaspoon dried oregano

1 teaspoon dried basil

1 teaspoon onion salt

1 teaspoon dried parsley

1 teaspoon granulated garlic

2 tablespoons Italian dressing mix

1 bay leaf

1 (2-pound) chuck roast

Homemade Italian Dressing Mix

You can find Italian dressing mix packets in the dressing aisle at most supermarkets, but if the ingredients aren't clean, you can make your own by combining 1 tablespoon garlic salt, 1 tablespoon onion powder, 1 tablespoon granulated erythritol, 2 tablespoons dried oregano, 1 teaspoon freshly ground black pepper, ¼ teaspoon dried thyme, 1 teaspoon dried basil, 1 tablespoon dried parsley, ¼ teaspoon celery salt, and 2 tablespoons sea salt. Use what you need and then store the rest in an airtight container.

1. Combine all ingredients, except chuck roast, in a medium saucepan over high heat and bring to a boil. Remove from heat.

2. Add roast to slow cooker and pour broth mixture over it.

3. Cover and cook on low 8 hours. Remove roast from slow cooker, shred with a fork, and return to slow cooker. Stir to combine and cook 1 more hour.

4. Allow to cool. Divide into six equal portions and transfer each portion to a separate airtight container. Store in the refrigerator until ready to eat, up to one week.

PER SERVING Calories: 249 | Fat: 8 g | Protein: 39 g | Sodium: 1,082 mg | Fiber: 0.5 g | Carbohydrates: 0.5 g | Sugar: 0 g | Net Carbohydrates: 0 g

Chicken Cacciatore

This dish pairs well with spaghetti squash or zucchini noodles. When meal prepping, use a storage container with separate compartments and put a serving of Chicken Cacciatore in one and the zoodles or spaghetti squash in another. When ready to eat, combine them and heat them in a saucepan over low heat.

INGREDIENTS | SERVES 6

2 pounds bone-in chicken thighs

1½ cups no-sugar-added marinara sauce

1 (6-ounce) can tomato paste

1 medium green bell pepper, seeded and diced

8 ounces sliced white mushrooms

1 small yellow onion, peeled and diced

3 tablespoons minced garlic

1 teaspoon dried oregano

⅛ teaspoon red pepper flakes

1. Place chicken in slow cooker. Top with remaining ingredients.

2. Cover and cook on low 8 hours. Allow to cool.

3. Divide into six equal portions and transfer each portion to a separate airtight container. Store in the refrigerator until ready to eat, up to one week.

PER SERVING Calories: 230 | Fat: 6 g | Protein: 32 g | Sodium: 367 mg | Fiber: 3 g | Carbohydrates: 5 g | Sugar: 2 g | Net Carbohydrates: 2 g

No-Crust Pizza

One of the most commonly missed foods on a keto diet is pizza, but with this recipe, you can enjoy all of the flavors without the carbohydrate-loaded crust.

INGREDIENTS | SERVES 6

1 tablespoon avocado oil

1½ pounds 85/15 ground beef

1 teaspoon salt

½ teaspoon freshly ground black pepper

½ teaspoon granulated garlic

½ teaspoon granulated onion

2½ cups shredded mozzarella cheese, divided

2 cups no-sugar-added pizza sauce

½ cup shredded provolone cheese

1. Heat avocado oil in a medium skillet over medium heat. Add beef and seasonings and cook until no longer pink, about 7 minutes. Remove from heat and stir in 2 cups mozzarella cheese.

2. Transfer cooked beef to bottom of a slow cooker and spread evenly.

3. Pour pizza sauce evenly over beef and sprinkle remaining cheese on top. Cover and cook on low 4 hours.

4. Allow to cool and divide into six equal portions. Transfer each portion to a separate airtight container and store in the refrigerator until ready to eat, up to one week.

PER SERVING Calories: 490 | Fat: 37 g | Protein: 33 g | Sodium: 972 mg | Fiber: 1.5 g | Carbohydrates: 3 g | Sugar: 1 g | Net Carbohydrates: 1.5 g

Spinach and Artichoke Chicken

When heating this Spinach and Artichoke Chicken, add a little chicken broth to a skillet with your portion, cover, and cook over low heat until it reaches the desired temperature.

INGREDIENTS | SERVES 6

1 teaspoon garlic powder

1 teaspoon onion powder

1 teaspoon sea salt

½ teaspoon freshly ground black pepper

1½ pounds boneless, skinless chicken breasts, cubed

¼ cup chicken bone broth

1 (10-ounce) package frozen chopped spinach, thawed and squeezed dry

1 (15-ounce) jar marinated artichoke hearts, chopped

8 ounces cream cheese

½ cup shredded Parmesan cheese

¾ cup shredded mozzarella cheese

1. Sprinkle garlic powder, onion powder, salt, and pepper all over chicken and place chicken in a slow cooker. Add chicken broth.

2. Cook on low 4 hours. Add spinach, artichokes, cream cheese, and Parmesan cheese. Cook 1 additional hour. Sprinkle mozzarella cheese on top and cover until cheese is melted.

3. Allow to cool. Divide into six equal portions and transfer each portion to a separate airtight container. Store in the refrigerator until ready to eat, up to one week.

PER SERVING Calories: 390 | Fat: 22 g | Protein: 37 g | Sodium: 767 mg | Fiber: 4.5 g | Carbohydrates: 10 g | Sugar: 2 g | Net Carbohydrates: 5.5 g

Fiber-Rich Artichokes

Artichokes don't get a lot of attention, but they're low-carb nutritional powerhouses that deserve a chance in the spotlight. Artichokes are packed with antioxidants and they're a good source of vitamin C, vitamin K, folate, and fiber. In fact, one medium artichoke has more fiber than a cup of prunes and only 12 grams of carbohydrates, a whopping 8 of which come from the fiber.

Spicy Cauliflower

Once you try cauliflower cooked this way in a slow cooker, you'll never go back to anything else. It's the perfect balance of creamy and spicy.

INGREDIENTS | SERVES 6

1 large head cauliflower, cut into florets

4 ounces cream cheese

¼ cup heavy cream

2 tablespoons grass-fed butter

3 cloves garlic, minced

1 teaspoon salt

½ teaspoon freshly ground black pepper

1 cup shredded pepper jack cheese

6 slices no-sugar-added bacon, cooked and chopped

1. Combine cauliflower, cream cheese, cream, butter, garlic, salt, and pepper in a slow cooker and stir to mix. Cook on low 3 hours.

2. Stir in pepper jack cheese and cook 1 more hour, or until cauliflower is tender.

3. Sprinkle bacon on top.

4. Allow to cool then divide into six equal portions. Transfer each portion to an airtight container and store in the refrigerator until ready to eat, up to one week.

PER SERVING Calories: 365 | Fat: 32 g | Protein: 12 g | Sodium: 816 mg | Fiber: 2 g | Carbohydrates: 5 g | Sugar: 2 g | Net Carbohydrates: 3 g

Garlic Parmesan Spaghetti Squash

A meal prep pro tip is to always have cooked spaghetti squash on hand. That way you can throw recipes like this together in just a few minutes and all you have to do is wait for it to cook.

INGREDIENTS | SERVES 6

6 cups cooked spaghetti squash strands

½ cup grass-fed butter

2 teaspoons minced garlic

¼ cup coconut cream

2 ounces cream cheese

⅓ cup grated Parmesan cheese

½ teaspoon sea salt

¼ teaspoon freshly ground black pepper

1. Combine all ingredients in a slow cooker, stir, cover, and cook on low 1 hour, stirring occasionally until melted and creamy. Allow to cool.

2. Divide into six equal portions and transfer each portion to a separate airtight container. Store in the refrigerator until ready to eat, up to one week.

PER SERVING Calories: 254 | Fat: 22 g | Protein: 4 g | Sodium: 336 mg | Fiber: 3 g | Carbohydrates: 11 g | Sugar: 2 g | Net Carbohydrates: 8 g

Chicken Thighs with Cream Sauce

Bone-in chicken thighs hold up really well to the cooking time of a slow cooker, but if you have only boneless chicken thighs or breasts or that's what's on sale, feel free to use that in their place.

INGREDIENTS | SERVES 6

1 teaspoon dried thyme

½ teaspoon dry mustard

½ teaspoon salt

¼ teaspoon freshly ground black pepper

2 pounds bone-in chicken thighs, skins removed

2 tablespoons grass-fed butter

¼ cup diced yellow onion

3 cloves garlic, minced

1¼ cups chicken bone broth

¾ coconut cream

¼ teaspoon arrowroot powder

1 teaspoon dried parsley

1 teaspoon dried basil

Breast or Thigh?

Both chicken thighs and chicken breasts are excellent sources of lean protein, but chicken thighs have three times the amount of fat. This fat adds flavor to recipes, especially when they're slow cooked and the fat is allowed to drip into the juices the chicken is being cooked in. Whether or not you want to choose chicken breasts or thighs is a personal preference, but chicken thighs can help you meet your fat needs a little more easily.

1. Sprinkle thyme, mustard, salt, and pepper all over chicken thighs.

2. Heat butter in a medium skillet over medium heat. Add onion and garlic and cook until softened, about 3 minutes. Add chicken thighs and cook 2 minutes on each side, to sear and brown.

3. Transfer chicken thighs to slow cooker and scrape contents of pan into slow cooker.

4. Add chicken broth, cover, and cook on low 6 hours or until thighs are cooked through.

5. Remove chicken from slow cooker with tongs and place equal portions into each of six separate airtight containers.

6. Transfer slow cooker ingredients to a medium saucepan over medium heat. Stir in coconut cream and arrowroot powder and whisk constantly until thickened, about 4 minutes. Stir in herbs. Allow to cool slightly.

7. Pour equal amounts of cream sauce over each chicken thigh and cover. Store in the refrigerator until ready to eat, up to one week.

PER SERVING Calories: 228 | Fat: 10 g | Protein: 30 g | Sodium: 356 mg | Fiber: 0 g | Carbohydrates: 2 g | Sugar: 0.5 g | Net Carbohydrates: 2 g

Pizza Meatballs

These Pizza Meatballs are like pizza on the go. They're easy to take with you and delicious cold, so they're the perfect option for when you have to take your prepped meals to work or somewhere that you might not have access to a stove or microwave to reheat them.

INGREDIENTS | SERVES 6 (MAKES 24 MEATBALLS)

1½ pounds meatloaf mix
¼ cup chopped fresh parsley
1 teaspoon dried oregano
1 teaspoon dried basil
1 large egg
2 cloves garlic, minced
1 teaspoon salt
1 (28-ounce) jar no-sugar-added marinara sauce
¾ cup chopped pepperoni
1 cup shredded mozzarella cheese
1 cup shredded provolone cheese

1. Grease the inside of a slow cooker with olive oil cooking spray.

2. In a medium bowl, combine meatloaf mix, parsley, oregano, basil, egg, garlic, and salt and mix with hands until fully incorporated. Shape into twenty-four meatballs and place meatballs in bottom of slow cooker.

3. Pour sauce on top and add pepperoni. Cover and cook on low 5 hours or until meatballs are cooked through.

4. Sprinkle cheeses on top, cover, and continue cooking an additional 30 minutes.

5. Remove from slow cooker, allow to cool, and divide into six equal portions. Transfer each portion to a separate airtight container and store in the refrigerator until ready to eat, up to one week.

PER SERVING Calories: 546 | Fat: 39 g | Protein: 35 g | Sodium: 1,289 mg | Fiber: 2.5 g | Carbohydrates: 5 g | Sugar: 2 g | Net Carbohydrates: 2.5 g

Pork Roast with Bacon and Mushrooms

Pair this pork roast with a side of sautéed greens or a fresh garden salad for a complete, perfectly macronutrient-balanced meal.

INGREDIENTS | SERVES 6

2 tablespoons grass-fed butter

1 (2-pound) pork shoulder

8 ounces sliced baby bella mushrooms

1 (15-ounce) can fire-roasted diced tomatoes

8 slices no-sugar-added bacon, cooked and chopped

½ cup chopped shallots

1 tablespoon minced garlic

1. Heat butter in a medium skillet over medium-high heat. Brown pork shoulder 2 minutes on each side and then transfer to a slow cooker.

2. Add remaining ingredients to the slow cooker and cover. Cook on low 8 hours or until pork is cooked through. Allow to cool.

3. Divide into six equal portions and transfer each portion to a separate airtight container. Store in the refrigerator until ready to eat, up to one week.

PER SERVING Calories: 430 | Fat: 29 g | Protein: 35 g | Sodium: 445 mg | Fiber: 2 g | Carbohydrates: 4 g | Sugar: 3 g | Net Carbohydrates: 2 g

CHAPTER 13

Pressure Cooker Meals

Sour Cream Pork Chops

Make sure to add sour cream after pressure cooking. If you put it in before, it will curdle. Stirring it in after will warm it up and make the sauce nice and thick.

INGREDIENTS | SERVES 6

1 teaspoon sea salt

½ teaspoon freshly ground black pepper

½ teaspoon dried thyme

6 (4-ounce) boneless pork chops

1½ tablespoons butter-flavored coconut oil

2 medium yellow onions, peeled and cut into strips

2 cloves garlic, minced

1½ cups beef bone broth

1½ teaspoons coconut aminos

1½ teaspoons arrowroot starch

2 teaspoons water

½ cup full-fat sour cream

It's about Thyme

Fresh and dried herbs give food lots of flavor, but they go far beyond that. According to research, thyme may help lower blood pressure in those with high blood pressure. It may also help reduce total cholesterol, triglycerides, and LDL (or "bad" cholesterol), while simultaneously increasing HDL (or "good" cholesterol). Experiment with using different herbs to flavor your foods and get used to incorporating them liberally into your cooking. Thyme pairs well with pork and poultry and makes a great flavor enhancer for soups.

1. Sprinkle salt, pepper, and thyme on pork chops.

2. Set pressure cooker to Sauté function and add coconut oil. Once coconut oil is hot, add onions and garlic and cook until softened, about 4 minutes.

3. Add pork chops to pan and cook 3 minutes on each side or until browned. Add bone broth and coconut aminos. Stir, scraping bottom of the pan to release browned bits.

4. Close and seal pressure cooker. Choose the manual setting and set for 8 minutes. Allow pressure to release naturally for 5 minutes then manually release any remaining pressure.

5. Remove pork chops from pot and place each chop in a separate airtight container.

6. In a small bowl, whisk together arrowroot powder and water and then pour into pressure cooker. Whisk until sauce thickens, about 3 minutes. Stir in sour cream.

7. Pour equal amounts of sauce over each pork chop and cover. Store in the refrigerator until ready to eat, up to one week.

PER SERVING Calories: 504 | Fat: 41 g | Protein: 26 g | Sodium: 722 mg | Fiber: 0 g | Carbohydrates: 5 g | Sugar: 2 g | Net Carbohydrates: 5 g

Buffalo Chicken Cauliflower

This Buffalo Chicken Cauliflower is a complete balanced meal that's easy to throw together and freezes well. Double up on it if you want to stock your freezer with some freezer meals. It will keep in the freezer up to six months.

INGREDIENTS | SERVES 6

1 large head cauliflower, chopped into florets

4 slices no-sugar-added bacon, cooked and chopped

2 cups cooked shredded chicken

½ cup Frank's RedHot sauce

¼ cup Jalapeño Ranch Dressing (Chapter 9)

½ teaspoon sea salt

¼ teaspoon freshly ground black pepper

4 ounces cream cheese, cubed

1 cup shredded Cheddar cheese

1 cup shredded pepper jack cheese

1. Combine cauliflower, bacon, chicken, hot sauce, dressing, salt, and pepper in pot of pressure cooker and stir. Choose the manual setting and set for 5 minutes. Allow pressure to release naturally.

2. Once pressure is fully released, stir in cream cheese until fully incorporated. Add shredded cheeses and stir until melted. Allow to cool slightly.

3. Divide into six equal portions and transfer each portion to a separate airtight container. Store in the refrigerator until ready to eat, up to one week.

PER SERVING Calories: 477 | Fat: 36 g | Protein: 29 g | Sodium: 828 mg | Fiber: 2 g | Carbohydrates: 7 g | Sugar: 3 g | Net Carbohydrates: 5 g

Philly Cheesesteak Soup

Ask your deli worker to slice your roast beef in thick cuts for you—that will give this soup a better texture. And check your ingredient lists on your roast beef to make sure there's no added sugar!

INGREDIENTS | SERVES 6

2 tablespoons grass-fed butter

6 cloves garlic, minced

1 medium sweet onion, peeled and diced

2 medium green bell peppers, seeded and diced

1 pound sliced roast beef, roughly chopped

3 cups beef bone broth

1 teaspoon sea salt

1 teaspoon freshly ground black pepper

¾ teaspoon garlic powder

¾ teaspoon onion powder

⅓ cup Paleo flour

2 cups half-and-half

2 cups shredded Monterey jack cheese

½ cup shredded provolone cheese

1. Set pressure cooker to Sauté and add butter. When butter is hot, add garlic and onions and cook until softened, about 4 minutes. Stir in bell peppers and cook another 5 minutes.

2. Add roast beef, broth, salt, pepper, garlic powder, and onion powder and stir. Cover and cook on manual for 10 minutes. Allow pressure to release naturally.

3. In a small bowl, whisk together flour and half-and-half and then stir into soup. Add cheeses and stir until melted and fully combined.

4. Allow to cool, then divide into six equal portions and transfer each portion to a separate airtight container. Store in the refrigerator until ready to eat, up to one week.

PER SERVING Calories: 526 | Fat: 37 g | Protein: 37 g | Sodium: 844 mg | Fiber: 5 g | Carbohydrates: 14 g | Sugar: 5 g | Net Carbohydrates: 9 g

Cauliflower Mashed Faux-Tatoes

These Cauliflower Mashed Faux-Tatoes taste just like garlic mashed potatoes.
They'll please even those who aren't following a keto diet.

INGREDIENTS | SERVES 6

1 cup chicken bone broth

1 large head cauliflower, cut into florets

4 tablespoons grass-fed butter

½ teaspoon sea salt

½ teaspoon freshly ground black pepper

½ teaspoon garlic powder

4 tablespoons chopped fresh chives

Immersion What?

An immersion blender, also called a stick blender or a hand blender, is a kitchen tool that's used to blend or purée foods in the container in which they're being prepared. Instead of pouring your ingredients into a countertop blender and making a mess (and creating more cleanup), an immersion blender makes it easy to quickly turn your recipes into a velvety smooth texture. They're fairly inexpensive and a worthwhile investment for your keto kitchen.

1. Pour chicken broth into pot of pressure cooker. Add steamer rack and arrange cauliflower florets on top.

2. Close and seal pressure cooker. Cook on manual for 4 minutes and release pressure manually.

3. Open and carefully remove cauliflower. Discard two-thirds of the chicken broth and then return cauliflower back to pot. Add butter, salt, pepper, and garlic powder and use an immersion blender to purée. Stir in chives.

4. Allow to cool. Divide into six equal portions and transfer each portion to a separate airtight container. Store in the refrigerator until ready to eat, up to one week.

PER SERVING Calories: 98 | Fat: 8 g | Protein: 3 g | Sodium: 236 mg | Fiber: 2 g | Carbohydrates: 5 g | Sugar: 2 g | Net Carbohydrates: 3 g

Creamy Tuscan Chicken

This recipe calls for baby bella mushrooms, which have a rich, deep flavor. If you prefer a milder mushroom flavor, you can swap the baby bellas for white mushrooms.

INGREDIENTS | SERVES 6

6 tablespoons olive oil, divided

6 cloves garlic, minced

3 teaspoons dried Italian seasoning

2 teaspoons sea salt, divided

2 teaspoons freshly ground black pepper, divided

6 (4-ounce) boneless, skinless chicken breasts

½ cup sliced baby bella mushrooms

2 tablespoons coconut aminos

¾ cup chicken bone broth

2 cups baby spinach

½ cup chopped sun-dried tomatoes

½ cup heavy cream

2 tablespoons cream cheese

⅓ cup grated Parmesan cheese

Young Mushrooms

Just like their name implies, baby bella mushrooms are immature portobello mushrooms. They're dark brown and firmer than white button mushrooms and have a richer, savorier flavor. Baby bella mushrooms are also sold under the name "cremini mushrooms." Weighing in at only 1 gram of carbohydrates per half cup, baby bella mushrooms make an excellent addition to any of your keto meals.

1. Combine 5 tablespoons olive oil, garlic, Italian seasoning, 1 teaspoon salt, and 1 teaspoon pepper in a small bowl. Spread mixture on each chicken breast, coating as much of the chicken as possible.

2. Set pressure cooker to Sauté function and heat remaining olive oil in the pot. Add chicken to the pot and brown 3 minutes on each side. Remove chicken and set aside.

3. Stir in mushrooms and remaining salt and pepper and cook until softened, about 5 minutes. Add coconut aminos and chicken broth to the pan, scraping the bottom of the pan while stirring to remove all the browned bits.

4. Place browned chicken in pot and cook on manual for 4 minutes. Allow pressure to release naturally for 10 minutes, then release any remaining pressure.

5. Open pressure cooker and remove chicken. Set aside.

6. Turn pressure cooker back to Sauté function and allow mixture to come to a boil. Stir in spinach and sun-dried tomatoes and cook 1 minute. Stir in cream, cream cheese, and Parmesan cheese and cook 1 more minute.

7. Add chicken back to pot and turn off. Let chicken sit in warm sauce 2 minutes. Remove each breast and transfer to a separate airtight container. Spoon equal amounts of sauce over each chicken breast. Allow to cool slightly.

8. Cover and store in the refrigerator until ready to eat, up to one week.

PER SERVING Calories: 389 | Fat: 27 g | Protein: 29 g | Sodium: 990 mg | Fiber: 1 g | Carbohydrates: 6 g | Sugar: 2 g | Net Carbohydrates: 5 g

Beef Bone Broth

Your days of simmering beef bone broth on the stovetop or in a slow cooker for 24 hours are over. With a pressure cooker, you can have gelatinous bone broth ready to go in just about 2 hours.

INGREDIENTS | SERVES 6

1 small carrot, peeled and roughly chopped

1 large onion, peeled and roughly chopped

3 medium stalks celery, diced

8 cloves garlic, crushed

3 pounds organic beef bones

2 chicken feet (ideally from pasture-raised chickens)

2 tablespoons apple cider vinegar

1 teaspoon sea salt

½ teaspoon whole black peppercorns

2 bay leaves

8 cups water

Stocked Up on Bone Broth

Bone broth is an absolute staple on the keto diet. Although you can use stock in any recipes, beef bone broth has a richer flavor and a significantly better nutrient profile. When cooked correctly, beef bone broth contains a high concentration of minerals and anti-inflammatory amino acids. It's also one of the only food sources of collagen and gelatin—two proteins that keep your gut healthy. It's a good idea to cook up a bunch of bone broth and freeze it in separate containers (Mason jars work well, but don't fill them all the way). That way, you always have some ready to go to use in recipes or drink straight up.

1. Place carrot, onion, celery, and garlic in the pot of a pressure cooker and pile bones and chicken feet on top. Pour apple cider vinegar over bones.

2. Add salt, peppercorns, bay leaves, and water and cover and seal pressure cooker.

3. Choose the manual setting and set pressure cooker to 120 minutes. Allow pressure to release naturally.

4. Strain the broth through a fine-mesh cheesecloth and discard bones. Allow to cool slightly.

5. Transfer the bone broth to an airtight container and store in the refrigerator up to one week, or the freezer up to six months.

PER SERVING Calories: 36 | Fat: 1 g | Protein: 6 g | Sodium: 430 mg | Fiber: 0 g | Carbohydrates: 0 g | Sugar: 0 g | Net Carbohydrates: 0 g

Noodle-Less Lasagna

This recipe uses the pot-in-pot (or PIP) method of pressure cooking. That means you'll compile all your ingredients in a dish that you'll place into the pressure cooker before cooking, which prevents burning. Keep that in mind and make sure to read through the entire recipe to see what you need before starting.

INGREDIENTS | SERVES 6

2 teaspoons butter-flavored coconut oil

2 cloves garlic, minced

1 small yellow onion, peeled and diced

8 ounces sliced white mushrooms

1½ pounds 85/15 ground beef

1 (28-ounce) jar no-sugar-added marinara sauce

1 cup whole milk cottage cheese

½ cup whole milk ricotta cheese

½ cup grated Parmesan cheese

1 large egg

2 tablespoons fresh chopped parsley

2 cups shredded mozzarella cheese

1 cup water

1. Turn pressure cooker to Sauté setting and heat coconut oil. Add garlic and onion and cook until softened, about 4 minutes. Add mushrooms and cook another 3 minutes. Crumble beef into pot and cook until no longer pink, about 7 minutes.

2. Pour marinara sauce into pot and stir to combine. Transfer half of the beef mixture to an oven-safe 1½–quart soufflé dish.

3. In a medium bowl, combine cottage cheese, ricotta cheese, Parmesan cheese, egg, and parsley.

4. Scoop half of the ricotta mixture on top of beef mixture and spread out evenly. Sprinkle half the mozzarella cheese on top.

5. Scoop in remaining beef mixture, top with remaining ricotta mixture, and sprinkle the rest of the mozzarella cheese on top.

6. Clean out inner pot of the pressure cooker and return to base. Pour 1 cup water into the pot then place steamer rack into pot. Place soufflé dish on steamer rack.

7. Cover and cook on manual setting for 8 minutes. Manually release steam and remove lid. Allow to cool and then carefully remove soufflé dish from pot.

8. Divide into six equal portions and transfer each portion to a separate airtight container. Store in the refrigerator until ready to eat, up to one week.

PER SERVING Calories: 592 | Fat: 40 g | Protein: 40 g | Sodium: 1,092 mg | Fiber: 3.5 g | Carbohydrates: 10 g | Sugar: 4 g | Net Carbohydrates: 6.5 g

Chicken Marsala

Because Marsala wine contains 56 grams of carbs per cup, it's out for a keto diet. This Chicken Marsala uses pinot noir, which contains only 11 grams of carbohydrates per cup, in its place. Although not a true Marsala, it does the trick!

INGREDIENTS | SERVES 6

6 (4-ounce) boneless, skinless chicken breasts

1 teaspoon sea salt

½ teaspoon freshly ground black pepper

2 tablespoons grass-fed butter

8 ounces sliced cremini mushrooms

4 cloves garlic, minced

1 cup keto-friendly pinot noir

1 cup heavy cream

2 tablespoons lemon juice

1 teaspoon dried oregano

1 teaspoon arrowroot powder

1 tablespoon water

What Is Keto-Friendly Wine?

When it comes to carbohydrates, all wines are not created equally. Carbohydrate count differs based on the types of grapes used, the growing conditions, and how the wine is fermented. In general, it's best to stick to dry to semidry wines, like pinot noir, cabernet sauvignon, merlot, pinot grigio, sauvignon blanc, chardonnay, Riesling, and champagne. Certain wine brands, like Dry Farm Wines and FitVine, market directly to the health-conscious consumer, offering wines that are lower in calories, sugar, and additives.

1. Pound chicken with a meat mallet to ½" thickness. Sprinkle salt and pepper over each breast.

2. Set pressure cooker to Sauté function and heat butter. Add mushrooms and garlic and cook 4 minutes, stirring frequently.

3. Pour in wine and stir to scrape off browned bits stuck to the bottom of the pan. Add cream, lemon juice, and oregano and stir. Add chicken breasts to pot.

4. Close and seal pressure cooker and cook on manual for 4 minutes. Manually release pressure. Once pressure is released, open pot and remove chicken.

5. Turn on Sauté function. In a small bowl, whisk together arrowroot powder and water and then stir into sauce in pot. Allow to simmer 3 minutes or until sauce thickens. Add chicken back to sauce and turn off pot. Allow to sit 5 minutes.

6. Transfer each chicken breast and equal amounts of sauce to each of six separate airtight containers. Store in the refrigerator until ready to eat, up to one week.

PER SERVING Calories: 343 | Fat: 21 g | Protein: 26 g | Sodium: 455 mg | Fiber: 0 g | Carbohydrates: 2 g | Sugar: 1 g | Net Carbohydrates: 2 g

Bacon-Smothered Pork Chops

Make sure you scrape the bottom of the pan with a wooden spoon after adding the beef broth. This will impart a deeper flavor, and also prevent your pressure cooker from giving you a burn warning.

INGREDIENTS | SERVES 6

1½ teaspoons dried thyme

¼ teaspoon dried rosemary

¾ teaspoon sea salt

½ teaspoon freshly ground black pepper

6 (4-ounce) boneless pork chops

2 tablespoons butter-flavored coconut oil

4 slices no-sugar-added bacon, chopped

3 cloves garlic, minced

½ cup sliced white mushrooms

1 cup beef bone broth

1 teaspoon onion powder

1 teaspoon garlic powder

1 cup chopped spinach

¾ cup full-fat coconut milk

1. Sprinkle thyme, rosemary, salt, and pepper over pork chops.

2. Set pressure cooker to Sauté function and heat coconut oil. When coconut oil is hot, add pork chops to pot and brown on all sides. Remove from pot and set aside.

3. Add bacon to pot and cook 3 minutes. Stir in garlic and mushrooms and cook 4 more minutes. Pour in beef broth and stir, scraping bottom of pan to remove browned bits. Add onion powder, garlic powder, and spinach.

4. Return pork chops to pot, cover, and seal. Cook on manual for 7 minutes. Allow pressure to release naturally for 10 minutes then release any remaining pressure manually.

5. Open pressure cooker and remove pork chops. Stir in coconut milk.

6. Transfer each pork chop to a separate airtight container. Pour equal amounts of sauce on top of each pork chop. Allow to cool slightly.

7. Cover and store in the refrigerator until ready to eat, up to one week.

PER SERVING Calories: 609 | Fat: 53 g | Protein: 29 g | Sodium: 674 mg | Fiber: 0.5 g | Carbohydrates: 4 g | Sugar: 0.5 g | Net Carbohydrates: 3.5 g

Ranch Chicken

To easily coat the chicken, put Homemade Ranch Seasoning in a resealable bag, add the chicken, and shake to cover completely.

INGREDIENTS | SERVES 6

6 (4-ounce) boneless, skinless chicken thighs

2 tablespoons Homemade Ranch Seasoning (see sidebar)

2 tablespoons butter-flavored coconut oil

1 small yellow onion, peeled and minced

8 tablespoons grass-fed butter, cut into chunks

1 cup half-and-half

½ teaspoon sea salt

1 cup shredded Cheddar cheese

1 cup shredded mozzarella cheese

Homemade Ranch Seasoning

The ranch seasoning packets that you can purchase in the store are often filled with artificial, and keto-unfriendly, ingredients. You can easily make your own ranch seasoning by combining some spices that you probably already have in your cabinet. Make a triple or quadruple batch and keep it in your spice cabinet for whenever you need it. To make it, combine 2 tablespoons dried parsley, 1½ teaspoons dried dill, 2 teaspoons garlic powder, 2 teaspoons onion powder, 2 teaspoons dried minced onion, 1 teaspoon dried chives, 1 teaspoon freshly ground black pepper, and 1 teaspoon salt.

1. Coat chicken in Homemade Ranch Seasoning, covering as much as possible.

2. Heat coconut oil in the pot of your pressure cooker using the Sauté function. Once hot, add onion and sauté until softened, about 4 minutes. Add chicken breasts and brown on each side.

3. Add butter, half-and-half, and salt. Cover and seal. Cook on manual setting for 4 minutes, then allow pressure to release naturally for 10 minutes. Release any remaining pressure manually.

4. Open pot and stir in shredded cheeses until smooth. Allow to cool.

5. Transfer each chicken breast and equal portions of sauce to six separate airtight containers. Store in the refrigerator until ready to eat, up to one week.

PER SERVING Calories: 516 | Fat: 41 g | Protein: 32 g | Sodium: 593 mg | Fiber: 0 g | Carbohydrates: 3 g | Sugar: 2 g | Net Carbohydrates: 3 g

Spinach and Artichoke Dip

This Spinach and Artichoke Dip is divine served alongside some Cheesy Crackers (Chapter 14), or you can use some slices of raw zucchini to dip.

INGREDIENTS | SERVES 6

1 (10-ounce) package frozen chopped spinach, thawed and squeezed dry

1 (14-ounce) can artichoke hearts, drained and roughly chopped

8 ounces cream cheese

½ cup full-fat sour cream

½ cup coconut oil mayonnaise

1 small white onion, peeled and chopped

½ cup chicken bone broth

4 cloves garlic, minced

½ teaspoon sea salt

½ teaspoon crushed red pepper

2 cups grated Parmesan cheese

1½ cups shredded Monterey jack cheese

1½ cups shredded mozzarella cheese

1. Combine spinach, artichokes, cream cheese, sour cream, mayonnaise, onion, chicken broth, garlic, salt, and red pepper in the pot of a pressure cooker.

2. Close and seal. Cook on manual setting for 4 minutes. Manually release pressure. Once pressure is released, open pressure cooker. Add cheeses, stirring until completely incorporated. Allow to cool.

3. Divide into six equal portions and transfer each portion to a separate airtight container. Store in the refrigerator until ready to eat, up to one week.

PER SERVING Calories: 704 | Fat: 58 g | Protein: 30 g | Sodium: 1,233 mg | Fiber: 4 g | Carbohydrates: 18 g | Sugar: 3 g | Net Carbohydrates: 14 g

Cashew Chicken

Whole cashews are often more expensive than their crushed counterparts. To make this recipe more budget-friendly, you can substitute the whole cashews with the pieces with no sacrifice to taste or quality.

INGREDIENTS | SERVES 6

½ cup coconut aminos

1 tablespoon fish sauce

2 teaspoons toasted sesame oil

2 teaspoons granulated erythritol

1 tablespoon apple cider vinegar

1 tablespoon minced fresh ginger

½ teaspoon crushed red pepper flakes

3 cloves garlic, minced

1 teaspoon sea salt

1 teaspoon freshly ground black pepper

1½ pounds boneless skinless chicken breasts, cut into 1" cubes

2 tablespoons butter-flavored coconut oil

¾ cup chicken bone broth

2 teaspoons arrowroot powder

3 tablespoons water

5 cups broccoli florets

1 large red bell pepper, seeded and sliced thinly

¾ cup whole cashews

2 scallions, chopped

1. Combine coconut aminos, fish sauce, sesame oil, erythritol, apple cider vinegar, ginger, red pepper flakes, and garlic in a medium bowl. Set aside.

2. Sprinkle salt and black pepper all over chicken.

3. Turn pressure cooker to Sauté function. Add coconut oil. When coconut oil is hot, add chicken and cook 3 minutes. Add prepared sauce and chicken broth. Cover and seal.

4. Cook on manual pressure for 4 minutes. Release pressure manually.

5. Turn pressure cooker back to Sauté function. In a small bowl, whisk together arrowroot powder and water and then stir into pressure cooker. Add broccoli and peppers and allow to simmer 5 minutes. Stir in cashews and scallions.

6. Remove from heat and allow to cool. Divide into six equal portions and transfer each portion to a separate airtight container. Store in the refrigerator until ready to eat, up to one week.

PER SERVING Calories: 329 | Fat: 19 g | Protein: 30 g | Sodium: 546 mg | Fiber: 3 g | Carbohydrates: 10 g | Sugar: 3 g | Net Carbohydrates: 7 g

The Good Fats

Toasted sesame oil contains almost a 1:1 ratio of monounsaturated fat and polyunsaturated fat. Monounsaturated fats can help lower your cholesterol levels and help your body develop new cells. Polyunsaturated fats also lower cholesterol and contribute omega-3 and omega-6 fatty acids, which contribute to brain and heart health.

Philly Cheesesteak–Stuffed Peppers

You can use whatever color bell peppers you want for this recipe. Make them all the same or incorporate some variety; it's up to you! Using different colors won't change the carbohydrate count significantly.

INGREDIENTS | SERVES 6

3 tablespoons olive oil

1 medium yellow onion, peeled and diced

1½ cups sliced white mushrooms

2 cups riced cauliflower

1½ pounds sliced roast beef, cut into chunks

1½ cups shredded provolone cheese

1½ cups shredded mozzarella cheese

½ teaspoon sea salt

¼ teaspoon freshly ground black pepper

3 medium red bell peppers, seeded and tops cut off

3 medium green bell peppers, seeded and tops cut off

½ cup water

1. Set pressure cooker to Sauté function and add oil to pot. When oil is hot, add onion and mushrooms and cook until softened, about 5 minutes.

2. Transfer onion and mushroom mixture to a bowl and add cauliflower, roast beef, cheeses, salt, and pepper. Stir to combine.

3. Stuff equal amounts of roast beef mixture into each pepper. Clean pressure cooker insert and pour water into pot.

4. Place trivet into pressure cooker and arrange peppers on top. Cover and seal.

5. Cook for 15 minutes on manual pressure and allow pressure to release naturally. Allow peppers to cool and carefully remove from pressure cooker.

6. Transfer each pepper to a separate airtight container and store in the refrigerator until ready to eat, up to one week.

PER SERVING Calories: 329 | Fat: 19 g | Protein: 30 g | Sodium: 546 mg | Fiber: 3 g | Carbohydrates: 10 g | Sugar: 3 g | Net Carbohydrates: 7 g

Butter Chicken

Butter Chicken, also called Murgh Makhani, originates from India. It's a fat-rich, creamy chicken dish that combines butter and yogurt with a mildly spiced tomato sauce.

INGREDIENTS | SERVES 6

1 tablespoon butter-flavored coconut oil

2 small shallots, minced

3 cloves garlic, minced

2 teaspoons minced fresh ginger

2 teaspoons curry powder

2 teaspoons garam masala

1 teaspoon chili powder

1 teaspoon sea salt

1 tablespoon chicken broth

1 (28-ounce) can tomato sauce

1 small head cauliflower, riced

1½ pounds boneless, skinless chicken breasts

2 tablespoons grass-fed butter

½ cup full-fat coconut milk

½ cup plain full-fat Greek yogurt

Greek versus Regular Yogurt

Greek yogurt is a more concentrated version of plain yogurt. It's strained three times to remove most of the liquid, which gives it a thicker consistency and a stronger sour flavor. Cup for cup, Greek yogurt contains more protein than regular yogurt. Because the liquid has been removed, Greek yogurt will give sauces and dressings a thicker texture, but you can use regular plain yogurt in its place if you prefer.

1. Turn pressure cooker to Sauté and add coconut oil. Add shallots and garlic and cook 3 minutes. Add ginger, curry, garam masala, chili powder, and salt and cook 30 seconds. Add chicken broth to pan and stir, scraping browned bits from the bottom of the pot.

2. Add tomato sauce and cauliflower and stir. Arrange chicken on top and place butter on top of chicken. Close and seal pressure cooker.

3. Cook on manual for 11 minutes then allow pressure to release naturally for 10 minutes. Release any remaining pressure manually.

4. Open pressure cooker and stir in coconut milk. Allow to cool for a few minutes then stir in Greek yogurt.

5. Divide into six equal portions and transfer each portion to a separate airtight container. Store in the refrigerator until ready to eat, up to one week.

PER SERVING Calories: 300 | Fat: 14 g | Protein: 30 g | Sodium: 913 mg | Fiber: 4.5 g | Carbohydrates: 8 g | Sugar: 1 g | Net Carbohydrates: 3.5 g

Picadillo

Traditionally, picadillo contains ground beef, but this version uses ground turkey in its place. If you want to up the fat content, you can swap it out for the beef instead.

INGREDIENTS | SERVES 6

1 tablespoon butter-flavored coconut oil

1 medium yellow onion, peeled and chopped

3 cloves garlic, minced

1½ pounds 85/15 ground turkey

1 teaspoon sea salt

½ teaspoon freshly ground black pepper

1 large tomato, diced

1 small red bell pepper, seeded and diced

½ cup tomato sauce

3 tablespoons water

1 teaspoon ground cumin

1 bay leaf

3 tablespoons chopped green olives

2 tablespoons olive brine (juice from the olive jar)

1. Turn pressure cooker to Sauté function and heat coconut oil. Add onion and garlic and cook until softened, about 4 minutes. Add ground turkey and cook until no longer pink, about 7 minutes.

2. Add remaining ingredients and stir to combine. Cover and seal. Use manual setting to cook for 15 minutes. Allow pressure to release naturally. Open pressure cooker and allow to cool.

3. Discard bay leaf, divide into six equal portions and transfer each portion to a separate airtight container. Store in the refrigerator until ready to eat, up to one week.

PER SERVING Calories: 216 | Fat: 11 g | Protein: 23 g | Sodium: 584 mg | Fiber: 1.5 g | Carbohydrates: 5 g | Sugar: 2 g | Net Carbohydrates: 3.5 g

Balsamic Beef

Low-carb herbs don't just give your food some intense flavor, they also all have individual benefits that keep your body healthy and happy. Use them liberally on your foods and don't be afraid to experiment with the amounts, types, and combinations.

INGREDIENTS | SERVES 6

4 cloves garlic, minced

1 teaspoon sea salt

½ teaspoon freshly ground black pepper

1 teaspoon dried rosemary

½ teaspoon dried thyme

¼ teaspoon dried parsley

2 pounds chuck roast

1 tablespoon butter-flavored coconut oil

2 tablespoons grass-fed butter

¼ cup balsamic vinegar

1 cup beef bone broth

The Power of Rosemary

Rosemary, a member of the mint family, along with thyme, basil, oregano, and lavender, is well noted for its ability to improve memory. According to research published in *Therapeutic Advances in Psychopharmacology*, even just smelling rosemary can improve concentration, performance, and mood.

1. In a small bowl, combine garlic, salt, pepper, rosemary, thyme, and parsley. Spread all over roast, covering as much as possible.

2. Turn pressure cooker on to Sauté function and add coconut oil. When hot, place roast in pot and brown on all sides. Remove roast and add remaining ingredients, stirring to scrape browned bits on the bottom of the pan.

3. Return roast to pan, cover, and seal. Cook on the manual setting for 40 minutes. When roast is done cooking, release pressure manually. Open and allow to cool.

4. Divide roast into six equal portions and transfer each portion, along with equal portions of liquid, into separate airtight containers. Store in the refrigerator until ready to eat, up to one week.

PER SERVING Calories: 310 | Fat: 14 g | Protein: 39 g | Sodium: 649 mg | Fiber: 0.5 g | Carbohydrates: 2 g | Sugar: 1 g | Net Carbohydrates: 1.5 g

Jerk Pork Roast

This pork roast isn't mean, but it sure is spicy! Jamaican Jerk seasoning is heavy on the cayenne and not for the fainthearted. If you're making your own and you want to dial it down, use less cayenne pepper in your blend.

INGREDIENTS | SERVES 6

2 tablespoons Jamaican Jerk spice blend
1 teaspoon dried thyme
1 teaspoon dried rosemary
2 pounds pork shoulder
2 tablespoons olive oil
½ cup beef bone broth

Homemade Jamaican Jerk Blend

It's easy to make your own Jamaican Jerk blend at home with spices that you probably already have in your cabinet. Combine 1 tablespoon garlic powder, 3 teaspoons cayenne pepper, 2 teaspoons onion powder, 2 teaspoons dried thyme, 2 teaspoons dried parsley, 2 teaspoons granulated erythritol, 2 teaspoons salt, 1 teaspoon paprika, 1 teaspoon ground allspice, ½ teaspoon freshly ground black pepper, ½ teaspoon crushed red pepper flakes, ½ teaspoon ground nutmeg, and ½ teaspoon ground cinnamon.

1. In a small bowl, combine Jamaican Jerk spice blend, thyme, and rosemary. Rub all over pork shoulder, covering as much as possible.

2. Turn pressure cooker to Sauté function and heat olive oil. Brown pork shoulder on all sides and remove from pot.

3. Stir in beef broth, using a wooden spoon to scrape up browned bits on bottom of pan. Return browned pork to pot.

4. Cover and seal. Cook on manual pressure for 40 minutes. Allow pressure to release naturally. Once pressure is released, open pot and allow to cool.

5. Remove roast and divide into six equal portions. Transfer each portion to a separate airtight container and store in the refrigerator until ready to eat, up to one week.

PER SERVING Calories: 263 | Fat: 15 g | Protein: 29 g | Sodium: 188 mg | Fiber: 0 g | Carbohydrates: 0 g | Sugar: 0 g | Net Carbohydrates: 0 g

Salsa Chicken

This Salsa Chicken is incredibly easy to make, but tastes like you spent hours in the kitchen. After reheating, top with shredded cheese, chopped avocado, and some fresh chopped cilantro.

INGREDIENTS | SERVES 6

2 tablespoons taco seasoning

1½ pounds boneless, skinless chicken thighs

4 ounces cream cheese, cubed

1 cup no-sugar-added salsa

¼ cup chicken bone broth

1. Sprinkle taco seasoning all over chicken, covering as much as possible.

2. Place chicken in pot of pressure cooker and add remaining ingredients. Cover and seal.

3. Cook on manual pressure then allow pressure to release naturally. Open and allow to cool.

4. Remove chicken and use an immersion blender to purée sauce.

5. Divide into six equal portions and transfer each portion to a separate airtight container. Store in the refrigerator until ready to eat, up to one week.

PER SERVING Calories: 224 | Fat: 11 g | Protein: 24 g | Sodium: 721 mg | Fiber: 1.5 g | Carbohydrates: 5 g | Sugar: 2 g | Net Carbohydrates: 3.5 g

Pork Stew

If you prefer your stew greens to have a tougher texture, use mature spinach, mature kale, or some Swiss chard in this Pork Stew instead of baby spinach.

INGREDIENTS | SERVES 6

1 large yellow onion, peeled and chopped

4 cloves garlic, minced

1 (14.5-ounce) can fire-roasted tomatoes

1 (4-ounce) can green chilies

1 teaspoon dried thyme

½ teaspoon dried rosemary

3 teaspoons Cajun seasoning blend

1½ pounds pork shoulder, cut into 2" cubes

¾ cup full-fat coconut milk

4 cups chopped baby spinach

Homemade Cajun Seasoning Blend

Cajun seasoning blend is popular in Southern cooking. It combines a little bit of spice with a little bit of smoky flavor and lot of herbs. To whip some up at home, combine 2 tablespoons garlic powder, 2 tablespoons Italian seasoning, 2 tablespoons paprika, 2 tablespoons sea salt, 1 tablespoon ground black pepper, 1 tablespoon cayenne pepper, 1 tablespoon dried thyme, and 1 tablespoon onion powder. Use what you need and then store the rest in an airtight container for later.

1. Combine onion, garlic, tomatoes, and chilies and put mixture into pot of pressure cooker.

2. In a small bowl, combine thyme, rosemary, and Cajun seasoning and then sprinkle over pork, covering as much as possible. Add pork to pressure cooker, close, and seal.

3. Cook on Meat setting for 20 minutes. Allow pressure to release naturally for 10 minutes, then release any remaining pressure.

4. Open pot and turn to Sauté function. Bring to a simmer and stir in coconut milk and spinach.

5. Allow to cool and divide into six equal portions. Transfer each portion to a separate airtight container. Store in the refrigerator until ready to eat, up to one week.

PER SERVING Calories: 258 | Fat: 14 g | Protein: 24 g | Sodium: 185 mg | Fiber: 2.5 g | Carbohydrates: 9 g | Sugar: 3 g | Net Carbohydrates: 6.5 g

Creamy Cabbage and Bacon

There's a reason cabbage is a staple on low-carb and "cleanse" diets. One cup of shredded cabbage contains only 4 grams of carbohydrates and around 93 percent water.

INGREDIENTS | SERVES 6

12 slices no-sugar-added bacon, diced
1 large yellow onion, peeled and diced
2 cups chicken bone broth
1 large head cabbage, chopped
2 bay leaves
1 cup full-fat coconut milk
¼ teaspoon ground nutmeg
1 teaspoon sea salt
½ teaspoon freshly ground black pepper
¼ cup chopped fresh parsley

1. Turn pressure cooker to Sauté function and add bacon and onion. Cook until onions are softened and bacon starts to crisp, about 6 minutes.

2. Stir in chicken broth, using a wooden spoon to scrape up the browned bits from the bottom of the pan. Stir in cabbage and bay leaves.

3. Close and seal pressure cover. Cook on manual pressure for 4 minutes. Release pressure manually.

4. Open and turn pressure cooker to Sauté function and stir in coconut milk, nutmeg, salt, and pepper. Simmer 3 minutes. Remove bay leaves and stir in fresh parsley. Turn off pressure cooker and allow to cool.

5. Divide into six equal portions and then transfer each portion to a separate airtight container. Store in the refrigerator until ready to eat, up to one week.

PER SERVING Calories: 368 | Fat: 30 g | Protein: 12 g | Sodium: 815 mg | Fiber: 4 g | Carbohydrates: 13 g | Sugar: 5 g | Net Carbohydrates: 9 g

CHAPTER 14

Appetizers and Snacks

Nacho Pepper Boats

These Nacho Pepper Boats give you all the nacho flavor without the carbs of corn chips. The bell peppers add a hint of sweet flavor, but if you prefer, you can use zucchini boats instead without increasing the carb count.

INGREDIENTS | SERVES 4

4 ounces cooked shredded chicken

1 cup salsa, drained, divided

1 cup full-fat sour cream, divided

1 cup shredded Mexican-style cheese blend, divided

1 tablespoon taco seasoning

1 (2.25-ounce) can chopped black olives

1 tablespoon minced jalapeño peppers

1 (8-ounce) package mini bell peppers, seeded and halved lengthwise

How Sweet It Is

Mini bell peppers are grown specifically for their size and flavor. They have thinner skins than mature peppers and a sweeter flavor. They're usually available in a bag that contains red, orange, and yellow varieties. Each whole mini pepper contains only 1.7 grams of carbohydrates, so they're an excellent way to get in the micronutrients you need without affecting ketosis.

1. Preheat oven to 350°F.

2. Combine shredded chicken, ½ cup salsa, ½ cup sour cream, ½ cup cheese blend, taco seasoning, olives, and jalapeños in a large mixing bowl and stir to mix.

3. Arrange pepper halves on a baking sheet and stuff as much chicken mixture into each pepper as you can.

4. Sprinkle remaining cheese over peppers and bake 20 minutes, or until peppers are softened and cheese is melted.

5. Remove from oven and top each pepper half with 1 tablespoon each of remaining salsa and sour cream. Allow to cool slightly.

6. Divide into six equal portions and transfer each portion to a separate airtight container. Store in the refrigerator until ready to eat, up to one week.

PER SERVING Calories: 337 | Fat: 24 g | Protein: 18 g | Sodium: 938 mg | Fiber: 3 g | Carbohydrates: 11 g | Sugar: 6 g | Net Carbohydrates: 8 g

Buffalo Chicken Dip

Make sure the ranch dressing you use in this dip is keto-friendly. Check your labels for added sugar and if there's any, make your own instead!

INGREDIENTS | SERVES 8

1 tablespoon butter-flavored coconut oil

1 medium stalk celery, diced

1 (8-ounce) package cream cheese

1½ cups ranch dressing

8 ounces cooked shredded chicken

½ cup Frank's RedHot sauce

1 cup shredded Cheddar cheese

1. Preheat oven to 350°F.

2. Heat coconut oil in a medium skillet over medium heat. Add celery and cook until softened, about 4 minutes. Add cream cheese and dressing to the skillet and stir until cream cheese is melted and mixture is smooth. Remove from heat and set aside.

3. Place chicken in the bottom of an 8" × 8" baking dish and pour hot sauce over chicken. Stir to combine and flatten in an even layer.

4. Pour dressing mixture over chicken. Sprinkle cheese on top.

5. Bake 30 minutes, or until dip is bubbly and cheese starts to brown.

6. Allow to cool and then divide into eight equal portions. Transfer each portion into an airtight container and store in the refrigerator until ready to eat, up to one week.

PER SERVING Calories: 423 | Fat: 39 g | Protein: 14 g | Sodium: 644 mg | Fiber: 0 g | Carbohydrates: 4 g | Sugar: 3 g | Net Carbohydrates: 4 g

Garlic Parmesan Chicken Wings

These chicken wings come out incredibly flavorful and crispy. Don't skip the step of boiling them in vinegar water before cooking. This allows the flavors to penetrate deep into the chicken and you'll be happy you took the extra time to do it!

INGREDIENTS | SERVES 8

12 cups water

⅓ cup balsamic vinegar

¼ cup plus ⅛ teaspoon sea salt, divided

1 bay leaf

1½ teaspoons dried thyme

1½ teaspoons dried oregano

4 pounds chicken wings

4 teaspoons granulated garlic

3 tablespoons olive oil

1 tablespoon freshly ground black pepper

2 teaspoons red pepper flakes

2 tablespoons almond meal

1 cup finely grated Parmesan cheese, divided

Almond Meal versus Almond Flour

The major difference between almond meal and almond flour is the size of the crumbs. Almond meal has a thicker texture similar to bread crumbs, while almond flour is processed more finely into a dust. You can easily and quickly make your own almond meal by grinding some almonds in a food processor until they form a thick, coarse texture. Be careful not to overdo it, though. If you process them too much, you'll end up with almond flour.

1. Preheat oven to 350°F. Coat a baking sheet with olive oil cooking spray and set aside.

2. Combine water, vinegar, ¼ cup salt, bay leaf, thyme, and oregano in a large stockpot and bring to a boil. Add chicken wings and allow to return to a boil. Cook 15 minutes.

3. Remove chicken from pot with a slotted spoon and transfer to a cooling rack. Allow to dry 15 minutes.

4. Combine remaining salt, granulated garlic, olive oil, black pepper, and red pepper flakes in a sealable bag and mix well. Add almond meal and ½ cup cheese and shake to combine.

5. Add chicken wings in batches and shake to coat. Transfer chicken wings to prepared baking sheet and sprinkle remaining cheese on top.

6. Bake 25 minutes, or until browned and crispy.

7. Remove from oven and allow to cool. Divide into eight equal portions and transfer each portion to a separate airtight container. Store in the refrigerator until ready to eat, up to one week.

PER SERVING Calories: 553 | Fat: 38 g | Protein: 45 g | Sodium: 3,583 mg | Fiber: 0 g | Carbohydrates: 6 g | Sugar: 1 g | Net Carbohydrates: 6 g

Reuben Dip

When it comes to corned beef, carbohydrates are almost nonexistent. The entire 12 ounces in this recipe contributes only 1.6 grams of carbohydrates to the whole dish.

INGREDIENTS | SERVES 8

½ cup coconut oil mayonnaise

¾ cup homemade Thousand Island Dressing (Chapter 9)

2 cups sauerkraut, squeezed dry

12 ounces shredded corned beef

1 cup shredded Swiss cheese

1 cup shredded mozzarella cheese

1. Preheat oven to 350°F.

2. Combine mayonnaise and Thousand Island Dressing in a medium bowl. Add sauerkraut and corned beef and stir until incorporated.

3. Transfer mixture to a 9" × 9" baking pan and sprinkle cheeses on top.

4. Bake 25 minutes or until dip is bubbly and cheese starts to brown.

5. Remove from oven and allow to cool. Divide into eight equal portions and transfer each portion to an airtight container. Store in the refrigerator until ready to eat, up to one week.

PER SERVING Calories: 427 | Fat: 36 g | Protein: 19 g | Sodium: 901 mg | Fiber: 1 g | Carbohydrates: 6 g | Sugar: 4 g | Net Carbohydrates: 5 g

Cauliflower Pizza Crust

This Cauliflower Pizza Crust provides the perfect low-carb base for any of your favorite pizza toppings. You can make a few at once and store the extras in the freezer tightly wrapped in plastic up to two months. When ready to use, just allow to thaw and proceed with your toppings and baking.

INGREDIENTS | SERVES 4

6 cups riced cauliflower
1 large egg
½ teaspoon dried oregano
½ teaspoon dried basil
½ teaspoon dried parsley
⅛ teaspoon sea salt
¼ teaspoon freshly ground black pepper
½ cup grated Parmesan cheese

Squeezing Cauliflower Dry

Like cabbage, cauliflower is made up of 93 percent water. When cooked, a lot of the water is released from the cauliflower. While this is okay when roasted or sautéing, you'll end up with soggy pizza crust if you don't squeeze out the excess water before you prepare it. All you have to do is wrap the cauliflower with cheesecloth or place it in a fine-mesh nut bag and squeeze as hard as you can. When you think you've squeezed out enough, squeeze a little more until no more water is released from the cauliflower.

1. Preheat oven to 450°F. Line a baking sheet with parchment paper and coat with olive oil cooking spray. Set aside.

2. Put cauliflower rice in a microwave-safe bowl and cover. Microwave for 3 minutes, remove and stir, and microwave 1 more minute. Allow to cool.

3. Transfer cooled cauliflower to fine-mesh cheesecloth and squeeze out excess liquid.

4. Combine remaining ingredients and cauliflower in a large mixing bowl and mix well with your hands.

5. Transfer cauliflower "dough" to baking sheet and flatten into the shape of a pizza crust.

6. Bake 20 minutes, flip crust over, and then bake 5 more minutes.

7. Store, covered, in the refrigerator up to three days.

8. When ready to eat, top with your favorite keto-friendly pizza toppings, and bake for 20 minutes in a 350°F oven.

PER SERVING Calories: 11 | Fat: 5 g | Protein: 8 g | Sodium: 364 mg | Fiber: 3 g | Carbohydrates: 10 g | Sugar: 3 g | Net Carbohydrates: 7 g

Pepper Poppers

These Pepper Poppers are reminiscent of jalapeño poppers, but instead of a spicy pepper base, the mini bell peppers impart a sweet taste that complements the spiciness of the pepper jack cheese perfectly.

INGREDIENTS | SERVES 6

6 mini sweet peppers, seeded and halved lengthwise

1 cup cream cheese, softened

½ teaspoon granulated garlic

½ teaspoon granulated onion

4 slices no-sugar-added bacon, cooked and chopped

½ cup shredded pepper jack cheese

1. Preheat oven to 350°F. Line baking sheet with parchment paper and arrange peppers on sheet cut side up.

2. Combine cream cheese, garlic, onion, and bacon in a medium bowl. Scoop 1 tablespoon cream cheese mixture into each pepper half.

3. Sprinkle cheese on top of peppers.

4. Bake 20 minutes or until cheese is melted and peppers are slightly softened.

5. Remove from oven and allow to cool. Transfer two pepper halves to each of six airtight containers. Store in the refrigerator until ready to eat, up to one week.

PER SERVING Calories: 280 | Fat: 24 g | Protein: 8 g | Sodium: 339 mg | Fiber: 2 g | Carbohydrates: 7 g | Sugar: 4 g | Net Carbohydrates: 5 g

BLT Dip

At only 3.5 grams of carbohydrates per cup, raw,
sliced zucchini coins are an ideal vessel for this BLT Dip.

INGREDIENTS | SERVES 6

½ pound no-sugar-added bacon, cooked
  and crumbled

4 ounces cream cheese, softened

⅛ cup mayonnaise

⅛ cup full-fat sour cream

⅛ cup shredded Cheddar cheese

1 teaspoon granulated onion

1 teaspoon dried minced garlic

¼ teaspoon smoked paprika

⅛ teaspoon sea salt

1 cup chopped iceberg lettuce

1 cup chopped tomatoes

1. Combine all ingredients, except lettuce and tomatoes, in a large bowl and mix until thoroughly incorporated.

2. Transfer mixture to an 8" × 8" baking pan. Sprinkle lettuce and tomatoes on top.

3. Divide into six equal-sized portions and transfer each portion to a separate airtight container. Store in the refrigerator until ready to eat, up to one week.

PER SERVING Calories: 280 | Fat: 26 g | Protein: 7 g | Sodium: 412 mg | Fiber: 0.5 g | Carbohydrates: 3 g | Sugar: 2 g | Net Carbohydrates: 2.5 g

Spaghetti Squash Pizza Bites

You can use any of your favorite low-carb pizza toppings for these Spaghetti Squash Pizza
Bites. Try them with ground pork sausage, green peppers, onions, and mushrooms.

INGREDIENTS | SERVES 6

1¼ cups cooked spaghetti squash
  "noodles"

1 large egg, beaten

½ cup no-sugar-added pizza sauce

½ cup chopped pepperoni

½ cup shredded mozzarella cheese

12 fresh basil leaves

1. Preheat oven to 400°F. Grease a muffin tin with olive oil cooking spray.

2. Combine spaghetti squash, egg, and pizza sauce in a medium bowl and mix well. Scoop equal amounts of spaghetti squash into each muffin well. Sprinkle with chopped pepperoni and mozzarella cheese and place a basil leaf on top of each.

3. Bake 25 minutes or until set.

4. Remove from oven and allow to cool. Transfer two bites to each of six separate airtight containers and store in the refrigerator until ready to eat, up to one week.

PER SERVING Calories: 100 | Fat: 7 g | Protein: 6 g | Sodium: 340 mg | Fiber: 1 g | Carbohydrates: 3 g | Sugar: 1 g | Net Carbohydrates: 3 g

Nacho Peppers

Instead of shredded chicken, these Nacho Peppers utilize ground beef with a homemade taco seasoning. They're delicious cold, but if you want to heat them up, place them under the broiler for a few minutes, but watch them closely so they don't burn.

INGREDIENTS | SERVES 6

6 mini sweet bell peppers, seeded and halved lengthwise

2 teaspoons coconut oil

1 pound 85/15 ground beef

1 teaspoon chili powder

1 teaspoon ground cumin

¼ teaspoon dried oregano

¼ teaspoon granulated garlic

¼ teaspoon granulated onion

½ teaspoon freshly ground black pepper

½ teaspoon sea salt

¾ cup no-sugar-added salsa

1 cup shredded Mexican-style cheese blend

1. Preheat oven to 375°F. Line a baking sheet with parchment paper and arrange peppers cut side up.

2. Heat coconut oil in a medium skillet over medium-high heat. Add ground beef and spices and cook until beef is no longer pink, about 8 minutes. Drain excess fat.

3. Add salsa to cooked beef and stir to mix well. Scoop equal amounts of beef mixture into pepper halves. Top with cheese blend.

4. Bake 15 minutes or until peppers start to soften and cheese is bubbly and golden. Remove from oven and allow to cool.

5. Transfer two pepper halves to each of six separate airtight containers and store in the refrigerator until ready to eat, up to one week.

PER SERVING Calories: 315 | Fat: 22 g | Protein: 20 g | Sodium: 652 mg | Fiber: 3 g | Carbohydrates: 8 g | Sugar: 4 g | Net Carbohydrates: 5 g

Jalapeño Popper Dip

Serve this Jalapeño Popper Dip with sliced raw zucchini, Cheesy Crackers (see recipe in this chapter), or freshly washed stalks of celery.

INGREDIENTS | SERVES 8

8 ounces cream cheese, softened

½ cup coconut oil or homemade mayonnaise

½ cup full-fat sour cream

½ cup minced jalapeño peppers

¾ cup cooked, crumbled no-sugar-added bacon

2 cups shredded Cheddar cheese, divided

Forego Conventional Mayonnaise

The mayonnaise that you typically find in grocery stores contains soybean oil, canola oil, and sugar. Ingredients that are not only unsuitable for a keto diet, but don't really fit into any healthy diet plan. Fortunately, food manufacturers like Primal Kitchen and Thrive Market are responding to the increasing demand for clean food products by producing mayonnaise made with avocado oil or coconut oil and no sugar. Use this kind of mayonnaise in any recipe that calls for it or if you prefer, make your own.

1. Preheat oven to 350°F.

2. Combine cream cheese, mayonnaise, sour cream, jalapeño peppers, bacon, and 1 cup cheese in a medium bowl and mix until incorporated.

3. Transfer to an 9" pie plate and sprinkle remaining cheese on top.

4. Bake 40 minutes or until dip is bubbly and cheese starts to turn golden brown.

5. Allow to cool slightly and divide into eight equal portions. Transfer each portion to an airtight container and store in the refrigerator until ready to eat, up to one week.

PER SERVING Calories: 432 | Fat: 42 g | Protein: 11 g | Sodium: 413 mg | Fiber: 0 g | Carbohydrates: 2 g | Sugar: 1 g | Net Carbohydrates: 2 g

Cheesy Ranch Cauliflower Bites

Ranch-inspired seasoning is a zesty complement to cauliflower in these tater tot–inspired low-carbohydrate cauliflower bites.

INGREDIENTS | SERVES 6

1 large head of cauliflower, cut into florets

2 large eggs

1¼ cups shredded Cheddar cheese, divided

1 tablespoon dried parsley

1 teaspoon dried dill

1 teaspoon granulated garlic

1 teaspoon granulated onion

1 teaspoon sea salt

⅓ teaspoon freshly ground black pepper

6 slices no-sugar-added bacon, cooked and chopped

2 teaspoons dried chives

1. Preheat oven to 375°F. Grease wells of a muffin tin with olive oil cooking spray. Set aside.

2. Place cauliflower florets into bowl of food processor and pulse until large crumbles form.

3. Transfer cauliflower to a fine-mesh cheesecloth and squeeze excess moisture out. Place cauliflower in a large mixing bowl and add eggs, 1 cup cheese, seasonings, bacon, and chives. Combine well.

4. Fill each muffin tin well with equal amounts of cauliflower mixture and top with remaining cheese.

5. Bake 20 minutes or until golden brown. Remove from oven and allow to cool.

6. Transfer two cauliflower bites to each of six separate airtight containers and store in the refrigerator until ready to eat, up to one week.

PER SERVING Calories: 281 | Fat: 22 g | Protein: 14 g | Sodium: 805 mg | Fiber: 2 g | Carbohydrates: 6 g | Sugar: 2 g | Net Carbohydrates: 4 g

Buffalo Chicken Jalapeño Poppers

Use cooked chicken from the Slow Cooker Whole Chicken (Chapter 12) for quick and easy prep.

INGREDIENTS | SERVES 6

6 jalapeño peppers, seeded and halved lengthwise

8 ounces cooked shredded chicken

⅓ cup Frank's RedHot sauce

4 ounces cream cheese, softened

4 ounces shredded sharp Cheddar cheese

6 slices no-sugar-added bacon, cut in half

1. Preheat oven to 375°F. Line peppers, cut side up, on a baking sheet lined with parchment paper.

2. Combine chicken, hot sauce, cream cheese, and Cheddar cheese in a medium skillet over medium heat and stir until cheeses are melted and ingredients are combined.

3. Remove from heat and scoop equal parts of chicken mixture into each jalapeño half.

4. Wrap a half slice bacon around each jalapeño half and secure in place with a toothpick.

5. Return to baking sheet and bake 25 minutes. Turn oven to broil and broil 1 minute. Remove from heat and allow to cool.

6. Transfer two poppers to each of six airtight containers and store in the refrigerator until ready to eat, up to one week.

PER SERVING Calories: 332 | Fat: 26 g | Protein: 20 g | Sodium: 406 mg | Fiber: 0.5 g | Carbohydrates: 2 g | Sugar: 1 g | Net Carbohydrates: 1.5 g

Cheesy Sausage Balls

Using pork breakfast sausage gives these Cheesy Sausage Balls a nice, sage-y flavor, but if you prefer, you can use hot Italian sausage or another sausage of your choice in its place without affecting the carbohydrate count significantly.

INGREDIENTS | SERVES 6 (MAKES 18 BALLS)

½ pound pork breakfast sausage
½ cup shredded Cheddar cheese
½ cup almond flour
⅛ cup grated Parmesan cheese
1 teaspoon baking powder
¼ teaspoon sea salt
¼ teaspoon freshly ground black pepper
1 large egg

Homemade Breakfast Sausage

If you can't find pork breakfast sausage that's made without sugar, you can create your own copycat version by combining a pound of ground pork with 1 teaspoon sea salt, ½ teaspoon dried parsley, ¼ teaspoon dried sage, ¼ teaspoon freshly ground black pepper, ¼ teaspoon dried thyme, ¼ teaspoon crushed red pepper flakes, and ¼ teaspoon coriander. If you want it spicy add ½ teaspoon cayenne pepper too. To make meal prep easier down the road, make a double or triple batch and freeze some of it (for up to six months) for use in recipes later.

1. Preheat oven to 375°F. Grease a baking sheet with olive oil cooking spray.

2. Combine all ingredients in a medium mixing bowl and mix with your hands until incorporated.

3. Form mixture into 1" balls and arrange in a single layer on prepared baking sheet.

4. Bake 18 minutes or until balls turn golden brown. Remove from oven and allow to cool.

5. Transfer three sausage balls to each of six airtight containers and store in the refrigerator until ready to eat, up to one week.

PER SERVING Calories: 244 | Fat: 16 g | Protein: 13 g | Sodium: 332 mg | Fiber: 0 g | Carbohydrates: 9 g | Sugar: 0 g | Net Carbohydrates: 9 g

Cauliflower "Mac" and Cheese Bites

When you try these Cauliflower "Mac" and Cheese Bites, you won't even miss the real macaroni. It has all the cheesy flavor without any of the carbohydrates.

INGREDIENTS | SERVES 6 (MAKES 12 BITES)

½ cup heavy cream

2 tablespoons grass-fed butter

1 cup shredded sharp Cheddar cheese, divided

6 slices no-sugar-added bacon, cooked and crumbled

3 cups frozen cauliflower, thawed and roughly chopped

2 large eggs

1. Preheat oven to 350°F. Spray each well of a muffin tin with olive oil cooking spray. Set aside.

2. Combine cream and butter in a small saucepan over medium heat and stir until melted. Add ⅔ cup cheese and stir into butter mixture. Remove from heat and continue stirring until cheese is melted.

3. Combine bacon and cauliflower in a large mixing bowl and pour cheese sauce over them. Stir to combine. Add eggs and use your hands to mix everything together.

4. Scoop equal amounts of mixture into each prepared muffin wells and sprinkle with remaining cheese.

5. Bake 35 minutes or until set and golden brown. Remove from oven and allow to cool.

6. Transfer two bites to each of six separate airtight containers and store in the refrigerator until ready to eat, up to one week.

PER SERVING Calories: 348 | Fat: 31 g | Protein: 12 g | Sodium: 374 mg | Fiber: 1.5 g | Carbohydrates: 4 g | Sugar: 2 g | Net Carbohydrates: 2.5 g

Mini Meatloaf Cups

The pork rinds used in this recipe give these Mini Meatloaf Cups a moist texture and help hold them together. You can omit them if you don't have any, but you'll end up with denser meat.

INGREDIENTS | SERVES 6 (MAKES 12 CUPS)

1 pound grass-fed 85/15 ground beef
¾ cup chopped yellow onion
1 large egg
1 cup crushed pork rinds
½ teaspoon granulated garlic
½ teaspoon granulated onion
¼ teaspoon dried basil
¼ teaspoon dried parsley
¼ teaspoon dried oregano
¼ teaspoon sea salt
¼ teaspoon freshly ground black pepper
6 tablespoons no-sugar-added ketchup

Fried Pig Skin

Pork rind, also sometimes referred to as cracklings, is the culinary term for the fried or roasted skin of a pig. During the frying or roasting process, the fat is cooked out of the skin, leaving a crispy pork-flavored snack behind. Pork rinds are an excellent keto-friendly alternative to bread crumbs because they have zero carbohydrates. When selecting pork rinds, choose companies that use pasture- or humanely raised pork.

1. Preheat oven to 350°F. Grease each well of a muffin pan with coconut oil cooking spray.

2. Combine all ingredients, except ketchup, in a large mixing bowl and use your hands to mix until fully incorporated.

3. Divide beef mixture into twelve equal portions and lightly press each portion into each well of the muffin pan. Top each with ½ tablespoon ketchup.

4. Bake 15 minutes or until meatloaves are cooked through.

5. Remove from oven and allow to cool. Transfer two mini meatloaves to each of six separate airtight containers. Store in the refrigerator until ready to eat, up to one week.

PER SERVING Calories: 213 | Fat: 14 g | Protein: 15 g | Sodium: 310 mg | Fiber: 0.5 g | Carbohydrates: 5 g | Sugar: 2 g | Net Carbohydrates: 4.5 g

Zucchini Pizza Bites

Don't skip the step of squeezing the zucchini dry! It helps ensure that these pizza bites will hold together and they'll last longer in the refrigerator without becoming soggy.

INGREDIENTS | SERVES 6 (MAKES 12 BITES)

2 cups shredded zucchini, squeezed dry

1 large egg

¼ teaspoon dried basil

¼ teaspoon dried oregano

¼ teaspoon dried parsley

⅛ teaspoon dried sage

⅛ teaspoon dried rosemary

½ teaspoon sea salt

¼ teaspoon freshly ground black pepper

1 cup shredded mozzarella cheese, divided

¼ cup grated Parmesan cheese

¼ cup chopped pepperoni

1. Preheat oven to 400°F. Grease each well of a muffin pan with coconut oil cooking spray.

2. Combine zucchini, egg, spices, ¼ cup mozzarella cheese, and Parmesan cheese in a large bowl and mix well. Divide into twelve equal portions and place each portion in a muffin well.

3. Top with remaining mozzarella cheese and then place pepperoni on top.

4. Bake 15 minutes or until pizza bites are set and cheese is bubbly and starts to turn golden.

5. Allow to cool and remove from muffin pan. Transfer two pizza bites to each of six separate airtight containers. Store in the refrigerator until ready to eat, up to one week.

PER SERVING Calories: 119 | Fat: 8 g | Protein: 8 g | Sodium: 498 mg | Fiber: 1 g | Carbohydrates: 2 g | Sugar: 1 g | Net Carbohydrates: 1 g

Bacon and Sun-Dried Tomato Dip

If you have only cottage cheese on hand, you can use that in place of the ricotta cheese. To make the texture more similar, strain the cottage cheese through a cheesecloth to remove the moisture and make it thicker.

INGREDIENTS | SERVES 6

1 (15-ounce) container whole milk ricotta cheese

¼ cup shredded Parmesan cheese

¼ cup shredded mozzarella cheese

2 tablespoons chopped sun-dried tomatoes

6 slices no-sugar-added bacon, cooked and chopped

¼ teaspoon crushed red pepper flakes

1. Preheat oven to 375°F.

2. Combine all ingredients in a large mixing bowl and stir until incorporated. Transfer to an 8" × 8" baking dish and bake 20 minutes or until bubbly and golden brown.

3. Remove from oven and allow to cool.

4. Divide into six equal portions and transfer each portion to a separate airtight container. Store in the refrigerator until ready to eat, up to one week.

PER SERVING Calories: 274 | Fat: 22 g | Protein: 14 g | Sodium: 344 mg | Fiber: 0 g | Carbohydrates: 3 g | Sugar: 1 g | Net Carbohydrates: 3 g

Chicken Enchilada Dip

If you prefer to use freshly cooked chicken instead of canned, use about a cup of shredded chicken to make this dip.

INGREDIENTS | SERVES 12

1 (12.5-ounce) can white chicken breast

1 tablespoon no-sugar-added fajita seasoning

4 ounces cream cheese, softened

½ cup full-fat sour cream

1 cup shredded Cheddar cheese

½ (4-ounce) can diced green chili peppers

½ medium-sized jalapeño, seeded and minced

1. Preheat oven to 350°F.

2. Combine chicken and fajita seasoning in a medium bowl and mix until chicken is coated.

3. Add remaining ingredients and stir to combine. Transfer to an 8" × 8" baking dish.

4. Bake 30 minutes or until cheese is bubbly and edges of dip are starting to brown.

5. Allow to cool. Divide into twelve equal-sized portions and transfer each portion to an airtight container. Store in the refrigerator until ready to eat, up to one week.

PER SERVING Calories: 127 | Fat: 9 g | Protein: 10 g | Sodium: 121 mg | Fiber: 0 g | Carbohydrates: 0.5 g | Sugar: 0.5 g | Net Carbohydrates: 0.5 g

Cauliflower Muffins

If you want to make these Cauliflower Muffins nut-free, you can replace the almond flour with Paleo flour, but doing so will increase the carbohydrate count by about 0.5 grams per muffin.

INGREDIENTS | SERVES 6 (MAKES 12 MUFFINS)

3 cups riced cauliflower

2 large eggs

¾ cup shredded Cheddar cheese, divided

¼ cup grated Parmesan cheese

¼ cup almond flour

½ teaspoon baking soda

¼ teaspoon dried basil

¼ teaspoon dried oregano

¼ teaspoon granulated garlic

¼ teaspoon granulated onion

½ teaspoon sea salt

4 slices no-sugar-added bacon, cooked and chopped

1. Preheat oven to 375°F. Grease each well of a muffin pan with coconut oil cooking spray.

2. In a large bowl, combine cauliflower, eggs, ½ cup Cheddar cheese, Parmesan cheese, almond flour, baking soda, and spices and mix well.

3. Divide into twelve equal portions and transfer each portion to the prepared muffin wells. Sprinkle remaining Cheddar cheese and bacon on top of each muffin.

4. Bake 20 minutes or until muffins are cooked through and cheese is hot and bubbly.

5. Remove from oven and allow to cool. Transfer two muffins to each of six separate airtight containers. Store in the refrigerator until ready to eat, up to one week.

PER SERVING Calories: 219 | Fat: 15 g | Protein: 11 g | Sodium: 643 mg | Fiber: 1.5 g | Carbohydrates: 7 g | Sugar: 1 g | Net Carbohydrates: 5.5 g

Cheesy Crackers

Although almond and coconut flour are both popular in keto baking, the two can't be used interchangeably. Coconut flour absorbs significantly more moisture than almond flour and doesn't produce the same results.

INGREDIENTS | SERVES 6

1 cup shredded Parmesan cheese
½ cup shredded Cheddar cheese
½ cup shredded mozzarella cheese
2 ounces cream cheese
1 cup almond flour
1 large egg
½ teaspoon sea salt
½ teaspoon dried chives
½ teaspoon granulated garlic

Making Coconut Flour Work

Although there's no explicit rule for substituting coconut flour for almond flour, it can be done with a few adjustments. Coconut flour is very absorbent and sucks in a lot of moisture from the other ingredients in the batter. When substituting coconut flour for almond flour, you have to adjust the ratios of both liquid and eggs. A good starting point is to substitute ¼ cup coconut flour for every 1 cup almond flour that a recipe calls for. Keep in mind that the texture won't come out exactly the same as the original recipe when you do this.

1. Preheat oven to 450°F. Line a baking sheet with parchment paper.

2. Combine all cheeses and almond flour in a medium saucepan over low heat. Stir constantly until cheese is just beginning to melt. Remove from heat and continue stirring until ingredients are fully combined.

3. Allow to cool 3 minutes. Add egg, sea salt, chives, and garlic and stir to combine.

4. Transfer cheese mixture to a piece of parchment paper and lay another piece of parchment paper on top.

5. Use a rolling pin to roll out the cheese mixture into a thin layer. Cut cheese mixture into 1" squares.

6. Transfer squares to prepared baking sheet and bake 5 minutes, flip each cracker over, and then bake another 5 minutes.

7. Allow to cool. Divide into six equal servings and then transfer to an airtight container. Store in the refrigerator until ready to eat, up to one week.

PER SERVING Calories: 247 | Fat: 15 g | Protein: 15 g | Sodium: 634 mg | Fiber: 0.5 g | Carbohydrates: 8 g | Sugar: 0.5 g | Net Carbohydrates: 7.5 g

CHAPTER 15

Fat Bombs

Vanilla Cheesecake Fat Bombs

These Vanilla Cheesecake Fat Bombs contain only four ingredients, but they taste just like little bites of cheesecake. They're perfect when you need a sweet snack and a little dose of fat.

INGREDIENTS | SERVES 12

6 ounces cream cheese, softened

1⅓ teaspoons vanilla extract

¼ cup granulated erythritol

⅔ cup heavy cream

1. Line a mini muffin tin with twelve cupcake liners.

2. Combine cream cheese, vanilla extract, and erythritol in a medium bowl and beat with a handheld mixer until smooth, about 2 minutes.

3. Beat in the heavy cream and mix on medium speed for 4 minutes, or until peaks start to form.

4. Divide mixture into twelve equal portions and scoop each portion into prepared muffin tin.

5. Refrigerate 1 hour or until set.

6. Store in the refrigerator until ready to eat, up to one week.

PER SERVING Calories: 95 | Fat: 9 g | Protein: 1 g | Sodium: 56 mg | Fiber: 0 g | Carbohydrates: 5 g | Sugar: 1 g | Net Carbohydrates: 5 g

Bacon and Cheese Fat Bombs

These savory fat bombs are perfect for when you need some extra fat and energy, but don't feel like having something sweet. Because of the cream cheese, you'll need to store them in the refrigerator so they can stay fresh all week.

INGREDIENTS | SERVES 12

6 ounces cream cheese, softened

¼ cup grass-fed butter, softened

¼ cup shredded Cheddar cheese

½ medium lime, juiced and zested

5 slices no-sugar-added bacon, cooked and chopped

2 serrano peppers, seeded and minced

1 clove garlic, minced

⅛ cup chopped cilantro

1. Beat cream cheese, butter, and Cheddar cheese together in a medium bowl. Add remaining ingredients and stir to combine.

2. Refrigerate until hardened, about 30 minutes.

3. Remove from refrigerator, divide into twelve equal parts, and roll into balls.

4. Store in the refrigerator until ready to eat, up to one week.

PER SERVING Calories: 141 | Fat: 14 g | Protein: 3 g | Sodium: 146 mg | Fiber: 0 g | Carbohydrates: 0 g | Sugar: 0.5 g | Net Carbohydrates: 0 g

Lemon Fat Bombs

If you want to up the lemony flavor of these fat bombs, you can add a little lemon juice and some lemon zest without significantly changing the carbohydrate content.

INGREDIENTS | SERVES 12

¾ cup coconut butter, room temperature

¼ cup butter-flavored coconut oil, room temperature

2 teaspoons lemon extract

3 tablespoons powdered erythritol

⅛ teaspoon sea salt

Storing Your Fat Bombs

These fat bombs aren't perishable, but if you don't store them in the refrigerator, they may melt or become gooey, depending on the temperature of your room. To be safe and ensure they keep their shape, store any fat bombs made with coconut oil in an airtight container in the refrigerator.

1. Line a mini muffin tin with twelve cupcake liners.

2. Combine ingredients in a medium bowl and beat with a handheld mixer until smooth, about 2 minutes.

3. Pour mixture evenly into prepared muffin tins and refrigerate until set, about 1 hour.

4. Remove from muffin tin and transfer to an airtight container. Store in the refrigerator until ready to eat, up to one week.

PER SERVING Calories: 159 | Fat: 18 g | Protein: 0 g | Sodium: 24 mg | Fiber: 0 g | Carbohydrates: 3 g | Sugar: 0 g | Net Carbohydrates: 3 g

Strawberry Cheesecake Fat Bombs

Strawberries are considered a low- to medium-carbohydrate fruit, containing around 12 grams of carbohydrates per cup. Although you have to monitor your intake on a keto diet, you can incorporate them without kicking yourself out of ketosis.

INGREDIENTS | SERVES 12

½ cup sliced frozen strawberries, room temperature

2 tablespoons powdered erythritol

2 teaspoons vanilla extract

¾ cup cream cheese, softened

¼ cup butter-flavored coconut oil, room temperature

1. Line a mini muffin tin with twelve cupcake liners. Set aside.

2. Place strawberries in a small bowl and mash with a fork until soupy. Add erythritol and vanilla extract and mix until smooth.

3. In a medium bowl, combine cream cheese and coconut oil and beat on low speed until smooth.

4. Fold strawberry mixture into cream cheese mixture and stir until smooth.

5. Divide into twelve equal parts and spoon each part into the prepared muffin tin.

6. Refrigerate until set, about 1 hour. Transfer fat bombs to an airtight container and store in the refrigerator until ready to eat, up to one week.

PER SERVING Calories: 94 | Fat: 9 g | Protein: 1 g | Sodium: 53 mg | Fiber: 0 g | Carbohydrates: 3 g | Sugar: 1 g | Net Carbohydrates: 3 g

Chocolate Fudge Fat Bombs

If you want to make these double-chocolate fat bombs, stir in some stevia-sweetened chocolate chips after the melted mixture has cooled and before you pour it into the muffin tin.

INGREDIENTS | SERVES 12

½ cup no-sugar-added sunflower seed butter

½ cup butter-flavored coconut oil, room temperature

¼ cup unsweetened raw cacao powder

3 tablespoons coconut flour

⅛ cup powdered erythritol

1/16 teaspoon sea salt

Silicone Molds

Lined muffin tins work perfectly well for making your fat bombs, but if you want to get a little creative—and you like fun shapes—you can use a silicone mold instead. Silicone molds are oven-safe and freezer-safe and they come in all kinds of different shapes and sizes. Plus, they're pliable, so you can easily remove the fat bombs from them once they set. They're also a lot less cumbersome than muffin pans, so you can store them more easily and work with several at a time when meal prepping.

1. Line a mini muffin tin with twelve cupcake liners. Set aside.

2. Combine sunflower seed butter and coconut oil in a medium saucepan and melt over medium heat. Stir until smooth.

3. Add remaining ingredients and stir until incorporated.

4. Remove from heat and allow to cool slightly. Pour equal portions into prepared muffin tin and transfer to the refrigerator.

5. Allow to cool until solidified, about 2 hours.

6. Remove from refrigerator and transfer to an airtight container. Store in the refrigerator until ready to eat, up to one week.

PER SERVING Calories: 117 | Fat: 11 g | Protein: 1.5 g | Sodium: 14 mg | Fiber: 2.5 g | Carbohydrates: 5 g | Sugar: 0 g | Net Carbohydrates: 2.5 g

Peanut Butter Cups

These Peanut Butter Cups taste like the conventional peanut butter cups that you probably know and love, but without any of the sugar or artificial ingredients.

INGREDIENTS | SERVES 12

¼ cup butter-flavored coconut oil

¼ cup unsweetened raw cacao powder

1 teaspoon vanilla extract, divided

2 tablespoons granulated monk fruit sweetener, divided

2 tablespoons coconut oil

¼ cup no-sugar-added creamy peanut butter

What Is Monk Fruit Sweetener?

Monk fruit, also called luo han guo or swingle, is an Asian vine-grown fruit that was first cultivated by Asian monks in the thirteenth century. The fruit's extract contains substances called mogrosides, which are 150 to 200 times sweeter than sugar, but contain none of the calories or carbohydrates. Because of its intense sweetness, monk fruit is used in small quantities, much like stevia. Monk fruit sweeteners are available as powders, liquids, and granulates.

1. Line a mini muffin tin with twelve cupcake liners. Set aside.

2. Combine coconut oil, cacao powder, ½ teaspoon vanilla extract, and 1 tablespoon monk fruit sweetener in a small saucepan over low heat. Stir until smooth.

3. Pour equal amounts of chocolate mixture into each prepared muffin tin. Freeze until set, about 15 minutes.

4. While chocolate is setting, combine remaining ingredients in small saucepan over low heat and stir until smooth.

5. Pour this peanut butter layer over chocolate layer and return to freezer until firm, about 1 hour.

6. Remove each fat bomb from muffin tray and transfer to an airtight container. Store in the freezer until ready to eat, up to two months.

PER SERVING Calories: 96 | Fat: 9 g | Protein: 1.5 g | Sodium: 23 mg | Fiber: 1 g | Carbohydrates: 2 g | Sugar: 0.5 g | Net Carbohydrates: 1 g

Caramel Apple Fat Bombs

Green apples are the lowest in carbohydrates of all the apple varieties, but one apple still contains around 20 grams of carbohydrates, 4 of which come from fiber. You can incorporate them into your keto diet, but make sure to stick to your portions and don't go overboard on your carbs for your other meals when you do.

INGREDIENTS | SERVES 12

2 tablespoons butter-flavored coconut oil

1 small green apple, peeled and sliced thinly

1 teaspoon ground cinnamon

⅔ cup coconut cream

½ cup coconut butter

15 drops caramel-flavored liquid stevia

⅛ teaspoon sea salt

Monk Fruit or Stevia?

You can replace stevia with monk fruit sweetener in any recipes that call for it, but you may have to adjust the amounts. Stevia is doubly as sweet as monk fruit sweetener, so you would have to use 2 tablespoons monk fruit sweetener for every 1 tablespoon stevia or two drops of monk fruit sweetener for every one drop of stevia. However, monk fruit sweetener is difficult to grow and importation is costly, so it may be more budget-friendly to stick with stevia or use erythritol in its place.

1. Line a mini muffin tin with twelve cupcake liners. Set aside.

2. Heat coconut oil in a medium saucepan over medium heat. Add apples and sauté until softened, about 6 minutes. Sprinkle cinnamon over apples and stir to coat.

3. Transfer apples, scraping down skillet to get all the coconut oil and cinnamon too, into a high-powered blender and add remaining ingredients.

4. Blend until smooth.

5. Pour equal portions of the apple mixture into prepared muffin tin and transfer to the refrigerator. Chill until set, about 2 hours.

6. After fat bombs have set, transfer to an airtight container and store in the refrigerator until ready to eat, up to two weeks.

PER SERVING Calories: 140 | Fat: 14 g | Protein: 0.5 g | Sodium: 26 mg | Fiber: 0.5 g | Carbohydrates: 3.5 g | Sugar: 2.5 g | Net Carbohydrates: 3 g

Coconut Berry Fat Bombs

You can use any combination of mixed berries for these fat bombs, just make sure to stay within the ½ cup portion size to avoid affecting the carbohydrate count too significantly.

INGREDIENTS | SERVES 12

1 cup coconut oil, melted
¼ cup frozen blueberries, thawed
¼ cup frozen raspberries, thawed
1 teaspoon vanilla extract
10 drops liquid stevia

1. Line a mini muffin tin with twelve cupcake liners. Set aside.

2. Combine ingredients in a high-powered blender or food processor and blend until smooth.

3. Pour equal amounts of berry mixture into each prepared muffin well. Transfer to the refrigerator and chill until set, about 2 hours.

4. Remove from muffin tin and transfer to an airtight container. Store in the refrigerator until ready to eat, up to two weeks.

PER SERVING Calories: 167 | Fat: 18 g | Protein: 0 g | Sodium: 1 mg | Fiber: 0.5 g | Carbohydrates: 2 g | Sugar: 1.5 g | Net Carbohydrates: 1.5 g

Pumpkin Pie Fat Bombs

The grass-fed collagen powder gives these fat bombs a boost of protein and essential amino acids, but if you don't have any, you can omit it without affecting the final outcome.

INGREDIENTS | SERVES 12

¾ cup coconut butter, melted
¼ cup coconut oil, melted
2 tablespoons grass-fed collagen powder
10 drops liquid stevia
⅛ teaspoon sea salt
⅓ cup pumpkin purée
2 teaspoons pumpkin pie spice
¼ teaspoon vanilla extract

1. Line a mini muffin tin with twelve cupcake liners. Set aside.

2. Combine all ingredients in a food processor. Process until smooth.

3. Pour equal parts of the mixture into prepared muffin wells and transfer muffin tin to the freezer. Freeze until set, about 1 hour.

4. Once set, remove from muffin wells and place in an airtight container. Store in the freezer until ready to eat, up to two months.

PER SERVING Calories: 142 | Fat: 16 g | Protein: 2 g | Sodium: 27 mg | Fiber: 0 g | Carbohydrates: 0 g | Sugar: 0 g | Net Carbohydrates: 0 g

Chocolate Peppermint Fat Bombs

This is a basic chocolate fat bomb recipe that can be easily adjusted to any flavor you want by changing the type of extract you use. You can swap peppermint extract for orange extract, maple extract, vanilla extract, or raspberry extract. Just make sure you're using a carbohydrate-free extract and not a flavored syrup.

INGREDIENTS | SERVES 12

½ cup plus 2 tablespoons coconut oil, melted

1 tablespoon powdered erythritol

¼ teaspoon peppermint extract

2 tablespoons unsweetened raw cacao powder

Extracts versus Flavorings

Extracts are made by placing some type of raw material, like vanilla beans or orange peels, in alcohol and water and letting the alcohol pull out the flavor. In pure extracts, nothing else is added. Flavored syrups are made from a mixture of water, sugar, natural and artificial flavors, and preservatives. There are sugar-free versions that technically meet the carbohydrate standards for the keto diet, but these contain artificial sweeteners that have been implicated in chronic health problems, so it's best to avoid them.

1. Line a mini muffin tin with twelve cupcake liners. Set aside.

2. Combine coconut oil, erythritol, and peppermint extract in a small bowl and stir until combined. Divide mixture in half and place into two separate bowls.

3. Add cacao powder to one of the bowls and stir until smooth.

4. Pour chocolate mixture evenly into each of the prepared muffin wells. Transfer to freezer and allow to set. Once set, pour coconut mixture evenly on top of each well. Place back in freezer until set, about 1 hour.

5. Once set, remove from muffin tin and transfer to an airtight container. Store in the freezer until ready to eat, up to two months.

PER SERVING Calories: 101 | Fat: 11 g | Protein: 0 g | Sodium: 1 mg | Fiber: 0.5 g | Carbohydrates: 1.5 g | Sugar: 0 g | Net Carbohydrates: 1 g

Jalapeño Popper Fat Bombs

You can store these Jalapeño Popper Fat Bombs in the freezer up to three months, so if you want to save some time down the road, double up on them, freeze them, and then take out what you need as you go.

INGREDIENTS | SERVES 12

6 ounces cream cheese, softened

½ cup unsalted grass-fed butter, softened

6 slices no-sugar-added bacon, cooked and chopped

½ cup shredded Cheddar cheese

2 small jalapeño poppers, seeded and minced

1. Line a baking sheet with parchment paper. Set aside.

2. Combine cream cheese and butter in a food processor and process until smooth.

3. Add remaining ingredients and stir until incorporated.

4. Refrigerate until mixture firms up, about 1 hour.

5. Divide into twelve equal portions and roll each portion into a ball and place on prepared baking sheet.

6. Chill in the freezer until set, about 2 hours. Transfer to an airtight container and store in the refrigerator until ready to eat, up to two weeks.

PER SERVING Calories: 197 | Fat: 19 g | Protein: 4 g | Sodium: 180 mg | Fiber: 0 g | Carbohydrates: 1 g | Sugar: 0 g | Net Carbohydrates: 1 g

Maple Almond Fat Bombs

These Maple Almond Fat Bombs use maple extract for their flavor instead of maple syrup, which contains too many carbohydrates to use on a keto diet.

INGREDIENTS | SERVES 12

½ cup no-sugar-added almond butter

¼ cup plus 2 tablespoons butter-flavored coconut oil

2 tablespoons powdered erythritol

½ teaspoon pure maple extract

1. Line a mini muffin tin with twelve cupcake liners. Set aside.

2. Combine all ingredients in a small saucepan and stir over low heat until melted and incorporated.

3. Pour equal parts of the mixture into each prepared muffin well and transfer to the freezer. Freeze until set, about 1 hour.

4. Store in the freezer until ready to eat, up to two months.

PER SERVING Calories: 123 | Fat: 12 g | Protein: 2.5 g | Sodium: 45 mg | Fiber: 0.5 g | Carbohydrates: 2 g | Sugar: 1 g | Net Carbohydrates: 1.5 g

Peanut Butter Fat Bombs

Storing these fat bombs in the freezer will help them keep their shape and make them last longer. They're also delicious as a sweet, frozen treat.

INGREDIENTS | SERVES 12

½ cup coconut oil

⅔ cup no-sugar-added creamy peanut butter

¼ teaspoon sea salt

2 teaspoons vanilla extract

3 tablespoons powdered erythritol

1. Line a mini muffin tin with twelve cupcake liners. Set aside.

2. Add all ingredients to a small saucepan and heat over medium heat until melted. Stir until combined.

3. Pour mixture evenly into each of the prepared muffin wells. Transfer to the freezer and freeze until set, about 1 hour.

4. Remove from muffin tin and transfer to an airtight container. Store in the freezer until ready to eat, up to two months.

PER SERVING Calories: 164 | Fat: 16 g | Protein: 3 g | Sodium: 109 mg | Fiber: 0.5 g | Carbohydrates: 3 g | Sugar: 1.5 g | Net Carbohydrates: 2.5 g

Bacon and Avocado Fat Bombs

The lime juice in these fat bombs helps preserve the avocado and keeps it from turning brown quickly. Even if the avocado does start to brown, it's still safe (and delicious) to eat!

INGREDIENTS | SERVES 6

½ large avocado, peeled and pitted

¼ cup grass-fed butter

2 cloves garlic, crushed

½ small white onion, peeled and minced

1 tablespoon fresh lime juice

¼ teaspoon sea salt

⅛ teaspoon freshly ground black pepper

4 slices no-sugar-added bacon, cooked and chopped

1. Combine all ingredients except bacon in a medium bowl and mash with a fork until evenly incorporated. Transfer to the refrigerator and chill 30 minutes.

2. Add bacon to bowl and mix until combined.

3. Divide mixture into six equal portions and roll into balls. Place in an airtight container and store in the refrigerator until ready to eat, up to six days.

PER SERVING Calories: 176 | Fat: 17 g | Protein: 3 g | Sodium: 223 mg | Fiber: 1.5 g | Carbohydrates: 2.5 g | Sugar: 0.5 g | Net Carbohydrates: 1 g

Mocha Fat Bombs

The brewed coffee or espresso in these fat bombs brings out the rich chocolate flavor of the raw cacao, so don't skip it! You can use what you need and then make some bulletproof coffee and drink the rest.

INGREDIENTS | SERVES 12

1 cup cream cheese, softened

4 tablespoons powdered erythritol

2 tablespoons unsweetened raw cacao powder

2 tablespoons coconut butter

4 tablespoons brewed espresso (or strong coffee), cooled

1. Combine all ingredients in a food processor and process until smooth.

2. Refrigerate until mixture firms slightly, about 1 hour. Remove from refrigerator and divide mixture into twelve equal portions. Roll each portion into a ball and transfer to an airtight container.

3. Freeze until set, about 2 hours. Store in the freezer until ready to eat, up to two months.

PER SERVING Calories: 88 | Fat: 8 g | Protein: 1.5 g | Sodium: 70 mg | Fiber: 0.5 g | Carbohydrates: 5 g | Sugar: 0.5 g | Net Carbohydrates: 4.5 g

Pizza Fat Bombs

There's almost nothing better than little pizza bites that you can easily take on the go. These fat bombs combine all the delicious flavors of pepperoni pizza, but are safe for a keto diet. Store them in the refrigerator so that they keep their shape.

INGREDIENTS | SERVES 6

4 ounces cream cheese, softened

¼ cup chopped pepperoni

¼ cup chopped black olives

2 tablespoons chopped fresh basil

2 tablespoons shredded Parmesan cheese

2 tablespoons no-sugar-added pizza sauce

Oleic Acid in Olives

Around 74 percent of the fat in olives is oleic acid, a monounsaturated fat that's credited with many of the health benefits of olive oil. Oleic acid has been linked to decreased chronic inflammation, a reduced risk of heart disease, and cancer prevention. In addition to their high fat content, olives are also low in carbohydrates containing only about 4 to 6 percent of their total volume. Of these carbohydrates 52 to 86 percent comes from fiber, making the net carbohydrate count negligible. Olives make a great addition to savory fat bombs, salads, cheese bakes, and burrito bowls.

1. Line a baking sheet with parchment paper.

2. Combine all ingredients in a medium bowl and beat with a handheld mixer on low speed until fully incorporated.

3. Refrigerate until chilled, about 30 minutes.

4. Remove from refrigerator and divide into six equal portions. Form each portion into a ball and transfer each ball to prepared baking sheet.

5. Chill in the refrigerator for 2 hours. Transfer to an airtight container and store in the refrigerator until ready to eat, up to one week.

PER SERVING Calories: 103 | Fat: 9 g | Protein: 3 g | Sodium: 247 mg | Fiber: 0.5 g | Carbohydrates: 1.5 g | Sugar: 0.5 g | Net Carbohydrates: 1 g

Coconut Matcha Fat Bombs

If you don't have matcha-flavored collagen, you can use powdered matcha, which provides the same flavor but will lower the protein count of these fat bombs.

INGREDIENTS | SERVES 12

¾ cup full-fat coconut milk, refrigerated overnight

¾ cup coconut butter

4 tablespoons coconut oil, melted

1½ teaspoons vanilla extract

1 teaspoon ground cinnamon

3 tablespoons powdered erythritol

4 tablespoons matcha-flavored collagen, divided

½ cup finely shredded unsweetened coconut

The Lowdown on Matcha

Matcha, which literally translates to powdered tea, comes from green tea that has been ground into a fine powder. The green tea is extremely rich in specific antioxidants called polyphenols, which help regulate blood pressure, reduce blood cholesterol, and fight heart disease and cancer. Polyphenols also have antiaging properties. You can purchase matcha powder on its own or combined with collagen powder, which makes the matcha protein rich. The powder can be used in recipes or mixed with hot water or milk to create a tea or a latte.

1. Combine all ingredients except 1 tablespoon matcha collagen and shredded coconut in a high-powered blender or food processor and process until smooth.

2. Place mixture in the refrigerator and allow to chill 1 hour.

3. While mixture is in the refrigerator, combine remaining matcha collagen and shredded coconut in a small bowl and stir until incorporated.

4. Remove mixture from refrigerator and divide into twelve equal-sized servings. Roll each portion into a ball.

5. Dip each ball into coconut mixture and roll until completely coated on the outside.

6. Transfer to an airtight container and store in the refrigerator until ready to eat, up to two weeks.

PER SERVING Calories: 200 | Fat: 22 g | Protein: 3 g | Sodium: 3 mg | Fiber: 0.5 g | Carbohydrates: 1 g | Sugar: 0.5 g | Net Carbohydrates: 0.5 g

Cookie Dough Fat Bombs

These fat bombs contain all the nostalgic goodness of raw cookie dough without the worry of salmonella from a raw egg—and you don't need to sneak a bite behind your mom's back while she's baking!

INGREDIENTS | SERVES 12

¼ cup unsalted grass-fed butter, softened

2 ounces cream cheese, softened

3 tablespoons powdered erythritol

½ teaspoon vanilla extract

¼ teaspoon sea salt

1 cup unblanched almond flour

⅓ cup stevia-sweetened chocolate chips

1. Combine butter, cream cheese, and erythritol in a medium bowl and beat on medium speed with a hand mixer until light and fluffy, about 2 minutes.

2. Beat in vanilla and salt. Slowly add almond flour, beating on low speed until incorporated. Fold in chocolate chips.

3. Refrigerate mixture until firm, about 1 hour. Divide into twelve equal portions and roll each portion into a ball.

4. Transfer to an airtight container and store in the freezer until ready to eat, up to two months.

PER SERVING Calories: 104 | Fat: 6 g | Protein: 1.5 g | Sodium: 66 mg | Fiber: 0.5 g | Carbohydrates: 6 g | Sugar: 1.5 g | Net Carbohydrates: 5.5 g

Zingy Ginger Fat Bombs

Ground ginger gives these fat bombs a spicy kick, but if you want to make them even zestier, use freshly grated ginger instead.

INGREDIENTS | SERVES 12

½ cup coconut butter

½ cup butter-flavored coconut oil

⅓ cup unsweetened shredded coconut

1 tablespoon granulated erythritol

1 teaspoon ground ginger

1. Line a mini muffin tin with twelve cupcake liners. Set aside.

2. Combine all ingredients in a food processor and process until smooth.

3. Pour equal parts of ginger mixture into prepared muffin wells and refrigerate until set, about 30 minutes.

4. Remove from muffin wells and transfer to an airtight container. Store in the refrigerator until ready to eat, up to two weeks.

PER SERVING Calories: 167 | Fat: 18 g | Protein: 0 g | Sodium: 1 mg | Fiber: 0 g | Carbohydrates: 1.5 g | Sugar: 0 g | Net Carbohydrates: 1.5 g

Almond Walnut Fat Bombs

Chai spice blend is made up of a mixture of ginger, cinnamon, cardamom, allspice, and cloves. If you don't have one already made, you can use a mixture of these spices to suit your tastes.

INGREDIENTS | SERVES 12

¾ cup coconut butter, melted

⅓ cup no-sugar-added almond butter

¾ cup butter-flavored coconut oil

¼ cup coconut cream

2 teaspoons vanilla extract

⅛ teaspoon almond extract

1 teaspoon chai spice blend

⅛ teaspoon sea salt

¼ cup raw walnuts, roughly chopped

The Lowdown on Coconut Butter

Unlike coconut oil, which is oil that's been extracted from coconut meat, coconut butter is made from coconut meat that's been blended into a spreadable paste, similar to nut butters. Coconut oil is all fat, while coconut butter contains fat and some carbohydrates, but the amounts are small. Two tablespoons of coconut butter contain 7 grams of carbohydrates, but 5 of those grams come from fiber, so the net carbohydrate count is only 1 gram per tablespoon.

1. Line a mini muffin tin with twelve cupcake liners. Set aside.

2. Combine all ingredients, except walnuts, in a food processor and process until smooth.

3. Pour equal amounts of mixture into prepared muffin wells. Sprinkle equal amounts of chopped walnuts into each muffin well and refrigerate until set, about 1 hour.

4. Remove from muffin tray and transfer to an airtight container. Store in the refrigerator until ready to eat, up to two weeks.

PER SERVING Calories: 310 | Fat: 33 g | Protein: 2 g | Sodium: 55 mg | Fiber: 1 g | Carbohydrates: 2 g | Sugar: 1 g | Net Carbohydrates: 1 g

CHAPTER 16

Desserts

Cheesecake Cupcakes

You can freeze these cupcakes and store them up to two months in the freezer. When you're ready to eat one, take it out of the freezer and let it thaw in the refrigerator.

INGREDIENTS | SERVES 12

½ cup almond meal

½ cup coconut flour

¼ teaspoon almond extract

¼ cup grass-fed butter, melted

2 (8-ounce) packages cream cheese, softened

¼ cup full-fat sour cream

2 large eggs

¾ cup granulated erythritol

1 teaspoon vanilla extract

1. Preheat oven to 350°F. Line a muffin tin with paper liners.

2. Combine almond meal, coconut flour, almond extract, and butter in a medium bowl and mix. Scoop equal parts of mixture into each muffin cup and press down to form a crust.

3. Bake 5 minutes and remove from oven.

4. While crust is baking, beat cream cheese, sour cream, eggs, erythritol, and vanilla extract together in a medium bowl until smooth. Pour equal amounts of mixture on top of each crust.

5. Bake 15 minutes or until filling is set. Allow to cool.

6. Transfer each cupcake to a sealable bag or an airtight container and store in the refrigerator until ready to eat, up to one week.

PER SERVING Calories: 208 | Fat: 18 g | Protein: 4 g | Sodium: 150 mg | Fiber: 3 g | Carbohydrates: 5 g | Sugar: 1 g | Net Carbohydrates: 2 g

Chocolate Peanut Butter Cups

You can store these Chocolate Peanut Butter Cups at room temperature if you prefer, but if the weather gets hot, they'll melt and won't hold their shape.

INGREDIENTS | SERVES 12

1 cup butter-flavored coconut oil
½ cup no-sugar-added creamy peanut butter
2 tablespoons coconut cream
1 tablespoon raw cacao powder
⅓ cup granulated erythritol
¼ teaspoon vanilla extract
⅛ teaspoon sea salt
2 tablespoons roasted peanuts

1. Line a muffin pan with cupcake liners. Set aside.

2. Melt coconut oil in a medium saucepan over low heat. Add peanut butter and stir until combined. Whisk in remaining ingredients.

3. Pour equal amounts of mixture into each prepared muffin well. Freeze until hardened, about 1 hour.

4. Transfer cups to a resealable bag or airtight container and store in the refrigerator until ready to eat, up to two weeks.

PER SERVING Calories: 230 | Fat: 24 g | Protein: 2.5 g | Sodium: 71 mg | Fiber: 0.5 g | Carbohydrates: 6 g | Sugar: 1 g | Net Carbohydrates: 5.5 g

Pumpkin Cheesecake Bars

When you try these Pumpkin Cheesecake Bars, you won't even miss the traditional pumpkin pie. They have all the same spicy flavor with hardly any of the carbs!

INGREDIENTS | SERVES 12

1 (8-ounce) package cream cheese, softened
1 cup pumpkin purée
5 large eggs, room temperature
1 cup granulated erythritol
1 teaspoon pumpkin pie spice
1 teaspoon ground cinnamon
1 teaspoon vanilla extract

1. Preheat oven to 350°F. Grease an 8" × 8" baking dish with butter.

2. Combine cream cheese and pumpkin purée in a medium bowl and beat until smooth. Add remaining ingredients and beat until combined. Pour batter into baking dish.

3. Bake 40 minutes or until filling is set. Allow to cool then cut into twelve equal-sized bars.

4. Transfer bars to resealable bags or an airtight container and store in the refrigerator until ready to eat, up to one week.

PER SERVING Calories: 96 | Fat: 8 g | Protein: 4 g | Sodium: 97 mg | Fiber: 0 g | Carbohydrates: 1.5 g | Sugar: 1 g | Net Carbohydrates: 1.5 g

Coconut Lime Bars

Use fresh lime juice instead of bottled for these bars. It's a little extra work, but the juice is worth the squeeze. You'll need about eight limes to get 1 cup of lime juice.

INGREDIENTS | SERVES 12

6 tablespoons grass-fed butter, melted

1½ cups fine almond flour

½ cup unsweetened shredded coconut

⅓ cup plus ½ cup granulated erythritol, divided

2 teaspoons lime zest, divided

¼ teaspoon sea salt

1 cup lime juice

½ cup full-fat coconut milk

5 large eggs, beaten

1. Preheat oven to 350°F. Grease an 8" × 8" baking dish.

2. Combine butter, almond flour, shredded coconut, ⅓ cup erythritol, 1 teaspoon lime zest, and salt in a medium mixing bowl and mix with a fork until fully incorporated. Press mixture into prepared baking dish.

3. Bake 10 minutes or until crust starts to brown.

4. Combine lime juice, 1 teaspoon lime zest, coconut milk, remaining erythritol, and butter in a medium saucepan over medium heat. Whisk until erythritol dissolves. Add beaten eggs slowly, whisking constantly until mixture foams and starts to thicken, about 6 minutes. Pour over crust.

5. Bake 12 minutes or until set. Remove from oven and allow to cool.

6. Cut into twelve squares and transfer each square to a separate airtight container. Store in the refrigerator until ready to eat, up to one week.

PER SERVING Calories: 172 | Fat: 11 g | Protein: 4.5 g | Sodium: 85 mg | Fiber: 1 g | Carbohydrates: 5 g | Sugar: 1 g | Net Carbohydrates: 4 g

Cream Cheese Brownies

If you want to save some time during your meal prep, you can skip the part where you dollop batter on top and swirl the layers together and just make these bars with two layers.

INGREDIENTS | SERVES 12

1 cup cream cheese, softened
1¼ cups granulated erythritol, divided
3 large eggs, divided
1 teaspoon vanilla extract
1 cup grass-fed butter
⅓ cup raw cacao powder
1 teaspoon salt
⅔ cup almond flour

1. Preheat oven to 350°F. Grease an 8" × 8" baking dish and set aside.

2. Beat cream cheese and ¼ cup erythritol in a medium mixing bowl until combined. Add 1 egg and vanilla extract and beat until incorporated. Set aside.

3. In a medium saucepan over low heat, combine butter, remaining erythritol, cacao powder, and salt and stir until incorporated, about 2 minutes. Remove from heat and allow to cool. Whisk in remaining 2 eggs, one at a time, until mixture thickens. Add almond flour and mix until incorporated.

4. Transfer brownie mixture to prepared pan, reserving ½ cup. Spread out evenly in pan. Top with cream cheese mixture. Drop dollops of remaining brownie mixture on top of cream cheese mixture and use a knife to swirl them together.

5. Bake 25 minutes or until brownies set. Remove from oven and allow to cool.

6. Cut into twelve equal-sized brownies and transfer each brownie to a separate airtight container or a resealable bag. Store in the refrigerator until ready to eat, up to one week.

PER SERVING Calories: 251 | Fat: 23 g | Protein: 4 g | Sodium: 284 mg | Fiber: 1 g | Carbohydrates: 5 g | Sugar: 0.5 g | Net Carbohydrates: 4 g

Cinnamon Almond Cookies

These cookies tend to crisp up as they sit, so take them out of the oven when they seem slightly under-baked so that they'll be perfect for the next few days.

INGREDIENTS | SERVES 12

2 cups blanched almond flour
½ cup grass-fed butter, softened
1 large egg
½ cup granulated erythritol
1 teaspoon vanilla extract
⅛ teaspoon almond extract
1 teaspoon ground cinnamon

The Concentration of Extracts

Not all extracts are equal in strength. They can often be used interchangeably, but you may have to adjust the amounts. For example, almond extract is about twice as potent as vanilla extract, so if replacing vanilla extract in a recipe, you would need only half as much almond extract. If you use too much, the flavor can be overpowering and off-putting.

1. Preheat oven to 350°F. Line a baking sheet with parchment paper.

2. Combine all the ingredients in a medium bowl and beat until combined.

3. Roll dough into 1" balls and arrange on prepared baking sheet. Flatten slightly.

4. Bake 12 minutes or until edges start to turn golden brown. Cool and then remove from baking sheet.

5. Transfer cookies to an airtight container and store in the refrigerator until ready to eat, up to one week.

PER SERVING Calories: 150 | Fat: 8 g | Protein: 2.5 g | Sodium: 7 mg | Fiber: 0.5 g | Carbohydrates: 5 g | Sugar: 0 g | Net Carbohydrates: 4.5 g

Key Lime Bars

These Key Lime Bars call for keto-friendly homemade Sweetened Condensed Milk (see recipe in this chapter). Don't try to use canned sweetened condensed milk in its place or your carbohydrate count will be thrown way off.

INGREDIENTS | SERVES 12

1¼ cups almond flour

⅓ cup granulated erythritol

¼ teaspoon sea salt

¼ cup grass-fed butter, melted

3 ounces cream cheese, softened

4 large egg yolks, room temperature

1 teaspoon lime zest

⅓ cup key lime juice

1 cup homemade Sweetened Condensed Milk (see recipe in this chapter)

Lime versus Key Lime

Although it seems like a lime is a lime, there are notable differences between a regular lime and a key lime. Key limes are smaller, with thinner rinds and a tarter, more acidic juice that has floral and herbal undertones. Because of their smaller size, key limes don't produce as much juice as regular limes—one key lime will give you about 1 tablespoon of juice, whereas a regular lime is good for 2 tablespoons. Key limes also tend to be more expensive for a smaller volume. That being said, the two limes may be used interchangeably without much difference, but of course, a key lime pie is not a true key lime pie without its main ingredient.

1. Preheat oven to 325°F.

2. Whisk almond flour, erythritol, salt, and melted butter together in a medium bowl until combined. Transfer to an 8" × 8" baking pan and press evenly into bottom. Bake 10 minutes or until slightly golden. Remove from oven.

3. Beat cream cheese in a medium bowl until smooth and fluffy, about 2 minutes. Add egg yolks and beat until fully incorporated. Beat in lime zest, lime juice, and Sweetened Condensed Milk until mixture is smooth.

4. Pour filling over crust and bake 15 minutes, or until just firm. Remove and allow to cool. Refrigerate 1 hour.

5. Cut into twelve equal-sized bars and transfer each bar to a resealable bag or airtight container. Store in the refrigerator until ready to eat, up to one week.

PER SERVING Calories: 205 | Fat: 10 g | Protein: 4 g | Sodium: 109 mg | Fiber: 0.5 g | Carbohydrates: 5 g | Sugar: 4 g | Net Carbohydrates: 4.5 g

Chocolate Mousse

Beating the cream mixture until peaks form is an essential step in making sure that the texture of this mousse comes out right, so take your time with it.

INGREDIENTS | SERVES 12

3¼ cups heavy cream, divided

¼ cup plus ⅓ cup plus 2 tablespoons powdered erythritol, divided

2 teaspoons vanilla extract, divided

8 ounces cream cheese, softened

⅓ cup raw cacao powder

Powdered versus Granulated

Erythritol is available in two forms— powdered and granulated. In simple terms, the powdered form is the blended or processed version of the granulated form. The texture of powdered erythritol is a lot finer than granulated, similar to the textures of powdered sugar and granulated sugar. In some recipes, granulated erythritol can leave a gritty texture, so you might want to use powdered instead. You can buy powdered erythritol ready to go, or you can make your own by processing granulated erythritol in a food processor for about 2 minutes, until a fine dust forms.

1. Combine ¼ cup heavy cream, ¼ cup powdered erythritol, ½ teaspoon vanilla extract, and cream cheese in a medium bowl and beat until smooth. Transfer to an 9" × 9" baking dish.

2. Combine 1½ cups heavy cream, ⅓ cup powdered erythritol, and 1 teaspoon vanilla extract in a medium bowl and beat with a handheld mixer until stiff peaks form, about 3 minutes. Slowly beat in cacao powder. Spread over cream cheese mixture.

3. Combine 1½ cups heavy cream, ½ teaspoon vanilla extract, and 2 tablespoons powdered erythritol in a medium bowl and beat with handheld mixer until stiff peaks form, about 4 minutes. Spread over chocolate layer.

4. Refrigerate 2 hours or until mousse is completely set.

5. Divide into twelve equal-sized portions and transfer each portion to an airtight container. Store in the refrigerator until ready to eat, up to one week.

PER SERVING Calories: 295 | Fat: 30 g | Protein: 3 g | Sodium: 93 mg | Fiber: 1 g | Carbohydrates: 8 g | Sugar: 2.5 g | Net Carbohydrates: 7 g

Cinnamon Roll Cheesecake Cupcakes

Like any good cinnamon roll, these cupcakes are best when served slightly warmed up. Right before you eat them, bake them at 250°F for a few minutes until they're heated through and frosting is melted.

INGREDIENTS | SERVES 6

½ cup almond flour

5 tablespoons granulated erythritol, divided

1 teaspoon ground cinnamon, divided

2 tablespoons grass-fed butter, melted

6 ounces cream cheese, softened

¼ cup full-fat sour cream

1¼ teaspoons vanilla extract, divided

1 large egg

2 tablespoons grass-fed butter, softened

3 tablespoons powdered erythritol

2 teaspoons heavy cream

1. Preheat oven to 325°F. Line six wells of a muffin pan with cupcake liners.

2. Combine almond flour, 2 tablespoons granulated erythritol, and ½ teaspoon cinnamon in a medium bowl. Mix well. Stir in melted butter until mixture becomes clumpy. Divide mixture evenly into prepared muffin tins and press into bottom. Bake 6 minutes and remove from oven. Allow to cool.

3. Reduce oven temperature to 300°F. In a medium bowl, beat cream cheese and 3 tablespoons granulated erythritol until fluffy and smooth, about 3 minutes. Beat in sour cream, 1 teaspoon vanilla extract, and egg. Pour equal amounts of mixture over crust and bake 15 minutes or until set. Remove from oven and allow to cool.

4. In a medium bowl, beat 2 tablespoons softened butter with 3 tablespoons powdered erythritol, until smooth, about 2 minutes. Add remaining vanilla extract and heavy cream and beat until combined. Drizzle over cupcakes. Allow frosting to set.

5. Transfer each cupcake to an airtight container or a resealable bag and store in the refrigerator until ready to eat, up to one week.

PER SERVING Calories: 238 | Fat: 20 g | Protein: 4 g | Sodium: 119 mg | Fiber: 0.5 g | Carbohydrates: 5 g | Sugar: 1.5 g | Net Carbohydrates: 4.5 g

Lemon Cream Pie

This Lemon Cream Pie needs to chill at least 4 hours, but overnight is even better. Keep that in mind when planning your meal prep.

INGREDIENTS | SERVES 8

8 tablespoons plus ¼ cup diced salted grass-fed butter, divided

¾ cup coconut flour

2 large eggs

1 cup heavy cream

4 large egg yolks

⅓ cup fresh lemon juice

2 teaspoons lemon zest

1 teaspoon lemon extract

½ cup powdered erythritol

1 cup full-fat sour cream

What Is Erythritol?

Contrary to what some people think, erythritol is not an artificial sweetener; it's a sugar alcohol that's made by fermenting corn or birch. Because erythritol is the byproduct of fermentation and not the corn or birch itself, it contains no calories or carbohydrates and is acceptable for a keto diet. It's generally the sweetener of choice because it's interchangeable in similar amounts to regular sugar and it doesn't have a bitter aftertaste that some people can detect with stevia or monk fruit sweeteners.

1. Cut 8 tablespoons butter into coconut flour using a fork or a pastry cutter until crumbly. Add in eggs and mix until dough forms.

2. Press dough into a 9" pie pan.

3. Combine cream, egg yolks, lemon juice, and lemon zest in a medium saucepan over medium-low heat. Whisk constantly 5 minutes or until mixture thickens.

4. Remove from heat and stir in ¼ cup diced butter, lemon extract, and erythritol until dissolved. Whisk in sour cream until smooth.

5. Pour lemon mixture into prepared crust and refrigerate at least 4 hours.

6. Store in the refrigerator until ready to eat, up to one week.

PER SERVING Calories: 369 | Fat: 37 g | Protein: 5 g | Sodium: 138 mg | Fiber: 6 g | Carbohydrates: 6 g | Sugar: 1.5 g | Net Carbohydrates: 0 g

Chocolate Tart

When making this Chocolate Tart, watch the crust closely to make sure it doesn't burn. You want it to turn a little golden, but not brown.

INGREDIENTS | SERVES 8

1¼ cups almond flour

¾ cup unsweetened shredded coconut

1 large egg

¼ cup butter-flavored coconut oil

¾ cup coconut cream

⅓ granulated erythritol

2 tablespoons raw cacao powder

1 teaspoon vanilla extract

⅛ teaspoon sea salt

1. Preheat oven to 350°F. Line a 9" pie plate with parchment paper.

2. Combine almond flour, shredded coconut, and egg in the bowl of a food processor and process until smooth. Press mixture into loaf pan and bake 15 minutes or until it starts to turn golden brown. Remove from oven and cool.

3. Melt coconut oil in a medium saucepan over medium heat. Add coconut cream, erythritol, cacao powder, vanilla extract, and salt and stir until smooth.

4. Pour into crust and refrigerate 2 hours or until set.

5. Cut into eight equal portions and transfer to a separate airtight container. Store in the refrigerator until ready to eat, up to one week.

PER SERVING Calories: 219 | Fat: 15 g | Protein: 3.5 g | Sodium: 50 mg | Fiber: 1.5 g | Carbohydrates: 7 g | Sugar: 1 g | Net Carbohydrates: 5.5 g

Sweetened Condensed Milk

Many keto dessert recipes call for sweetened condensed milk. With this simple recipe, you can keep some on hand for whenever you need to whip something up quickly, or you can put it in your coffee in the morning for a sweet treat.

INGREDIENTS | SERVES 12 (MAKES 1½ CUPS)

2 cups heavy cream

2 tablespoons unsalted grass-fed butter

⅓ cup erythritol

1. Combine all ingredients in a medium saucepan. Bring to a boil, reduce heat to low, and simmer until reduced by half, about 20 minutes, stirring regularly.

2. Remove from heat and allow to cool. Transfer to a sealed glass jar and store until ready to use, up to two weeks.

PER SERVING Calories: 154 | Fat: 16 g | Protein: 1 g | Sodium: 15 mg | Fiber: 0 g | Carbohydrates: 1 g | Sugar: 0 g | Net Carbohydrates: 1 g

No-Bake Chocolate Almond Butter Cookies

These no-bake cookies are perfect for the warm weather months when you don't feel like turning on the oven, but you want to prepare some sweet treats for your meal prep.

INGREDIENTS | SERVES 8

1⅓ cups creamy no-sugar-added almond butter

2 teaspoons vanilla extract

2 tablespoons unsweetened cocoa powder

2 cups unsweetened shredded coconut

2 tablespoons butter-flavored coconut oil

1. Line a baking sheet with parchment paper.

2. Combine all ingredients in a medium mixing bowl and stir until incorporated. Divide into eight equal portions and scoop onto prepared baking sheet. Form into cookie shapes.

3. Freeze 1 hour or until cookies set.

4. Transfer cookies to an airtight container and store in freezer until ready to eat, up to two months.

PER SERVING Calories: 361 | Fat: 32 g | Protein: 10 g | Sodium: 186 mg | Fiber: 4.5 g | Carbohydrates: 9 g | Sugar: 1 g | Net Carbohydrates: 4.5 g

Pumpkin Cinnamon Roll Coffee Cake

Pumpkin gets a lot of attention in October, but it's divine any time of the year, especially in this high-fat, low-carbohydrate coffee cake. Make sure you're purchasing pumpkin purée, which contains only pumpkin, and not pumpkin pie filling, which contains added sugar and has a higher carb count.

INGREDIENTS | SERVES 12

3 cups finely ground almond flour, divided

1½ cups granulated erythritol, divided

5 teaspoons pumpkin pie spice, divided

2 teaspoons baking powder

¼ teaspoon baking soda

½ teaspoon and ⅛ teaspoon sea salt, divided

½ cup grass-fed butter, melted

4 tablespoons full-fat sour cream

2 large eggs

¾ cup pumpkin purée

1 teaspoon vanilla extract

½ cup coconut flour

½ cup crushed walnuts

½ cup grass-fed butter, chilled

Homemade Pumpkin Pie Spice

Many spice manufacturers have premade pumpkin pie spice available for purchase, but you can make your own with spices that you probably already have in your spice cabinet. Just combine 4 teaspoons ground cinnamon, 2 teaspoons ground ginger, 1 teaspoon ground cloves, and ½ teaspoon ground nutmeg. Use what you need then store the rest in an airtight container for whenever you need it.

1. Preheat oven to 350°F. Grease a 9" × 9" baking dish with grass-fed butter.

2. In a medium bowl, combine 2 cups almond flour, 1 cup granulated erythritol, 3 teaspoons pumpkin pie spice, baking powder, baking soda, and ½ teaspoon sea salt and mix well.

3. Combine melted butter, sour cream, eggs, pumpkin purée, and vanilla extract in a separate medium bowl and mix well. Fold pumpkin mixture into almond flour mixture and mix until just incorporated. Transfer to prepared baking dish.

4. Combine remaining almond flour, remaining erythritol, coconut flour, walnuts, remaining pumpkin pie spice, and ⅛ teaspoon salt in a bowl. Cut chilled butter into the mixture with a fork or a pastry cutter until crumbly.

5. Sprinkle crumb mixture evenly over the top of cake batter. Bake 30 minutes or until a toothpick inserted in the center comes out clean.

6. Allow to cool then cut into twelve equal-sized portions. Transfer each portion to a separate airtight container or resealable bag and store at room temperature until ready to eat, up to one week.

PER SERVING Calories: 281 | Fat: 17 g | Protein: 5 g | Sodium: 245 mg | Fiber: 4 g | Carbohydrates: 6 g | Sugar: 0.5 g | Net Carbohydrates: 2 g

Chocolate Chip Pumpkin Blondies

If you don't have stevia-sweetened chocolate chips, you can make these blondies without them and add any of your favorite keto-friendly mix-ins. Shredded coconut, crushed walnuts, and macadamia nuts work well.

INGREDIENTS | SERVES 12

1¾ cups Paleo flour

1 cup granulated erythritol

½ teaspoon baking soda

½ teaspoon sea salt

1 tablespoon pumpkin pie spice

½ cup grass-fed butter, melted

⅓ cup pumpkin purée

1 large egg

1 teaspoon vanilla extract

½ cup stevia-sweetened chocolate chips

1. Preheat oven to 350°F. Grease an 8" × 8" pan with grass-fed butter.

2. Combine Paleo flour, granulated erythritol, baking soda, sea salt, and pumpkin pie spice in a medium bowl and mix well.

3. In a separate medium bowl, combine melted butter, pumpkin purée, egg, and vanilla extract and stir until incorporated.

4. Fold wet ingredients into dry ingredients. Add chocolate chips and stir until mixed well.

5. Transfer to prepared baking dish and bake 20 minutes or until a toothpick inserted in the center comes out clean. Allow to cool.

6. Cut into twelve equal-sized pieces and transfer each piece to a separate airtight container or resealable bag. Store at room temperature until ready to eat, up to one week.

PER SERVING Calories: 130 | Fat: 11 g | Protein: 3 g | Sodium: 156 mg | Fiber: 10 g | Carbohydrates: 15 g | Sugar: 0.5 g | Net Carbohydrates: 5 g

Lemon Pound Cake

Don't skip the lemon zest in this pound cake! It may seem like a small addition, but it's responsible for a lot of the lemon flavor.

INGREDIENTS | SERVES 12

1¼ cups almond flour

1 teaspoon baking powder

¼ teaspoon sea salt

4 tablespoons grass-fed butter, softened

¾ cup granulated erythritol

4 ounces cream cheese, softened

1 teaspoon lemon extract

2 teaspoons lemon zest

4 large eggs

Zesting a Lemon

When zesting a lemon, it's helpful to use a small, fine grater called a microplane. You want to zest only the yellow part of the skin and avoid the white layer underneath, which is called the pith. The pith has a bitter flavor and can be off-putting in recipes. To zest, rub the lemon against the microplane in one direction and turn the lemon as you go, so you don't get too deep.

1. Preheat oven to 350°F. Grease a loaf pan with grass-fed butter.

2. In a medium bowl, combine almond flour, baking powder, and salt and set aside.

3. In a separate medium bowl, beat butter and erythritol together until combined and airy, about 2 minutes. Beat in cream cheese, lemon extract, and lemon zest until smooth, about 2 minutes. Beat eggs in one at a time.

4. Stir in almond flour mixture until well incorporated. Transfer to prepared loaf pan and bake 30 minutes or until a toothpick inserted in the center comes out clean. Remove from oven and allow to cool.

5. Cut into twelve equal slices and transfer each slice to a separate airtight container or resealable bag. Store at room temperature until ready to eat, up to one week.

PER SERVING Calories: 137 | Fat: 8 g | Protein: 4 g | Sodium: 147 mg | Fiber: 1 g | Carbohydrates: 8 g | Sugar: 0.5 g | Net Carbohydrates: 7 g

Cream Cheese Frosting

This Cream Cheese Frosting makes a great accompaniment to the Lemon Pound Cake or the Pumpkin Cinnamon Roll Coffee Cake (see recipes in this chapter). You can drizzle a little on right after baking to take your dessert up a notch. To adjust the consistency, add more or less heavy cream.

INGREDIENTS | SERVES 12 (MAKES 1½ CUPS)

8 ounces cream cheese
1 cup powdered erythritol
¼ cup heavy cream
1 teaspoon vanilla extract

1. Beat cream cheese in a medium bowl with a handheld mixture until light and airy, about 3 minutes. Add erythritol and beat until combined. Beat in heavy cream and vanilla.

2. Store in the refrigerator in an airtight container until ready to use, up to two weeks.

PER SERVING Calories: 81 | Fat: 8 g | Protein: 1 g | Sodium: 70 mg | Fiber: 0 g | Carbohydrates: 1 g | Sugar: 1 g | Net Carbohydrates: 1 g

No-Bake Chocolate Chip Cookie Dough

Finally, a chocolate chip cookie dough that's safe to eat raw! This recipe contains no eggs, so you can eat this cookie dough straight from the bowl or use it as a dip.

INGREDIENTS | SERVES 8

½ cup heavy cream
¼ cup coconut cream
½ cup granulated erythritol
¾ cup coconut flour
¾ cup grass-fed butter, melted
1 teaspoon vanilla extract
¼ teaspoon sea salt
⅓ cup stevia-sweetened chocolate chips

1. Combine all ingredients except chocolate chips in a medium bowl and stir until well blended. Stir in chocolate chips.

2. Divide into eight equal portions and transfer each portion to a resealable bag. Store in the refrigerator until ready to eat, up to one week.

PER SERVING Calories: 266 | Fat: 26 g | Protein: 2 g | Sodium: 81 mg | Fiber: 7 g | Carbohydrates: 23 g | Sugar: 3 g | Net Carbohydrates: 16 g

Cannoli Cheesecake

Unlike collagen, which increases nutritional value but can be omitted from most recipes, gelatin is a nonnegotiable ingredient in this cheesecake. Gelatin allows the cheesecake mixture to harden and set and without it, the mixture would be too liquid-y.

INGREDIENTS | SERVES 12

1¼ cups almond flour

⅓ cup plus ½ cup granulated erythritol, divided

¼ teaspoon sea salt

8 ounces cream cheese, softened

1½ cups whole milk ricotta cheese

1 teaspoon ground cinnamon

1 teaspoon vanilla extract

2 teaspoons grass-fed gelatin

1 cup heavy cream

Collagen versus Gelatin

Collagen and gelatin have an identical nutritional profile, but their properties have an importance difference. While collagen dissolves in liquid, gelatin thickens liquid, turning it into a gel. Gelatin, which is actually just the cooked form of collagen, is often used as a thickener in soups, gravies, desserts, and homemade Jell-O. The two cannot be used interchangeably.

1. Preheat oven to 350°F.

2. Combine almond flour, ⅓ cup granulated erythritol, and salt in a bowl with a fork until crumb mixture forms. Press into the bottom of a 9" pie plate. Bake 10 minutes.

3. In a medium bowl beat cream cheese in a bowl until light and airy, about 2 minutes Add ricotta and beat until smooth, another 1 minute. Beat in cinnamon, vanilla, and gelatin.

4. In a chilled small bowl, beat heavy cream until stiff peaks form, about 3 minutes. Fold cream into cream cheese mixture until just combined.

5. Pour mixture on top of prepared crust. Refrigerate until set, about 4 hours.

6. Divide into twelve equal portions and transfer each portion to a separate airtight container. Store in the refrigerator until ready to eat, up to one week.

PER SERVING Calories: 240 | Fat: 17 g | Protein: 7 g | Sodium: 153 mg | Fiber: 0.5 g | Carbohydrates: 10 g | Sugar: 1 g | Net Carbohydrates: 9.5 g

5-Layer Bars

After cutting, you can store these 5-Layer Bars in the freezer for safekeeping up to six months. When ready to eat, you can transfer them to the refrigerator the night before, or just enjoy them right from the freezer.

INGREDIENTS | SERVES 12

1 cup almond flour

¼ teaspoon sea salt

¼ teaspoon baking powder

1 large egg

2 tablespoons grass-fed butter, melted

2 cups stevia-sweetened chocolate chips, divided

1 cup chopped walnuts

1 cup chopped almonds

1 cup shredded unsweetened coconut

Your Brain on Walnuts

Your brain is composed of about 60 percent fat. Walnuts contain about 65 percent fat. Approximately 8 to 14 percent of the fat in walnuts is in the form of alpha-linoleic acid, or ALA—polyunsaturated fat that helps reduce inflammation and gets converted to DHA, which is essential for brain health. Healthy fats, like the ones in walnuts, also provide your body with the raw materials it needs to promote cell turnover and prevent degeneration of the brain cells.

1. Preheat oven to 300°F. Grease an 8" × 8" baking dish with grass-fed butter.

2. Combine almond flour, salt, and baking powder in a medium bowl and mix well. Beat in egg and melted butter until combined, about 2 minutes. Press mixture into the bottom of pan. Bake 20 minutes and remove from oven.

3. Increase oven temperature to 350°F.

4. Spread 1 cup chocolate chips on top of prepared crust. Sprinkle walnuts and almonds on top. Cover with remaining chocolate chips. Sprinkle coconut on top.

5. Bake 10 minutes or until chocolate has melted. Remove from oven and allow to cool.

6. Cut into twelve equal-sized bars and transfer each bar to a separate airtight container. Store at room temperature until ready to eat, up to one week.

PER SERVING Calories: 313 | Fat: 21 g | Protein: 6 g | Sodium: 67 mg | Fiber: 4 g | Carbohydrates: 10 g | Sugar: 11 g | Net Carbohydrates: 6 g

CHAPTER 17

Weekend Gourmet Meals

Tomato-Basil Feta–Stuffed Chicken

This Tomato-Basil Feta–Stuffed Chicken is restaurant worthy but takes only a few ingredients and about 30 minutes to prepare. It's perfect for when you want to impress, but don't want to spend extra time in the kitchen.

INGREDIENTS | SERVES 6

6 (4-ounce) boneless, skinless chicken breasts
1 cup crumbled feta cheese
½ cup chopped sun-dried tomatoes
½ cup chopped fresh basil
½ cup almond meal
1½ teaspoons Italian seasoning
2 large eggs, lightly beaten

1. Preheat oven to 350°F. Spray a 9" × 13" baking dish with olive oil.

2. Butterfly chicken breasts and use a meat mallet to pound chicken to ¼" thickness.

3. Combine feta cheese, tomatoes, and basil in a small bowl. In a separate small bowl, mix together almond meal and Italian seasoning.

4. Scoop equal amounts of feta mixture into the middle of each chicken breast. Fold chicken in half and secure with a toothpick.

5. Dip each chicken breast in egg and then roll in almond mixture. Transfer to baking dish.

6. Bake 30 minutes or until chicken is no longer pink. Remove from oven and cool.

7. Transfer each chicken breast to a separate airtight container and store in the refrigerator until ready to eat, up to one week.

PER SERVING Calories: 274 | Fat: 10 g | Protein: 32 g | Sodium: 314 mg | Fiber: 1 g | Carbohydrates: 11 g | Sugar: 2 g | Net Carbohydrates: 10 g

Chicken with Spicy Cream Sauce

If you're not a fan of the slight sweetness of coconut in savory dishes (and you can tolerate dairy), you can use cream or half-and-half in place of the coconut cream in this recipe.

INGREDIENTS | SERVES 6

1 teaspoon sea salt

¾ teaspoon freshly ground black pepper

¾ teaspoon paprika

6 (4-ounce) boneless, skinless chicken thighs

2 tablespoons butter-flavored coconut oil

2 small shallots, minced

1½ cups chicken bone broth

3 tablespoons lime juice

1½ tablespoons minced garlic

½ teaspoon ground cumin

½ teaspoon crushed red pepper flakes

3 tablespoons minced jalapeños

3 tablespoons grass-fed butter

⅓ cup coconut cream

3 tablespoons chopped fresh cilantro

Shallots or Onions?

Both shallots and onions belong to the allium family of vegetables, but their flavors are different. Different color onions have different flavor profiles, but they all share an underlying characteristic of that zingy, sulfuric bite and fragrance. Shallots have a mild onion flavor, but also have flavors of garlic and sweeter undertones. Shallots and onions can be used interchangeably in cooked dishes, but you'll have to use more shallots. Three small shallots are the equivalent of one small onion. When it comes to raw dishes, if it calls for shallots, stick to the recipe. Raw onions may be too potent in some cases.

1. Preheat oven to 375°F.

2. Sprinkle salt, black pepper, and paprika over chicken thighs.

3. Heat coconut oil in a large oven-safe skillet over medium-high heat. Add chicken and cook 3 minutes on each side to brown. Remove from skillet.

4. Reduce heat to medium and add shallots, chicken broth, lime juice, minced garlic, cumin, and red pepper flakes. Stir, scraping brown bits from the bottom of the pan, and cook 15 minutes or until reduced by half.

5. Whisk in jalapeños and butter and stir until butter melts. Remove from heat and stir in coconut cream.

6. Add chicken back to pan and put skillet in the oven 7 minutes or until chicken is completely cooked. Remove from oven and cool. Sprinkle cilantro on top.

7. Transfer equal amounts of chicken and sauce to six separate airtight containers and store in the refrigerator until ready to eat, up to one week.

PER SERVING Calories: 274 | Fat: 18 g | Protein: 23 g | Sodium: 517 mg | Fiber: 1 g | Carbohydrates: 3 g | Sugar: 0.5 g | Net Carbohydrates: 2 g

Mozzarella Chicken

If you use a bottled marinara sauce, this recipe comes together extremely quickly, but it's still fancy enough to impress your mother-in-law! Just make sure to read the ingredients and make sure there's no added sugar.

INGREDIENTS | SERVES 6

1 teaspoon sea salt

1 teaspoon freshly ground black pepper

1 teaspoon garlic powder

6 (4-ounce) boneless, skinless chicken breasts

2 tablespoons butter-flavored coconut oil

1 small yellow onion, peeled and chopped

2 cups no-sugar-added marinara sauce

6 slices mozzarella cheese

Sugar by Another Name

Unfortunately, sugar isn't always listed as "sugar" on an ingredient list, so you'll have to do some detective work to figure out if a bottled item contains added sugar. There are more than fifty-six names for sugar that you might find on a label. Some of the most common include cane juice, rice syrup, barley malt, dextrose, sucrose, maltose, glucose, fructose, high-fructose corn syrup, golden syrup, maple syrup, honey, and molasses. Get familiar with these names and the other names for sugar and avoid them.

1. Preheat oven to broil.

2. Combine salt, pepper, and garlic powder and sprinkle over chicken.

3. Heat coconut oil in a large oven-safe skillet over medium heat. Add onion and cook until softened, about 4 minutes. Add chicken to pan and cook 5 minutes on each side or until chicken is completely cooked through.

4. Pour marinara sauce over chicken and allow to heat through. Place one slice of cheese on top of each chicken breast. Move skillet into oven and broil 2 minutes or until cheese starts to bubble and turn golden brown.

5. Remove from oven and allow to cool. Transfer each chicken breast and equal amounts of sauce to each of six separate airtight containers. Store in the refrigerator until ready to eat, up to one week.

PER SERVING Calories: 266 | Fat: 13 g | Protein: 31 g | Sodium: 616 mg | Fiber: 0 g | Carbohydrates: 2 g | Sugar: 0 g | Net Carbohydrates: 2 g

Cottage Pie

This keto-approved Cottage Pie replaces mashed potatoes with puréed cauliflower. It's a veggie-rich meal that's totally complete all by itself.

INGREDIENTS | SERVES 6

1 tablespoon butter-flavored coconut oil

1 small yellow onion, peeled and diced

3 cloves garlic, minced

1½ pounds 85/15 ground beef

1 small zucchini, seeded and diced

3 tablespoons tomato paste

2 teaspoons sea salt, divided

2 teaspoons freshly ground black pepper, divided

1 large head cauliflower, cut into florets, lightly steamed

3 tablespoons grass-fed butter

1 tablespoon olive oil

½ cup chicken bone broth

¼ teaspoon granulated garlic

1. Preheat oven to 350°F.

2. Heat coconut oil in a medium skillet over medium heat. Add onion and garlic and cook until softened, about 4 minutes. Crumble beef into skillet and cook until no longer pink, about 8 minutes. Add zucchini, tomato paste, 1 teaspoon salt, and 1 teaspoon pepper and cook 2 more minutes.

3. Transfer mixture to a 9" × 13" baking dish.

4. Combine remaining ingredients in a food processor and process until smooth. Spread cauliflower mixture over beef mixture.

5. Bake 25 minutes or until hot and bubbly and top starts to turn golden brown. Remove from oven and allow to cool.

6. Divide into six equal portions and transfer each portion to a separate airtight container. Store in the refrigerator until ready to eat, up to one week.

PER SERVING Calories: 399 | Fat: 31 g | Protein: 23 g | Sodium: 948 mg | Fiber: 3 g | Carbohydrates: 9 g | Sugar: 3 g | Net Carbohydrates: 6 g

Gouda and Bacon–Stuffed Pork Tenderloin

The best way to reheat this pork tenderloin is to add some chicken broth to a skillet over low heat, add the pork, and cover. Let it come to temperature over low heat and then sprinkle some Gouda and fresh parsley on top.

INGREDIENTS | SERVES 6

1½ pounds pork tenderloin

1½ teaspoons sea salt, divided

½ teaspoon freshly ground black pepper, divided

¼ teaspoon dried sage

⅔ cup shredded smoked Gouda cheese

12 slices no-sugar-added bacon, cooked and crumbled

¾ cup chopped fresh parsley

1 tablespoon olive oil

1. Preheat oven to 400°F.

2. Butterfly pork tenderloin and pound with a meat mallet to ¼" thickness.

3. Sprinkle ½ teaspoon sea salt, ¼ teaspoon pepper, and dried sage on inside of pork.

4. Combine Gouda, bacon, parsley, and ¼ teaspoon pepper in a small bowl. Spread cheese mixture on inside of pork, leaving ¾" from the sides empty. Roll pork up, starting with the short side, and secure with kitchen twine. Drizzle pork with olive oil and sprinkle remaining salt on top.

5. Roast 20 minutes or until pork is cooked through. Remove and allow to cool.

6. Cut in six equal-sized portions and transfer each portion to a separate airtight container. Store in the refrigerator until ready to eat, up to one week.

PER SERVING Calories: 438 | Fat: 31 g | Protein: 34 g | Sodium: 1,100 mg | Fiber: 0 g | Carbohydrates: 1 g | Sugar: 0.5 g | Net Carbohydrates: 1 g

Bacon-Wrapped Pork Loin

If you want to save some time during your meal prep, you can skip the step of cooking the bacon in the skillet, but the bacon in your finished pork loin won't be as crispy if you do. After reheating this pork loin, let it sit under the broiler for a couple minutes to crisp.

INGREDIENTS | SERVES 6

1 tablespoon garlic powder

1 teaspoon sea salt

1 teaspoon dried basil

1 teaspoon dried oregano

¼ teaspoon dried rosemary

¼ teaspoon dried thyme

12 slices no-sugar-added bacon

1½ pounds pork tenderloin

Loin or Tenderloin?

Pork tenderloin is the leanest cut of meat that comes from the pork. It comes from the meat that runs from the pig's hip to shoulder, which is where pork chops are taken from too. It's typically the most expensive cut of pork because it's so tender. When you're following a recipe that's slow cooked, you can usually replace pork tenderloin with pork loin to save a little money, but in recipes that are cooked more quickly, you might want to stick to pork loin for a more tender finished product.

1. Preheat oven to 400°F.

2. Combine garlic powder, salt, basil, oregano, rosemary, and thyme in a small bowl. Set aside.

3. Place bacon in a medium oven-safe skillet and cook over medium-high heat until lightly browned, but still flexible, about 5 minutes. Remove bacon from pan and place on a paper towel–lined plate. Reserve grease in pan.

4. Wrap pork in bacon strips, securing with toothpicks. Slice wrapped pork into six medallions.

5. Sprinkle seasoning mixture on each side of each pork medallion.

6. Place pork in skillet with bacon grease and cook 4 minutes on each side or until pork is cooked through. Allow to cool.

7. Transfer each medallion to a separate airtight container and store in the refrigerator until ready to eat, up to one week.

PER SERVING Calories: 361 | Fat: 24 g | Protein: 30 g | Sodium: 818 mg | Fiber: 0 g | Carbohydrates: 2 g | Sugar: 0.5 g | Net Carbohydrates: 2 g

Parmesan-Crusted Pork Chops

You can replace the almond meal with crushed pork rinds in this recipe. It will still give you that crisp texture, but without any of the carbohydrates, as pork rinds are all fat.

INGREDIENTS | SERVES 6

¼ cup Paleo flour
1 teaspoon sea salt
½ teaspoon freshly ground black pepper
2 cups almond meal
2 teaspoons Italian seasoning
1½ cups grated Parmesan cheese
1 tablespoon dried sage
6 (4-ounce) boneless pork chops
2 large eggs, lightly beaten
3 tablespoons butter-flavored coconut oil

1. Preheat oven to 425°F.

2. Combine Paleo flour, salt, and pepper in a medium bowl. Combine almond meal, Italian seasoning, Parmesan cheese, and sage in another medium bowl.

3. Dip each pork chop into flour mixture, then egg, then almond meal mixture to coat. Transfer to a 9" × 13" baking dish and dot ½ tablespoon coconut oil on top of each pork chop.

4. Bake 12 minutes or until pork is cooked through. Remove from oven and allow to cool.

5. Transfer each pork chop to a separate airtight container and store in the refrigerator until ready to eat, up to one week.

PER SERVING Calories: 772 | Fat: 51 g | Protein: 39 g | Sodium: 965 mg | Fiber: 4 g | Carbohydrates: 10 g | Sugar: 0 g | Net Carbohydrates: 6 g

Chicken Cordon Bleu with Creamy Lemon Butter Sauce

If you want a richer flavor, you can use chicken thighs instead of chicken breasts. This will also double the fat content of each serving, as chicken thighs are much higher in fat.

INGREDIENTS | SERVES 6

6 (4-ounce) boneless, skinless chicken breasts

6 slices Swiss cheese

6 slices no-sugar-added deli ham

3 tablespoons Paleo flour

1 teaspoon paprika

1 cup plus 2 tablespoons grass-fed butter, divided

½ cup keto-friendly white wine

2 shallots, minced

½ cup heavy cream

3 tablespoons lemon juice

Save Money with Thighs

Chicken thighs don't get as much love as chicken breasts, but they're an excellent source of both protein and fat. When cooked, the fat renders from the chicken thigh into the sauce in which it's being cooked and gives it a richer flavor than chicken breasts. Plus, chicken thighs tend to be cheaper and go on sale more often, especially the bone-in, skin-on varieties. You can use chicken thighs in any recipes that call for chicken breasts. If the recipe calls for skinless, you can save money by buying it with the skin on and then removing before cooking.

1. Pound chicken with a meat mallet to ½" thickness. Place one slice of cheese and ham on each breast and fold chicken over, securing with a toothpick.

2. Combine Paleo flour with paprika in a medium bowl. Dip each chicken breast in flour mixture and set aside.

3. Heat 2 tablespoons butter in a large skillet over medium heat. Add chicken breasts and cook 5 minutes on each side or until chicken is cooked through.

4. While chicken is cooking, combine wine and shallots in a small saucepan. Bring to a boil and reduce until 2 tablespoons of liquid remain.

5. Reduce heat to low and whisk in remaining butter, stirring constantly until butter is incorporated. Remove from heat and whisk in cream and lemon juice.

6. Pour sauce over chicken and cook 1 more minute. Remove from heat.

7. Transfer one chicken breast and equal amounts of sauce to each of six separate airtight containers. Store in the refrigerator until ready to eat, up to one week.

PER SERVING Calories: 686 | Fat: 55 g | Protein: 39 g | Sodium: 441 mg | Fiber: 2.5 g | Carbohydrates: 6.5 g | Sugar: 1.5 g | Net Carbohydrates: 4 g

Lemon Chicken with Buttery Mushroom Sauce

If you want to up the nutrition of this recipe, throw some trimmed asparagus stalks in with the chicken while it bakes. They soak in the lemon flavor and make a perfect accompaniment to the chicken and the sauce.

INGREDIENTS | SERVES 6

2 tablespoons butter-flavored coconut oil

6 (4-ounce) boneless, skinless chicken breasts

2 tablespoons lemon juice

1 teaspoon lemon pepper

½ medium lemon, thinly sliced

¼ cup grass-fed butter

2 cups sliced white mushrooms

2 tablespoons Paleo flour

½ cup chicken bone broth

1. Preheat oven to 400°F.

2. Drizzle coconut oil in an 8" × 8" baking dish. Arrange chicken breasts in dish and pour lemon juice over chicken breasts. Sprinkle lemon pepper on top and place a lemon slice on each chicken breast.

3. Bake 40 minutes or until chicken is cooked through.

4. While chicken is baking, melt butter in a medium skillet over medium heat. Add mushrooms and cook until softened, about 5 minutes. Add flour and stir to coat mushrooms. Add chicken broth and stir. Simmer and allow to reduce until sauce thickens.

5. Allow to cool slightly. Transfer each chicken breast to a separate airtight container. Spoon equal amounts of sauce over each breast and cover. Store in the refrigerator until ready to eat, up to one week.

PER SERVING Calories: 256 | Fat: 15 g | Protein: 27 g | Sodium: 59 mg | Fiber: 3 g | Carbohydrates: 5 g | Sugar: 1 g | Net Carbohydrates: 2 g

Prosciutto-Wrapped Spinach and Feta–Stuffed Chicken Breasts

You can use bacon to wrap these chicken breasts, but it's often easier to find prosciutto without sugar added and since it's so thin, prosciutto tends to crisp up better in the oven.

INGREDIENTS | SERVES 6

¾ cup coconut oil mayonnaise

1 (10-ounce) package frozen chopped spinach, thawed and drained

1 cup crumbled feta cheese

3 cloves garlic, minced

6 (4-ounce) boneless, skinless chicken breasts

1 teaspoon garlic powder

1 teaspoon onion powder

6 slices prosciutto

1. Preheat oven to 375°F.

2. Combine mayonnaise, spinach, feta, and garlic in a medium bowl and stir until incorporated. Set aside.

3. Cut a slit into each chicken breast and spoon equal amounts of feta mixture into slit. Sprinkle garlic powder and onion powder on chicken and wrap a slice of prosciutto around each chicken breast and secure with a toothpick.

4. Arrange chicken breasts in a 9" × 13" baking dish. Cover and cook for 1 hour or until chicken is cooked through. Remove from oven and allow to cool.

5. Transfer each chicken breast to a separate airtight container and store in the refrigerator until ready to eat, up to one week.

PER SERVING Calories: 533 | Fat: 40 g | Protein: 36 g | Sodium: 903 mg | Fiber: 1 g | Carbohydrates: 5 g | Sugar: 1.5 g | Net Carbohydrates: 4 g

Garlic-Roasted Prime Rib

Prime rib may sound intimidating, but it's actually fairly simple to make. Just rub in a garlic, oil, and herb mixture and let it roast in high heat before lowering the oven temperature. Serve this with a side of Cauliflower Risotto (Chapter 10) and a fresh salad for a meal that's worthy of five stars.

INGREDIENTS | SERVES 6

4 cloves garlic, minced

3 teaspoons olive oil

1 teaspoon sea salt

1 teaspoon freshly ground black pepper

1 teaspoon dried thyme

1 teaspoon dried rosemary

1 (3-pound) prime rib roast

1. Preheat oven to 500°F.

2. Combine garlic, olive oil, salt, pepper, thyme, and rosemary in a small bowl. Sprinkle seasonings on fatty side of roast and place on a roasting pan with seasoned side up.

3. Bake 20 minutes, then reduce oven temperature to 325°F. Bake another 45 minutes or until internal temperature reaches 135°F. Remove from oven and allow to rest.

4. Cut roast into six equal portions and transfer each portion to a separate airtight container. Store in the refrigerator until ready to eat, up to one week.

PER SERVING Calories: 732 | Fat: 63 g | Protein: 36 g | Sodium: 511 mg | Fiber: 0.5 g | Carbohydrates: 1 g | Sugar: 0 g | Net Carbohydrates: 0.5 g

Marinated Flank Steak

This recipe requires you to marinate the flank steak at least 6 hours before cooking, so keep that in mind when scheduling your meal prep. It's an important step for flank steak, since it tends to be tough and is best after marinating.

INGREDIENTS | SERVES 6

1 clove garlic, minced

1 teaspoon sea salt

2 tablespoons coconut aminos

2 tablespoons lemon juice

3 teaspoons no-sugar-added ketchup

2 teaspoons olive oil

½ teaspoon freshly ground black pepper

¼ teaspoon dried oregano

½ teaspoon garlic powder

3 pounds flank steak

1. Combine garlic, salt, coconut aminos, lemon juice, ketchup, olive oil, pepper, oregano, and garlic powder in a small bowl.

2. Score meat and rub garlic mixture all over. Wrap tightly in foil and refrigerate 6 hours, or overnight.

3. Preheat grill to high heat. Lightly oil grill grate.

4. Cook 5 minutes on each side or until steak reaches desired doneness. Remove from grill and allow to rest.

5. Cut meat into strips and divide into six equal portions. Transfer each portion to a separate airtight container and store in the refrigerator until ready to eat, up to one week.

PER SERVING Calories: 366 | Fat: 17 g | Protein: 47 g | Sodium: 535 mg | Fiber: 0 g | Carbohydrates: 1.5 g | Sugar: 0.5 g | Net Carbohydrates: 1.5 g

Grilled Sirloin with Garlic Butter

All you need for the perfect grilled sirloin is some butter, garlic, and a few seasonings. This is a recipe you can whip up at any time with ingredients you probably have on hand. Just stock up on some sirloin steaks whenever they go on sale and have them ready to go in your freezer.

INGREDIENTS | SERVES 6

½ cup grass-fed butter

2 teaspoons garlic powder

3 cloves garlic, minced

½ teaspoon dried parsley

1 teaspoon sea salt

1 teaspoon freshly ground black pepper

6 (4-ounce) sirloin steaks

Types of Cuts

Sirloin is typically divided into two types of cuts: top cut (also referred to as top butt or sirloin butt) and bottom cut (or bottom sirloin or tri-tip). Top cut steaks are more suited for high-heat grilling than bottom cuts, which are leaner and don't hold up to heat as well.

1. Preheat grill to high heat.

2. Combine butter, garlic powder, garlic, and parsley in a small saucepan over medium-low heat. Stir until melted. Set aside.

3. Sprinkle salt and pepper all over steaks. Grill 4 minutes on each side or until steaks reach desired level of doneness.

4. Remove from heat and brush garlic butter over each steak. Allow to rest.

5. Transfer one steak to each of six separate airtight containers. Store in the refrigerator until ready to eat, up to one week.

PER SERVING Calories: 284 | Fat: 20 g | Protein: 24 g | Sodium: 456 mg | Fiber: 0.5 g | Carbohydrates: 1.5 g | Sugar: 0 g | Net Carbohydrates: 1 g

Blackened Salmon

This salmon has some serious kick and is not for the weakhearted. If you want to take it down a notch, reduce the cayenne pepper or omit it completely. You'll still get that blackened salmon flavor but without the spice.

INGREDIENTS | SERVES 6

2 tablespoons ground paprika

1 tablespoon cayenne pepper

1 tablespoon onion powder

1 tablespoon sea salt

1 teaspoon ground white pepper

½ teaspoon freshly ground black pepper

½ teaspoon dried oregano

½ teaspoon dried thyme

6 (4-ounce) salmon filets

¾ cup grass-fed butter, melted, divided

1. Combine spices in a small bowl and mix well.

2. Brush salmon filets on both sides with ¼ cup melted butter. Sprinkle spice mixture over each filet, covering as much as possible.

3. Heat cast iron skillet over high heat. Drizzle ¼ cup butter on one side of salmon and place buttered side down in skillet. Drizzle remaining butter on top. Cook 3 minutes, flip, and then cook another 4 minutes or until outsides are blackened and salmon flakes easily with a fork. Remove from heat. Allow to cool slightly.

4. Transfer each salmon filet to a separate airtight container and store in the refrigerator for up to four days or the freezer for up to four months, until ready to eat.

PER SERVING Calories: 406 | Fat: 31 g | Protein: 27 g | Sodium: 1,225 mg | Fiber: 1.5 g | Carbohydrates: 3 g | Sugar: 0 g | Net Carbohydrates: 1.5 g

Pesto Chicken Pinwheels

This recipe uses a basil pesto made with walnuts instead of pine nuts, which gives it a richer, nuttier flavor. If you want to make a traditional pesto, replace the walnuts with equal amounts of pine nuts.

INGREDIENTS | SERVES 6

3 cups packed fresh basil leaves

¾ cup grated Parmesan cheese

¾ cup extra virgin olive oil

½ cup chopped walnuts

4 cloves garlic, minced

½ teaspoon sea salt

¼ teaspoon freshly ground black pepper

6 (4-ounce) boneless skinless chicken breast halves, pounded to ¼" thickness

6 slices mozzarella cheese

Freezing Pesto

Pesto freezes really well and it's an easy way to add a delicious fat source to any protein. When you're preparing pesto, it's a good idea to make extra and freeze it so that when you need it for your next recipe, you don't have to go through the process of making it. To divide it into smaller portions, divide prepared pesto into ice cube trays and then freeze. Once frozen, remove from the ice cube trays and transfer the frozen pesto into an airtight container. Use what you need and store the rest in the freezer for nine to twelve months.

1. Preheat oven to 350°F. Grease a 9" × 13" baking dish with olive oil cooking spray.

2. Combine basil, Parmesan cheese, olive oil, walnuts, garlic, salt, and pepper in a food processor and process until smooth.

3. Scoop equal amounts of pesto onto flattened side of each chicken breast. Place one slice of cheese on top and roll chicken breasts into a pinwheel. Secure with toothpicks.

4. Transfer chicken breasts to prepared baking dish and bake 45 minutes or until chicken is cooked through. Remove from oven and allow to cool.

5. Transfer each chicken breast to a separate airtight container. Store in the refrigerator until ready to eat, up to one week.

PER SERVING Calories: 582 | Fat: 46 g | Protein: 37 g | Sodium: 649 mg | Fiber: 1 g | Carbohydrates: 4 g | Sugar: 0.5 g | Net Carbohydrates: 3 g

Lemon Butter Salmon

This salmon makes a great addition to any of the Mason jar salads, and there's no need to heat it up! Just flake with fork and add it to the bottom of the jar before layering your ingredients on top.

INGREDIENTS | SERVES 6

¼ cup grass-fed butter, melted

2 cloves garlic, minced

⅓ cup lemon juice

1 teaspoon lemon zest

2 teaspoons dried dill

½ teaspoon sea salt

¼ teaspoon freshly ground black pepper

6 (4-ounce) salmon filets

6 slices lemon

1. Preheat oven to 350°F. Grease a 9" × 13" baking dish.

2. Combine butter, garlic, lemon juice, lemon zest, dill, salt, and pepper in a bowl and whisk until incorporated.

3. Arrange salmon in prepared baking dish and pour butter mixture over salmon. Place a slice of lemon on top of each salmon filet.

4. Bake 20 minutes or until salmon flakes easily with a fork. Remove from oven and allow to cool.

5. Transfer each filet to a separate airtight container and store in the refrigerator until ready to eat, up to one week.

PER SERVING Calories: 582 | Fat: 46 g | Protein: 37 g | Sodium: 649 mg | Fiber: 1 g | Carbohydrates: 4 g | Sugar: 0.5 g | Net Carbohydrates: 3 g

Beef Tenderloin

With only three ingredients, this recipe seems extremely basic, but the taste is anything but. The coconut aminos and butter combine to give the meat an umami flavor that rivals five-star restaurant quality.

What Is Umami?

Umami is difficult to explain, but it's described by the Umami Information Center as "a pleasant savory taste imparted by glutamate, a type of amino acid, and ribonucleotides…which occur naturally in many foods including meat, fish, vegetables, and dairy products." Mushrooms, cabbage, tomatoes, and green tea are also described as having an umami flavor.

1. Preheat oven to 350°F.

2. Place tenderloin in a 9" × 13" baking dish. In a small bowl whisk together coconut aminos and butter and pour over tenderloin.

3. Bake 40 minutes, basting occasionally, or until meat reaches desired level of doneness. Remove from oven and allow to rest.

4. Cut into six equal portions and transfer each portion to a separate airtight container. Store in the refrigerator until ready to eat, up to one week.

PER SERVING Calories: 337 | Fat: 22 g | Protein: 33 g | Sodium: 64 mg | Fiber: 0 g | Carbohydrates: 0 g | Sugar: 0 g | Net Carbohydrates: 0 g

Parmesan Chicken with Spinach Cream Sauce

When ready to eat, heat this Parmesan chicken in a covered baking dish at 300°F. If you cook it too quickly, the sauce will dry out and the chicken will lose its moisture.

INGREDIENTS | SERVES 6

½ cup grated Parmesan cheese

½ teaspoon Italian seasoning

½ teaspoon sea salt

¼ teaspoon freshly ground black pepper

6 (4-ounce) boneless, skinless chicken breasts

2 tablespoons grass-fed butter

¼ cup chopped scallions

2 cloves garlic, minced

1 tablespoon Paleo flour

⅓ cup heavy cream

⅓ cup full-fat sour cream

1 (10-ounce) package frozen chopped spinach, thawed and squeezed dry

½ cup chopped roasted red peppers

1. Preheat oven to 350°F.

2. Combine Parmesan cheese, Italian seasoning, salt, and pepper in a small bowl. Set aside.

3. Use a meat mallet to pound chicken breasts to ½" thickness. Coat chicken in cheese mixture and transfer to a 9" × 13" baking dish.

4. Heat butter in a medium saucepan over medium heat. Add scallions and garlic and cook until softened, about 2 minutes. Whisk in flour and then add cream and sour cream and whisk until smooth. Add spinach and roasted red peppers and reduce heat to low. Simmer 3 minutes.

5. Remove from heat and pour sauce over chicken breasts. Sprinkle any remaining cheese mixture on top. Bake 30 minutes or until chicken is cooked through. Remove from oven and cool.

6. Transfer each chicken breast to a separate airtight container and store in the refrigerator until ready to eat, up to one week.

PER SERVING Calories: 290 | Fat: 16 g | Protein: 29 g | Sodium: 443 mg | Fiber: 2 g | Carbohydrates: 6 g | Sugar: 1.5 g | Net Carbohydrates: 4 g

Bacon and Goat Cheese–Stuffed Chicken Breasts

If goat cheese isn't your thing, you can use equal amounts of crumbled feta cheese or some smoked Gouda in its place.

Cow or Goat?

Cow milk and goat milk have similar amounts of fat—but the fat globules in goat milk are smaller and easier to digest for most people. Goat's milk also has a higher proportion of medium-chain fatty acids (or MCFAs), which are also found in coconut products, than cow milk. MCFAs have been shown to improve metabolism and digestive problems.

1. Preheat oven to 350°F.

2. Add 6 slices bacon to a medium skillet and cook over medium high heat for 5 minutes. Remove when bacon starts to brown but is still flexible. Transfer to a paper towel–lined plate. Add remaining 6 slices bacon to pan and cook 5 minutes on each side or until crispy. Transfer to paper towel–lined plate and allow to cool. Roughly chop the 6 slices crispy bacon. Set remaining, flexible 6 slices aside.

3. Combine olive oil, lemon juice, garlic, oregano, salt, and pepper in a small bowl and whisk until combined.

4. Combine goat cheese and chopped bacon in a separate small bowl.

5. Cut a slit into each chicken breast and stuff equal parts goat cheese and bacon mixture into slit. Wrap each chicken breast in one piece of flexible bacon and secure in place with a toothpick.

6. Arrange chicken in a 9" × 13" baking dish. Pour olive oil mixture over chicken and bake 25 minutes or until chicken is cooked through. Remove from oven and allow to cool.

7. Transfer each chicken breast to a separate airtight container and store in the refrigerator until ready to eat, up to one week.

PER SERVING Calories: 675 | Fat: 57 g | Protein: 36 g | Sodium: 869 mg | Fiber: 0.5 g | Carbohydrates: 2 g | Sugar: 1 g | Net Carbohydrates: 1.5 g

Filet Mignon with Balsamic Glaze

The balsamic glaze adds a little bit of sweet flavor without adding too many carbohydrates. Just make sure to stick to the amounts listed and don't overdo it on the vinegar or the carbohydrate counts will change.

INGREDIENTS | SERVES 6

1½ teaspoons freshly ground black pepper

1 teaspoon sea salt

6 (4-ounce) filet mignon steaks

1 tablespoon butter-flavored coconut oil

¼ cup balsamic vinegar

¼ cup keto-friendly red wine

1. Sprinkle pepper and salt all over steaks. Heat coconut oil in a large skillet over medium-high heat.

2. Sear steaks, cooking 1 minute on each side. Reduce heat to low and add balsamic vinegar and wine. Cover, cook 4 minutes, baste with vinegar mixture, then flip and cook an additional 4 minutes. Remove steaks from heat and allow to rest.

3. Transfer filets to each of six separate airtight containers and spoon equal amounts of glaze on top. Store in the refrigerator until ready to eat, up to one week.

PER SERVING Calories: 317 | Fat: 22 g | Protein: 21 g | Sodium: 903 mg | Fiber: 0 g | Carbohydrates: 2 g | Sugar: 1.5 g | Net Carbohydrates: 2 g

Two-Week Menu Plan

WEEK 1	Monday	Tuesday	Wednesday	Thursday	Friday	Saturday	Sunday
Breakfast	Beef and Egg Skillet	Beef and Egg Skillet	Beef and Egg Skillet	Beef and Egg Skillet	Beef and Egg Skillet	Beef and Egg Skillet	Banana Nut Muffins
Lunch	Feta Cheese Turkey Burgers	Feta Cheese Turkey Burgers	Feta Cheese Turkey Burgers	Feta Cheese Turkey Burgers	Spinach and Cheese Turkey Pinwheels	Spinach and Cheese Turkey Pinwheels	Cottage Pie
Snack	Lemon Fat Bombs	Lemon Fat Bombs	Lemon Fat Bombs	Nacho Pepper Boats	Nacho Pepper Boats	Nacho Pepper Boats	Nacho Pepper Boats
Dinner	Spinach and Cheese Turkey Pinwheels	Spinach and Cheese Turkey Pinwheels	Spinach and Cheese Turkey Pinwheels	Spinach and Cheese Turkey Pinwheels	Feta Cheese Turkey Burgers	Feta Cheese Turkey Burgers	Lemon Butter Salmon
Dessert	Cheesecake Cupcakes	Cheesecake Cupcakes	Cheesecake Cupcakes	Cheesecake Cupcakes	Key Lime Bars	Key Lime Bars	Key Lime Bars
WEEK 2	Monday	Tuesday	Wednesday	Thursday	Friday	Saturday	Sunday
Breakfast	Banana Nut Muffins	Banana Nut Muffins	Banana Nut Muffins	Ham and Cheese Hash Brown Casserole	Ham and Cheese Hash Brown Casserole	Ham and Cheese Hash Brown Casserole	Ham and Cheese Hash Brown Casserole
Lunch	Cottage Pie	Cottage Pie	Sausage, Spinach, and Pepper Soup	Sausage, Spinach, and Pepper Soup	Sausage, Spinach, and Pepper Soup	Sausage, Spinach, and Pepper Soup	Garlic Parmesan Spaghetti Squash
Snack	Bacon and Cheese Fat Bombs	Bacon and Cheese Fat Bombs	Bacon and Cheese Fat Bombs	Mini Meatloaf Cups	Mini Meatloaf Cups	Mini Meatloaf Cups	Mini Meatloaf Cups
Dinner	Lemon Butter Salmon	Spinach and Artichoke Chicken	Spinach and Artichoke Chicken	Spinach and Artichoke Chicken	Garlic Parmesan Spaghetti Squash	Garlic Parmesan Spaghetti Squash	Bacon and Goat Cheese–Stuffed Chicken Breasts
Dessert	No-Bake Chocolate Almond Butter Cookies	No-Bake Chocolate Almond Butter Cookies	No-Bake Chocolate Almond Butter Cookies	No-Bake Chocolate Almond Butter Cookies	Pumpkin Cinnamon Roll Coffee Cake	Pumpkin Cinnamon Roll Coffee Cake	Pumpkin Cinnamon Roll Coffee Cake

Standard US/Metric Measurement Conversions

VOLUME CONVERSIONS

US Volume Measure	Metric Equivalent
⅛ teaspoon	0.5 milliliter
¼ teaspoon	1 milliliter
½ teaspoon	2 milliliters
1 teaspoon	5 milliliters
½ tablespoon	7 milliliters
1 tablespoon (3 teaspoons)	15 milliliters
2 tablespoons (1 fluid ounce)	30 milliliters
¼ cup (4 tablespoons)	60 milliliters
⅓ cup	80 milliliters
½ cup (4 fluid ounces)	125 milliliters
⅔ cup	160 milliliters
¾ cup (6 fluid ounces)	180 milliliters
1 cup (16 tablespoons)	250 milliliters
1 pint (2 cups)	500 milliliters
1 quart (4 cups)	1 liter (about)

WEIGHT CONVERSIONS

US Weight Measure	Metric Equivalent
½ ounce	15 grams
1 ounce	30 grams
2 ounces	60 grams
3 ounces	85 grams
¼ pound (4 ounces)	115 grams
½ pound (8 ounces)	225 grams
¾ pound (12 ounces)	340 grams
1 pound (16 ounces)	454 grams

OVEN TEMPERATURE CONVERSIONS

Degrees Fahrenheit	Degrees Celsius
200 degrees F	95 degrees C
250 degrees F	120 degrees C
275 degrees F	135 degrees C
300 degrees F	150 degrees C
325 degrees F	160 degrees C
350 degrees F	180 degrees C
375 degrees F	190 degrees C
400 degrees F	205 degrees C
425 degrees F	220 degrees C
450 degrees F	230 degrees C

BAKING PAN SIZES

American	Metric
8 × 1½ inch round baking pan	20 × 4 cm cake tin
9 × 1½ inch round baking pan	23 × 3.5 cm cake tin
11 × 7 × 1½ inch baking pan	28 × 18 × 4 cm baking tin
13 × 9 × 2 inch baking pan	30 × 20 × 5 cm baking tin
2 quart rectangular baking dish	30 × 20 × 3 cm baking tin
15 × 10 × 2 inch baking pan	38 × 25 × 5 cm baking tin (Swiss roll tin)
9 inch pie plate	22 × 4 or 23 × 4 cm pie plate
7 or 8 inch springform pan	18 or 20 cm springform or loose bottom cake tin
9 × 5 × 3 inch loaf pan	23 × 13 × 7 cm or 2 lb narrow loaf or pâté tin
1½ quart casserole	1.5 liter casserole
2 quart casserole	2 liter casserole

Index

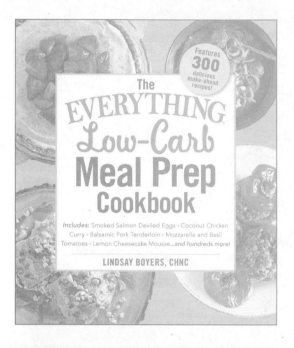
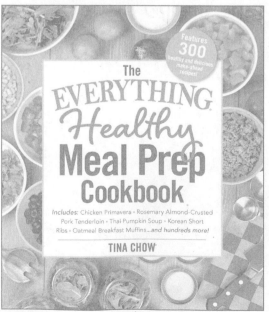